ABOUT THE AUTHOR

Born in Cuba to British diplomat parents, Clara started travelling as a baby and hasn't stopped since. She's lived in eleven countries on five continents, and visited nearly 70. She will soon be on her way to country number twelve – South Africa. Along the way, Clara has picked up a husband and produced two daughters. She's worked as a journalist, a diplomat, a writer, a press officer, an antenatal teacher, a customer service advisor, a PA, a coffee shop waitress and a school cook. Which only lasted for a day.

If Clara had any spare time she would spend it diving and getting better at taking photographs. In reality, she spends her days writing, looking out of the window and picking things up off the floor.

Follow Clara:
expatpartnersurvival.com
@strandedatsea
https://www.facebook.com/expatpartnersurvival

ISBN-13: 978-1505448887
ISBN-10: 1505448883

DISCLAIMER

This book is designed to act as a guide for people moving overseas with their partners. This information is provided and sold with the knowledge that the author does not offer any legal or other professional advice. This book does not contain all information available on the subject. This book has not been created to be specific to any individual's or organisations' situation or needs. Every effort has been made to make this book as accurate as possible. However, there may be typographical and or content errors. Therefore, this book should serve only as a general guide and not as the ultimate source of subject information. This book contains information that might be dated and is intended only to educate and entertain. The author and publisher shall have no liability or responsibility to any person or entity regarding any loss or damage incurred, or alleged to have incurred, directly or indirectly, by the information contained in this book.

clara@expatpartnersurvival.com

The Expat Partner's Survival Guide

Clara Wiggins

Table of Contents

This book is dedicated to:

My mother, Rowena, for going through it all when it was so much harder than it is now.

My husband, Keith, for taking us there.

And my daughters Emma and Martha, for coming with us.

INTRODUCTION

So What Is An Expat Partner?

Islamabad, August 2008, sometime in the early hours of the morning:

My husband, Keith, crawls into bed beside me, too excited by his night out to let me sleep. He starts his story about the 'lamb man', a story that's been repeated many times, which starts with the ritual cooking of the lamb over stones in his colleague's back garden, continuing with a great long description of exactly how old the lamb man looked and how his hands shook as he passed round little lamb titbits at the start of the feast, and goes on to describe, in painstaking detail, every course and every piece of lamb consumed that night. I see myself probably falling asleep somewhere around the soaking up of the lamb juices with naan bread, waking up again to find him still bubbling with enthusiasm for the local culture he'd been privileged to experience that night.

I'm not particularly amused.

He might have had a great night out with his colleagues, been introduced to new people and places, not to mention food. But I had been condemned, once again, to staying in. We had no one to leave the children with, plus, as a woman, I would not have been invited to the men-only party anyway.

All evening, I'd been hacking up great globules of green pus – an unpleasant reminder that a bad cold caused by continually going from forty two degree heat to chillingly cold air conditioning, had finally turned into a chest infection. The baby had cried herself awake several times already that night and I was exhausted.

We had only been in Pakistan a few weeks, but already I was feeling the stresses of living in such a suffocatingly close community

1

on the diplomatic compound. The frequent suicide bombings on the other side of the protective gates were a real worry, meaning taking the children out anywhere always felt like too big a risk.

But for my husband, the worker, the one whose job had brought us to this difficult, troubled but fascinating country, the first few weeks in Islamabad were exhilarating, learning about a new job and meeting the people who would help him do it. For me, it was boring, lonely, frustrating and tiring in equal measures.

At this point I would like to reassure you that whilst our time in Pakistan was a particularly negative one, brought abruptly to the end by the violent bomb attack on Islamabad's Marriott Hotel, even in these circumstances I could see potential for this posting to have turned into a wonderful period of my life. Yes it was dangerous and hot and there weren't many places to go with small children. But there was a huge expat community, a good British school right there on our compound, and we got to eat delicious curries as often as we liked.

What my time in Pakistan did highlight, though, was the very different experiences two people that move to the same country at the same time can have.

Until recently, most people were more familiar with the term 'trailing spouse' to describe what we now more commonly refer to as an expat or accompanying partner. The definition of a trailing spouse was someone who followed their husband, wife or partner on an overseas posting – but the word 'trailing' brought with it associations of following behind, somehow being the lesser of the two in the partnership.

These days many prefer the term 'expat', or 'accompanying' spouse or partner, and certainly this conjures up more of an equal partnership – which is how it should be. But whichever term you use, more and more global employers are starting to understand that the key to keeping their employees happy is keeping their partners and families happy.

Unfortunately, this isn't always straightforward. I would argue that the accompanier is the one with the hard job, the one who has to find their own way, get through each day alone or perhaps with children in tow, the one who is usually put in charge of organising schooling, finding the local doctor, working out where the best place to buy a decent piece of meat is or how to get hold of the required school uniform. Whilst the worker will have a routine, a structure to their day, the accompanier will be left with hours to fill, often stranded without transport at the beginning of a posting, sometimes with no one to talk to until their spouse arrives back in the evening.

Of course, no-one's experiences will be the same. But hopefully through this book I will show how different people, mostly women, but also men, accompanying their spouses on overseas postings, have faced the various challenges thrown at them and have (mostly) managed to come out fighting.

It is not intended as a self-help book, although it is full of hopefully useful information, more of a support book: a book to show you that whatever you are going through you are not alone, many have been where you are and will continue to go where you are, and that their stories, advice and information can help make your 'trailing experience' a positive one.

I was first inspired to write this book after meeting a number of women on our last posting, to St Lucia. This was the one that we were given after our early exit from Pakistan, supposedly the sop to make up for our experience in Islamabad.

St Lucia was a posting that most would assume would be a relaxed mix of sun, sand and rum cocktails. In reality, it was harder than even I, already knowledgeable about life in the Caribbean after a stint in Jamaica, would have imagined. A beautiful but small, very hot country, with few obvious activities for the children, it was not an easy country to settle or make friends in.

However, what I did find was that I was better prepared than many of the other accompanying spouses I met, women (and the odd man) who seemed to be as much victims of shell shock as culture shock. These were women who perhaps had never lived away from their home countries before, or who had had little preparation and even less support for their postings. These were not women whose partner's worked for the usual large posting organisations like the Foreign Office or a financial institution, but whose husbands were in the catering or tourism industry or who maybe weren't even on an official 'posting' but had been offered a job and had to do all the work of getting there and settling in without any help at all. Women who, no doubt, were strong, intelligent and capable, who had held down jobs while raising children in their own countries but who, in these new surroundings, were suddenly left exposed and desperate, scared of venturing out and socially isolated.

When I met these women, what struck me most was how unprepared they were for their posting, and, when they arrived, how little support they were able to access to help them settle in. Even the most well-travelled, culturally-astute person will suffer some form of culture shock on arrival in a new country, but those with experience will be able to recognise it for what it is: a totally normal reaction to living in a completely new environment. But for those who not only have no experience of overseas life, as well as little preparation, culture shock can be much longer lasting and much more damaging.

So who are these expat partners – who are YOU, and where are you moving to?

It's hard to build up an exact picture of the transient worker – there are statistics which show how many people leave the country every year, and how many Brits there are living in various countries, but these don't show how many of these are permanent settlers and how many are temporary. It's also hard to know exactly what they are doing – although the type of work available overseas is as varied as in this country and will include diplomats, aid workers, people working in the oil industry, banking and finance, hotel, catering and tourism, missionaries, law enforcement…the list goes on.

The kind of packages each of these workers will be on will vary. Some will be on generous relocation packages, which might include the shipping of their goods, flights home every year, all accommodation and bills paid for, even schooling. Others, however, will have to make their own way – for these people, there may be a lot more anxiety caused by things like finding housing and paying their own electricity bills; but on the other hand they might find themselves integrating into local life in their new country a little quicker than someone who has all of that done for them.

But despite not knowing exactly how many people are making a temporary move overseas, the basic answer is that there are people of all nationalities moving more or less everywhere in the world, and very often bringing their partners and families along with them.

Taking my own home country the United Kingdom as an example and according to the BBC's special report about British nationals who have moved overseas, which is titled (rather uninspiringly) Brit's Abroad (http://news.bbc.co.uk/1/shared/spl/hi/in_depth/brits_abroad/html/default.stm), there are around 5.5 million British people living overseas, with the most popular countries being Australia, Spain, America and Canada. But look on any forum aimed at British expats and you will see posts from the Middle East, from the Caribbean, South America, Eastern Europe…

I currently know of British people living in or who have recently lived in countries as diverse as the Philippines, Saudi Arabia, Jamaica, Martinique, Colombia, the Netherlands and many more. There are many surveys showing expats living all over the world. For example, a NatWest International Personal Banking survey (http://www.natwestinternational.com/nw/global/quality-of-life-study.ashx) found there were around three quarters of a million British nationals travelling abroad to work annually, with an average posting of 5.4 years. Another report, for the Economist's Intelligence Unit (http://graphics.eiu.com/upload/eb/lon_pl_regus_web2.pdf), talks about the expansion overseas following stagnation in the Western markets and mentions, in particular, emerging markets such as China, India, the Middle East and Russia. This report also notes that cultural and family pressures present the greatest difficulties to these workers – and that spouse's needs have become more important than ever.

A survey in 2005 (http://www.expatresearch.com/) of 264 trailing spouses from twenty eight different countries (including Britain), found that almost all the spouses were women and married, that just over half were under forty, that almost forty per cent were on their first posting and that fifty seven per cent had children with them. It also showed that almost sixty five per cent of them had to give up a career in order to relocate, and that over half of them could not work in their new country because of work permit or visa restrictions.

So looking at these statistics, your typical accompanying partner would be a married woman under forty, with children, who had possibly already been on a posting, who had given up a career to move overseas and who now couldn't work in her new country.

This pretty much summed me up when we moved to Pakistan – although it was my first posting as a spouse (having already been on my own posting as a diplomat to Jamaica) and I turned forty within a few weeks of arriving.

However, I was by no means a newcomer to expat life. As a child, I accompanied my parents on their postings (my father was a diplomat with the British Foreign Office) to countries including the Philippines, Nigeria, Venezuela and Gibraltar. In Manila, my three brothers and I attended the International School (an experience which has left me with a great knowledge of the American coin system...) and then later went to boarding school in the UK.

So although I came to the 'trailing' part of my expat experience relatively late on in my life, I had already had extensive experience of living overseas and had a good idea of what to expect when we were posted as a family for the first time. But even I, with my background knowledge, was hit harder than I had ever experienced by culture shock, by isolation and alienation and just the sheer hard work of trying to integrate into a whole new life.

Of course, growing up overseas in the 1970s and '80s was very different from life today. When we went, we went: we spent two years in the Philippines without one trip back home, and telephone calls were a rare treat. People communicated by writing letters (an almost forgotten art these days) – in our case, weekly through the diplomatic bag. Babies could be born, learn to walk and to talk before they ever even met their grandparents. If a close family member was ill or even died while you were abroad, the cost of flights meant it was unlikely you would be going home to see them or attend their funeral. It was a different life back then – although in many ways, it was a more settled one as it can be easier to establish your life in a new country without the constant to-ing and fro-ing cheap air travel affords us, and the technology which means life can feel like you've never left home.

Nowadays, we can be in almost constant communication with someone in another country – Skype or FaceTime, in particular, is a very popular way for grandparents to keep up with their grandchildren and feel like they are not missing out too much. And there is great comfort in knowing that, were you to need it, you can usually find a flight home from most destinations within twenty-four hours in the case of an emergency.

An increase in the number of British or other English-speaking schools overseas also makes it easier to keep your children with you on a posting, a huge improvement for those who would rather not send them to board back home.

But just because you can instant message your friends all day long if you want to, that you know you could be home by the next morning if you really needed to, and have your children with you throughout your time overseas, this doesn't necessarily mean you won't still go through many of the same emotions and worries as earlier generations.

My overseas experiences would be unrecognisable to my mother. But much of what she would have gone through – the anticipation and trepidation before the start of the posting, the feelings of disorientation on arrival, the loneliness but also the joy of discovery and thrill of the new – would have been the same. Similarly, she lived in completely different countries to me, but whether you are sent to Paris or

Pnom Penh, Washington or Warsaw, everyone is likely to experience some, if not all, of the same emotions before, during and even after their posting.

Stories from me, as well as my mother, will feature in this book, alongside those of many more women and men who have accompanied, or are still accompanying, their other halves overseas. Each chapter will cover a different subject or theme, from preparing for a posting to what to do if it all goes wrong. Although I can't cover every country in the world, hopefully there will be enough to show that experiences can be similar wherever you are and that support is also always available. I also couldn't put absolutely EVERYTHING in – right up to the last edit I kept thinking of more I wanted to add, but I had to stop somewhere. Throughout the book you'll find lots of references to help you access that support, and some suggestions for other ways to help your experience to be a positive one. Ultimately, though, it is up to you to make the most of your time overseas, to see it as an opportunity, grab it in both hands and run with it. There will be ups and there will be downs, but, as long as you are prepared for what lies ahead, you should be ready to meet every challenge thrown at you.

And, finally, remember what I was told by one friend weeks before setting off on our first posting as a family: 'Just because you hate it at first, doesn't mean you'll hate it forever. Give it time, give it patience and give it love. Hopefully, eventually, you'll get back as much as you put in.'

Note

Throughout this book I inter-change the phrases expat partner, accompanying partner and trailing spouse. I realise that a lot of people aren't spouses and no one wants to think of themselves as 'trailing'. But the term is just so much more evocative than the far duller 'expat partner'. I have had many discussions with fellow expats and re-pats (which is an ex-expat...) about this term and many refuse to use it – but I quite like it so will continue to throw it in from time-to-time.

CHAPTER ONE

Before You Go

Moving overseas starts long before you get there. If you're lucky, you'll get plenty of notice. If you're not, your preparations might be a little more hurried. Whichever way it is, in this chapter I look at what sort of things you can do, practically and emotionally, to get ready for the move – and to help those not coming with you to prepare as well. This includes actually making the decision to go, telling others about your imminent departure (and trying to ignore their reaction), researching and – if possible – even visiting your new home.

Whether it comes in the form of a hesitant conversation opener, a jollied up email, a cryptic message or a stark statement of fact, the first time you hear that your other half has applied for, or possibly already accepted, an overseas job will almost certainly be a life-changing moment.

Even if it was something you'd been expecting, even if the two of you had poured over websites together, endlessly discussed the benefits of living 'there' over living 'here', there is no doubt that when it suddenly, or possibly finally, becomes a reality, you'll probably panic. It's not that there's 'no going back' – after all, they can always say no. It's more that you probably realise this is the first step on a long, exciting but also probably pretty stressful, and possibly fairly lonely, journey into a physical and emotional un-known. Welcome to your new life as an expat partner.

Should we stay or should we go?

There are many different reasons why people move abroad these days. It could be they want to leave the 'rat race' behind and try out life in another country. They might be getting sent abroad by their employers – the world is becoming increasingly global these days and overseas 'postings' are no longer simply the realm of diplomats and the military. Or perhaps they see a foreign job as a sensible career move, a way to gain new skills by moving into a new market.

The majority of partners I spoke to in the course of researching this book told me that the decision about whether to take a foreign posting was very definitely a joint one. Most workers realise that they are unlikely to have a successful posting if their other half is not happy and part of being happy is being involved, right from the start.

For some, of course, the decision is already a fait accompli – perhaps the overseas move is a natural part of a career progression or too good to turn down, or, as in the case of Chellie, one wife I spoke to whilst researching this book, her husband's job in the army meant that they simply weren't given a choice. She always knew moving was part of the life she married into and was mentally prepared well in advance of every new posting. But for many, things aren't quite so straightforward, and throw things like the loss of a second career, schooling, relocation costs, health issues, aging parents, even pets into the mix and often you are left with more questions than answers.

When I first found out my husband had been offered our posting to Islamabad in 2007, I was living in the UK, pregnant with my second daughter and refused to make a decision about whether we would go or not until she was safely born. The fact that he had applied at all was all a bit of a blur to me and I can still remember the surprise when he told me the news. He had applied for a number of posts and I don't recall Pakistan even being one of the options, so it was certainly not a place that was on my radar. It was possibly a slightly surprising choice for a man with a wife, a toddler and another baby on the way – certainly, I can't recall much but stunned silence from anyone I told about it. But my entire upbringing was one big adventure after another, so I took this strange turn in our lives in my stride.

As we decided not to take the final decision until after our baby was born, we had plenty of time to research and plan, to find out about medical facilities, schooling, housing and – crucially for this posting – security. I spoke to parents who were already there, emailed the on-compound British nurse, read the Foreign Office's detailed post report and trawled through any other online resources I could find. Eventually we made the decision to go, and Keith was lucky enough to get a paid 'recce' visit to check out houses, what the school was like and what sort of things were available in the local shops. I'm glad he did as it meant that we were a lot more prepared than we otherwise would have been – even to the point that we not only took our own bread maker, but we also took enough of the right kind of flour, as well as yeast (a difficult commodity to buy in a Muslim country), to last us at least through our first year.

So our decision for this posting was made. But it hadn't been an easy one. And when we needed to make another decision about another posting not that long afterwards (following our evacuation from Islamabad after the Marriott bombing), things were made even more difficult by the fact that we were putting our children through two very big moves in a very short space of time.

When Kate C was faced with the dilemma about a move with her husband and their family to New York, she knew that she would have some regrets whichever decision she finally made. On the one hand, they would be moving to New York! On the other hand, she had a family and the responsibilities that went with it to worry about. Visions of dancing 'til dawn in Manhattan bars, shopping trips to 5th Avenue department stores and picnics in Central Park vied with the more practical issues of schools, housing costs and what sort of relocation package they were likely to be offered. 'Our heads were turned by the glamour of it all,' she said. 'The relocation package was generous, but that was what it was: the means to get us there. Once in the US, we would be financially responsible for all housing costs and schooling.

'Initially, we agreed that we'd go for two years and then come back to the UK. This seemed fine to us, because, since the downturn, generous, expat deals were the exception rather than the rule. But when we drilled down into the detail, we were looking at housing costs two-and-a-half times what we were already paying, $15,000 per annum nursery fees for our pre-schooler and the possibility of school fees for the other two children if we were unable to get them into the state system.

'Despite all our doubts, we were ready for an adventure and were all set to say yes when we found out that when the two years was up we'd need to get back to the UK under our own steam. It was then that we decided the numbers just didn't add up. We do really regret the decision, we think that we should have just said "sod it" and gone and worried about the consequences later. But we knew our kids wouldn't thank us if we spent the next five years recovering from a two-year adventure in another country.'

So in the end, Kate and her family decided not to make the move and she tried to forget the life she could have led and enjoy the one she had. But it wasn't an easy decision, and whichever way you go, you'll probably always have moments when you wonder what might have been if you had chosen the other route. The trick is to promise yourself not to regret your decision, whatever it is, and to ensure you completely embrace whichever direction your life is taking.

Telling others

So you've made the decision, you're getting used to the idea of turning your life upside down; now to tell all the other people in your life. For some, this is the hardest thing of all – especially when there are children or elderly parents involved. My granny almost stopped speaking to my mother when she told her we were moving to Lagos. There seemed to be no particularly good reason why this was any harder for her to deal with than the other postings my parents had taken us on; but sometimes a particular place or a particular time in someone's life can have a greater impact than you might be expecting, so don't be too surprised or upset if people's reactions aren't quite as positive as you were hoping.

Most people told me they were met with general support from the majority of their friends – and those who were taking off for the Caribbean were, unsurprisingly, given a particularly positive reaction. ('Great holidays for them,' said Ange, who moved to Jamaica with her husband Neil and their baby daughter Mollie.) However, the words 'disappointed' and 'sad' came up a lot in relation to one group of people – grandparents.

A first move abroad often coincides with the time a couple starts a family. If the woman (and it usually is the woman – although, of course, not always) is going to give up her career, it might as well be the time she's taking a few years off to have a baby or two. But for the grandparents who have been looking forward for such a long time to finally having grandchildren to play with, the announcement that you're taking those precious babies hundreds of miles away to an unknown or what could potentially be a dangerous country can be heart breaking. Add to this the fact that they might be getting quite elderly and in need of more care and you have a potentially very difficult situation.

This was certainly something that Jules found when she went to tell her mother that they were moving abroad: it was such a stressful discussion that she found herself having a rare nosebleed, moments after she got the words out that they were leaving. Then the second time they moved, she found it so hard to tell anyone that she bottled it all up – to the extent that her friends thought she must have some dreadful terminal illness!

But she sums up the thoughts of many when she says, 'My parents are in their 70s and the smiles and comforting words are wearing thin. They always insist they are happy for us and that they are glad we can have this experience, but as the years go by, I know that's not true anymore and I long to be home for them as much as for myself.'

Others found they faced a mixture of emotions when they told their nearest and dearest about their plans. Morwenna described how her dad, whose own career was an international one, was thrilled for them when they were first posted overseas – but at the same time he was sad to see them go, as they were taking his young and only grandson with them.

Like Morwenna's father, many have found the reaction of others does depend on how well travelled – or not – their friends and relations are.

Jenny's family have a military background and thought their move to America was a 'good idea to take every opportunity you can, with the thinking that you can always regret not taking opportunities more than the ones you do'. Her husband's family, on the other hand, had a very different mind-set and were 'definitely against it as they were taking their only grandchildren 6,000 miles away'.

It's a similar story with friends – those that have moved around themselves tend to be more supportive than those who have never even contemplated it. But sometimes, a negative reaction is the outward sign of inward jealousy – taking a decision to make such a life-changing move is something not everyone has the opportunity to do, and there are some people who might enjoy making you doubt your own decision.

Haylee, who moved to Islamabad a year or so before us, recalled how some of her friends in the UK felt. She said: 'They weren't exactly chuffed with us – they couldn't understand how we could uproot our children and live abroad, only to be uprooted three years down the line to come back to the UK…not only that but they couldn't understand how we could put ourselves and our children in danger and go to a posting like Islamabad.'

For some, the reactions to their news about moving is made all the more difficult by the fact that they had little choice in the matter. Adele's pilot husband was made redundant by the airline he flew for in the UK and then needed to take whatever job he could find in the middle of a recession-struck, shrinking market. It so happened that the sole job open to him was in Qatar – the only other option was for him to be out of work. However, despite it being a difficult decision in the first place, things were made worse by the reaction of family members who, according to Adele, didn't seem to realise that they really had no choice. 'They implied that he had chosen to go there, and still didn't seem to grasp that getting a job back in the UK wasn't possible...there was lots of tears and worries,' she said.

In some circumstances, the reaction to the news of a move overseas is perhaps more understandable. Chesney left everything she knew behind when she followed her partner to Mongolia – having never previously even left continental United States. 'Everyone thought I was crazy,' she recalled. 'Flying halfway round the world to Outer Mongolia by myself to pursue a relationship that may or may not work out was just nuts for everyone in my life, although I think that a lot of people thought that it was an incredibly brave thing to do as well.' Yes, Chesney, I think you get the award for bravery – and nuttiness!

The other important person or persons you will need to tell your news to pretty soon after you make the decision to go (or even before you make it) are your children. I deal more with this in the specific chapters on children, including hearing from some in their own words about life on the move. But it's worth stressing here that this can be the toughest call of all – especially if they are well settled and not expecting a sudden and total upheaval in their lives.

It's up to you to judge how much you should tell your children in advance of the posting becoming a definite – a lot will depend on them, their ages, whether you have moved before and how long you have lived in your present home. Generally, my advice would be for any child younger than say ten or eleven, is not to tell them anything until it's definite. What you really don't want to do is worry them needlessly (or get their hopes up – depending on where you are going/what sort of child you have). If they are older than this, you might want to involve them in the decision – again, this is totally up to you and whether you want to risk them being completely against the idea and then getting cross when you go ahead with it anyway.

For younger children, from around the age of five or six up to eleven, it's probably better to tell them as soon as you know yourself where and when you are going. This way, they'll have time to get used to the idea but as long as you're not expected to leave immediately, the actual event will still seem like such a long way away they won't panic too much when you first break the news.

Very young children don't need to be told at all until much nearer the leaving date – little children can't comprehend time in the same way as we can and will have no idea what 'next year' or even 'next month' actually means. It's better to drop the news into conversation every now and then, mentioning it more often the closer you get to when you leave, until it's something they accept as an on-going part of their lives (in a similar way to how you might get them used to the idea of a new sibling or starting school).

Finally, when the time comes to tell children the news, be ready with your 'weapons' in case they don't take the news well. Think of all the positive things about the country you will be moving to in advance. All the exciting things you will be able to do, all the adventures you'll have. If they've been pleading for a pet, perhaps this is the time to tell them you'll get one. And then hope they'll forget you said that (in our case – no chance! Although my elder daughter is still tossing up whether she would prefer a dog or a giant tortoise).

But if all else fails and your children do seem genuinely upset at the thought of leaving behind their school, their friends and everything they know, do take comfort in the fact that children – especially young children – get used to change a lot quicker than we do.

16

Assuming that you have made the decision that you definitely are moving whatever others say, how do you deal with negative reactions?

When it comes from grandparents who are understandably upset about you taking their precious grandchildren far from their reach, the answer is gently and with as much tact and sympathy as possible. Remind them that the world is a much smaller place these days thanks to the Internet, emails and things like Skype. Point out that you are likely to be home for holidays fairly regularly (if this is true) and will be able to spend extended periods with them when you are over. And that of course they can visit whenever they like (again, if this is true...if you really don't think you could cope with long visits from the in-laws, it's probably better to manage their expectations from the outset).

As far as everyone else is concerned, the negative reactions should be treated with the contempt they deserve. You might know what you're doing is crazy, scary and possibly even dangerous – but you don't need other people to tell you this. As Carole, a seasoned traveller who so far has accompanied her husband on postings to Tokyo, Berlin and Pretoria put it, 'I took very little notice of other people's reactions, to be frank – it was our life.'

Preparing to go

So you've made the decision to go, you've broken the news to your loved ones (and dealt with the fall out) – what now?

For some, the answer is not much, depending on how long you have between discovering that you're going and actually getting on the plane. In fact, it can be such a long time there can be a definite feeling of anti-climax as you wait for the day you can finally start packing.

Emily, moving to Vienna with her husband and two young sons, found one of the hardest things about the move was being left in limbo for so long: the process of applying and getting the job took about eighteen months. 'Then,' she added, 'when we told them we needed four months before we could move, they were grumpy that we were "taking so long"!'

We also hated being left in limbo after being evacuated from Islamabad – we knew we would be offered another posting but it took my husband's department months to find somewhere suitable. In the meantime, I felt like my entire life was on hold. The frustration of waiting, not knowing what the future held, was harder for me than the actual evacuation from Pakistan.

For others though, things can happen in much more of a rush. Sharon and her partner Mark, only had six weeks' notice for their first postings to Dhaka. For Sharon, who hadn't even decided whether to accompany her then boyfriend on his first overseas job with the Department for International Development (DfID), things were even more stressful as she had to sort out some pretty life-changing issues such as resigning from her job and selling her share in a house, all in a very short space of time.

But assuming you do have time to do at least a bit of research how is the best way to prepare?

For those lucky enough to have a trip funded or be able to fund it themselves, a pre-move recce to check out things like housing, schools and what is available in the local shops is invaluable.

Farah, who was posted to the Netherlands with her husband and children, said they were able to travel around with their relocation contacts who showed them different house and school opportunities. 'I felt very prepared after coming here and seeing what our possibilities might be,' she said about the trip.

Anabelle, who moved to Germany, said they were able to visit twice thanks to the proximity of their new home to where they were living (in the UK): 'I did find it useful to visit it, of course, although had it been further, I don't think I would have done it twice,' she said. 'I think nowadays with Google maps, the internet and other web tools, you can find so much information online it is easier. But no matter how many small visits you make, living there is nothing like what you imagine.'

If visiting in advance is an option for you, make a list of what you want to know before you go and, if possible, plan the trip to make sure you cover all bases. If the main reason to go is to find accommodation, factor in enough time to see plenty of houses – and if you can, book all the appointments before you get there. It's also really important to have a feel for what sort of things are avail-able on your budget and where the areas you either want – or really don't want – to live are. There's nothing worse than feeling like you have to make a rushed decision about something as impor-tant as where you are going to live.

One word of warning about visiting a country before moving their permanently – which also holds true if you're basing your decision on a previous holiday there – remember, living some-where is a very, very different experience to vacationing there.

'Never muddle tourism and immigration,' said Viktor, who has so far moved from his homeland in Russia to Kazakhstan, England and Saudi Arabia with his wife and sons. 'Indeed you will have an absolutely different impression about a country after a short visit and after being there a long time.'

Wise words indeed – even we, seasoned travellers, found it hard not to be overwhelmed by the beauty of St Lucia on our pre-posting visit. We managed to stay grounded in reality through the fact that we had both lived in the Caribbean before and knew that life there certainly wasn't a beach. But many a family have fallen foul of the lure of places like Australia after a back-packing trip in their twenties or watching those amazing 'So Where Are You?' ads, only to find that the problems you have at home tend to come with you. Although sometimes they are easier to deal with when the sun is shining and the sea is so blue!

Even if you aren't going to get the chance to visit but your partner is, ask them to take photos and write down everything they see each day. I wasn't able to visit Islamabad before our posting, since I had only just had our second daughter and the thought of taking them both all that way was too much to contemplate. (They both came with us when we went house-hunting in St Lucia – but they were older and it was a much easier country to take small children to.) But to make up for the fact that I wouldn't get the chance to help him house hunt or visit the school on the British High Commission compound, my husband kept an amazingly detailed diary of his time in Islamabad on his visit, which was a huge help in imagining what life would be like for us when we got out there. He also walked around the compound with a video camera, showing us things like the playground and swimming pools – making talking about the move much easier with our then nearly-three-year-old daughter. These days, of course, you could use FaceTime or Skype in much the same way, to really make your new home come alive for those not with you.

However, for most people, a pre-post visit is a luxury neither they nor their employers can afford. So where to turn for information?

In my parents' day, pre-internet, the best option was to speak to people who had recently returned from living in that country – and this is still an excellent way to get a proper feel for the place and to ask all those questions niggling at the back of your mind. Of course nowadays you don't have to wait for someone to actually return from the country to speak to them – the magical power of the telephone, Skype or the Internet makes it easy to contact people actually living in the country.

I, for example, gained some very useful information about bringing a baby to Pakistan from the wife of one of my husband's future colleagues. Others tap into their predecessor and their partner – although it's better to find someone in a similar situation to yourself (e.g. has small children/older children/no children; is working/not working etc.) to get the best idea of what life will be like.

If you are lucky enough to have access to a post report, especially an up-to-date one, then that is another obvious source of information. The Foreign Office have internal reports for every city they post people to – although they vary in terms of accuracy and detail. But for everyone else, you can also access online reports at

Tales From a Small Planet, the excellent website set up by US Foreign Service Spouses (http://www.talesmag.com/). Books, including guidebooks and fiction, are all useful for your research. And more and more of us are using Google Maps as a way to 'virtually' visit locations before we visit in real-life. But of course in this day and age, the one place most people turn to straight away when they hear where they might be posted are expat websites, forums and blogs on the Internet.

Over the course of writing this book I have found countless numbers of blogs and websites dedicated to the expat experience. I have listed a few of the more 'general' ones below, which might appeal to a wide variety of people, wherever they are going and I will list more in each chapter. All of these links, as well as links to other expat blogs, can be found on my own blogsite which can be found at http://expatpartnersurvival.com/. But my best advice, especially as the Internet is such a fast-moving place, is simply to type the word 'expat' or 'trailing spouse' or 'living overseas' into your chosen search engine along with the country or city where you are going and see what comes up.

Despite the enormous wealth of information out there, there are still those who would rather not know too much before they move. 'I tend not to research a country as I prefer to remain open minded and not reliant on other people's views,' said Carole.

And Sharon said she preferred to remain 'blissfully naïve' for their first posting, 'happier to trust that everything would be okay'.

This, of course, is easier when it's just the two of you: the amount of preparation and planning you do tends to increase with the number of dependents (children, pets...) you are taking with you. But certainly, with the amount of online information now available, it would be hard to imagine someone moving abroad with absolutely NO idea about what to expect...

Hopefully by the time you've read this far you're starting to feel a little more prepared for your move. You've told everyone you're going (or at least, those that need to know), you've done your research, made some online contacts, perhaps read up on a few travel opportunities. You're feeling good about this, you think you'll actually be able to do it. In the next chapter, I will start looking at the practical side of the move itself – and encourage you to start making a very long list.

Useful Websites to Look at Before You Leave

NOTE: These links and all the links throughout this book can be found on my blogsite expatpartnersurvival.com under the book links tab. I will try and keep them as up to date as possible but please let me know if you find any of the links are broken.

UK Foreign Office travel advice: always worth keeping an eye on, as well as checking for information about things like driving abroad, renewing your passport etc.: https://www.gov.uk/foreign-travel-advice

General travel advice to read up on before you go anywhere: https://www.gov.uk/knowbeforeyougo

And for more info from the UK Government about moving or living abroad: https://www.gov.uk/browse/abroad

Specific 'living-in' guides from the UK Government for a number of different countries (including some of the more exotic ones, such as Afghanistan and Zimbabwe) https://www.gov.uk/government/collections/overseas-living-in-guides

Tales from a Small Planet: A fantastic resource of information, stories, post reports, school reports and more, initially started by US foreign service spouses but now used and contributed to by a huge variety of expats: http://www.talesmag.com/

Britishexpats.com: a whole smorgasbord of advice from fellow expats: http://britishexpats.com/

Country reports from the Economist magazine's Intelligence Unit: http://country.eiu.com/All

A list of easy to download books about living overseas, in various different locations: http://www.escapefromamerica.com/category/ebooks-for-expats/

Destination guides for some of the most popular expat countries and cities including Singapore, Dubai, Shanghai, South Africa and Tokyo: http://www.expatandoffshore.com/city-guides

The CIA World Factbook: lots of useful information about (almost) every country in the world, including facts about history, politics, the economic situation, transportation, communication: https://www.cia.gov/library/publications/the-world-factbook/

Country guides, great info, columns written by people like ME! : http://www.expatfocus.com/

A website offering a whole host of useful information for the expat in locations around the world. Include specific information for the 'trailing spouse': http://www.global-xpats.com/

Robin Pascoe is one of the 'expert expat's' who has been around and knows a thing or two about this peripatetic life. She has written some books and also made some videos for YouTube: http://www.expatexpert.com/

Need some help with relocation? This website offers coaching or mentoring in cross-cultural training, as well as repatriation assistance: http://www.expatknowhow.com/menus/main.asp

A website dedicated to Brits moving abroad – includes information like wage comparisons in different countries, job information, petrol price comparisons etc.: http://www.byebyeblighty.com/1/

The Telegraph's comprehensive expat section:
http://www.telegraph.co.uk/expat/

More support for what this site calls 'smart expats':
http://expatriateconnection.com/

This website promises that you will 'feel at home abroad: fast':
http://www.expatinfodesk.com/

The 'adventurers guide to moving, living and working abroad':
http://myinternationaladventure.com/

More country guides, written by expats in the locations:
http://www.expatarrivals.com/article/expat-city-and-country-guides

Magazine for expats: http://globallivingmagazine.com/

Lots of 'top 5' hints and tips for expat living:
https://expatexplorer.hsbc.com/hintsandtips/lists

Lots more resources for expat 'wives':
http://areyouanexpatwife.com/recent/

Sign up for the destination you're moving to. I get to see lots of pictures of wild animals every time I log in because I've joined the South Africa section: http://www.expat-blog.com/

CHAPTER TWO

The Move

'We have always taken everything – mostly to help the children feel at home. As the years have gone by, I hate how moving makes you acutely aware of how much junk you accumulate and "can't live without" – but my son can burst into tears just looking at his baby photos so I think we have done the right thing allowing them to have all their familiar belongings and memories around them.' Jules, moved three times.

'I take everything to make sure it feels like home, and add things along the way. I like to think that my house has an eclectic mix but others may think it's just cluttered.' Heather, two kids, two dogs, getting divorced.

'I wish we had taken everything. Because we had intended to be here for only two years, we left a lot of stuff behind. Now that we're going to be here longer, we're missing most of it!' Emily, two sons aged two and four. Just signed up for another two years in Vienna.

'I wish I hadn't taken so much crap with me! I mean, why on earth did I think I needed two boxes of geological specimens…? Yeah, rocks!' Carole, on her third move.

So, you know you're definitely going, you've researched your destination, found out what you need to take...now is the time to get planning. And for most people this means lists, lists and more lists. But in this chapter I will also look at some of the practicalities of an overseas move, including ensuring you start your planning early enough, what to pack – and what to leave behind, and where to find more information about things like taking your car abroad and renting out your home.

How much preparation you do depends on a few things:

- how long you're going for;
- how many of you are going;
- how much support you have (from your partner or otherwise); and
- where exactly you are going.

A short hop across the channel to France will probably take a little less planning than a move to a country where very little is available to buy and it might be a while before you get the chance to replenish stocks. But wherever you are going, and for however long the posting is, one thing is for sure: you will have to be very, very organised.

There are plenty of websites, experts, relocation companies, agents and consultants who can help you with your move, but whether you use them or not probably depends on how much time you have to do the work yourself, as well as how much you can afford (a lucky few will have experts provided by their company). Many people I spoke to were very pleased they used a relocation specialist – certainly they can be invaluable for those who aren't moving with a large company or Government department and have to do all the work themselves.

Unfortunately, the Catch 22 is that often the countries where you really need extra assistance – those in the developing world or more remote places where it might be harder to find information over the Internet for example – are those that are unlikely to have relocation companies available at the other end. However, they should be able to offer you advice, support and all sorts of extras before you go – some companies even offer spouses things like pre-move counselling and help with looking for a job in your new location. Other things they offer include help with selling or renting your house, help storing your furniture, school searches, short-term accommodation, language training and sorting out visas. It goes without saying that the more you can afford, the more you can get – but certainly for those who have absolutely no other support whatsoever and especially those who are up to their eyeballs in other things (work, children, international modelling career...whatever), their services can be worth their weight in gold.

Farah, who used the services of a relocation company to help in advance of their move, used them again for the actual move: 'The relocation contacts that we have worked with are amazing,' she said. 'They assisted us with every detail – down to ordering the necessary furniture (beds, sofa, kitchen table) and their delivery prior to our arrival. They even had a few staples in the kitchen for us and have been more than willing to help with doctors, cleaning help, and so much more. We never would have had half as smooth an experience without them.'

So some people will have the luxury of a company to help them with their move, others will get support from their partner's employers. But what about those who have to do it more or less on their own?

You might fall into this category if you're moving under your own steam – perhaps your partner has their own business or is moving overseas without a 'package'. Or their employers might just not have the funds to pay for you to have that sort of support. Whatever the reason, now is the time to get a piece of paper and a pen and sit down to make your first list.

Some of us are born list-makers. I, for example, seem to make lists for everything. I am even one of those annoying people who writes things on lists that I've already done just for the satisfaction of seeing that it's been accomplished. Others, however, prefer to live life a little more on the hoof. Unfortunately, an international move probably isn't one of those things that can be done without at least some planning. So if you are one of those unorganised types you might have to act out of character just a bit. Go on, get that pen and paper and start to jot down everything that comes into your head that needs doing before you leave for your new life abroad.

Again, there are plenty of websites that can help you here and in fact those relocation companies I have already mentioned are quite useful at pointing you in the direction of all the things you need to get done before you go. The best place to start is with some timescales – which obviously depends how long you have until you go – but perhaps your list should look something like my list below. And, by the way, when I say 'you', I mean a collective 'you' – you, your partner as well as any more support you can muster. This should be a joint effort and a good place to start, once you've written your list, is by divvying up the tasks.

Approximately six months before D (departure) Day

- If you own your own house, decide whether you want to sell or rent it out while you're away; contact estate agents and decide who you are going to use; arrange the timescale for them to let out/sell your home.
- Start shopping around for international movers and book them in (if this isn't being arranged by your partner's employers or relocation company). Don't forget they will need to come and do an estimate of how much it will cost to move you and all your belongings abroad.
- Identify and book flights (if flying).
- Check if you need vaccinations and if so book these.
- If you need to find schools, start looking as soon as you know you are going – including contacting any you are interested in to find if they have a waiting list (more on this in the chapter on schools).
- If you are taking a pet, find out about how to transport them (again, more in the pets chapter).
- Check your passports aren't about to expire and have at least a year to run; do you need visas? Who will be sorting these?
- If you're taking a car, contact DVLA (or your local car licensing authority if not in the UK) and fill in all the necessary documents. Check which importation

documents you need, as well as tax, insurance etc. at the other end.

- Contact HMRC to find out if you need to keep paying National Insurance contributions while you are overseas. (For non-British readers, check if there are any financial contributions you will need to keep paying in your home country).

Approximately three months before D-Day

- Start thinking about what you want to take, what you want to get rid of, what you want to store etc. This doesn't have to be a detailed list but should at least give you some idea of what you need to think about in terms of storage rental e.g. for furniture. See below for tips on what to bring and what to leave.

- Also start thinking about what you are going to send ahead (e.g. by ship), what you will leave until nearer the time (air freight) and what you will take with you on the plane. Make sure none of the important stuff – which should include things like documents, medication, glasses, certificates, children's favourite toys/blankets etc. and possibly a stress ball or two – goes on the wrong pile. Also don't do what one of my friends did and pack the air beds they were all meant to sleep on, on their last night, into the shipping container.

- If you need to buy much to take with you (e.g. toiletries etc.) start buying now. Every time you do a shop, buy a favourite shampoo, or suntan cream, or packet of tampons or whatever it is you don't think you'll be able to get at your destination. Of course this very much depends on where you are going (some countries will sell everything you need) and how much you can take with you.

- Start packing! I realise three months is a long time, especially for those who like to throw everything together at the last moment, but you will be surprised at how much time this can take – especially if this is your first move and you have a lot of stuff to clear out/get rid of. Or if you have small children you need to work around.

- If you're working, give in your notice. If you have children and they are at school, tell the school you'll be leaving. If possible, ask for a report that can be sent to the new school so that they are placed in the appropriate class. Tell anyone else who needs telling (cleaners? clubs? mother-in-law?). Hopefully by this point it will be too late for anyone to try and persuade you not to go.

- Arrange for your post to be forwarded through the Royal Mail and start informing all and sundry of your address change – banks, subscriptions, any charity you contribute to. In the old days, I would have included friends and family but as everyone communicates by email, text, Facebook, FaceTime etc. these days, you probably don't need to bother, especially if you are going somewhere where the post isn't mightily reliable. If you are not yet sure what your address will be, or if you are moving somewhere without a reliable post system, can you use a PO Box address in the meantime, or a family member?

- Do you need to open a bank account in your country of destination? Is this something you need to do now or can it wait until you arrive? Sometimes it's useful to do it in advance so you can transfer money across; sometimes it's not worth it at all if you can still use your UK bank account in the new country.

- Do you need references for anything in your new country – e.g. accommodation, bank accounts etc.? If so, whom can you get these from? It usually needs to be someone you have known for a number of years so it's unlikely to be someone you have just met.

- Arrange dental and health check-ups. Unless you are going somewhere where this will be easier and cheaper than in the UK/your home country. Inform your doctor's surgery that you will be moving but ask if you can remain on their list as sometimes it is hard to get back into a surgery once you have left. This is particularly useful if you intend to return to your home country on a regular – e.g. annual – basis as this is a good time to go in and get any niggles checked over.

One-two months before D-Day
- Start thinking about selling your car (if you are going to). You also need to think about how to get to the airport – are you going to take a taxi? You are likely to be taking a lot of suitcases with you so the logistics can sometimes be quite complicated.
- Contact your insurers e.g. car insurers, breakdown services, house content insurers etc. Can you get some of your money back? Also check if you can get a letter from your car insurers telling you how many years of no-claims you have.
- Do you have travel insurance? If not, get some now. Make sure it covers everything you need. Including things like dangerous sports – that is, if you intend to do any.
- Cancel your TV licence and contact your utility companies. Arrange for them to stop billing you from the day you leave. If you are letting your house, make sure you get the bills transferred to the new occupants or the letting company. Do the same with Council Tax.
- Back up your computers onto a hard drive. Keep that somewhere safe. Or keep them all in a cloud storage system such as Dropbox. For the REALLY important stuff (I don't know what – perhaps first editions of famous books or a personally signed copy of an original Take That poster) there are also companies who keep all your documents safe for you and forward them on wherever you are in the world, e.g. Vital Documents: http://www.vitaldocuments.co.uk/

- If you're sending anything ahead by ship, make sure you know EXACTLY what is going where. If necessary, pack everything you know will be coming with you in separate suitcases and put them well out of the way (in your car? A neighbour's house?) on the day the packers come. Buy some Bach Rescue Remedy and try not to get too worried when you see the packers wrapping your priceless Wedgewood dinner set in one flimsy piece of newspaper. They know what they're doing. You hope.
- Make sure arrangements at the other end are in place. Will you have someone to meet you at the airport? Somewhere to stay? A car? Do you also have money for those first few days – or can you get that when you arrive?
- Make sure you have got your head around the local currency at your destination. If possible, get a feel for how much things should cost. This might sound silly but it's very easy to be ripped-off by an unscrupulous taxi driver in the first few days after you arrive because you haven't worked out how many noughts there should be on the money note he's asking you for. You don't want to be handing out the equivalent of £60 instead of £6…
- If you're having a leaving party, arrange it. Or hope someone else arranges a surprise one! It never happened to us...

The week of departure
- If necessary, move into a hotel or in with family members for the last few days. You might need to be around for the handover of the house, to check the final clean etc. is done. But it's better to get everything out before the day of departure.
- Buy any last minute things for the journey and if necessary the first few days after arrival. If you've got children, think particularly about what they might need.

- Finish packing for the journey. Unpack to get at the thing you really need right at the bottom of your case. Re-pack. Repeat.
- Start eating everything in the fridge – don't forget the freezer. Drink all your wine. Why not make it the party you didn't manage to arrange? You could give away your houseplants as going-away presents.

The day of departure

- Depending on how you're getting to your destination, you might find the best way to leave is to spend the last night at an airport hotel. This way you can say all your goodbyes the day before you actually go. Leaving for an overseas posting can be a deeply emotional experience; it can be easier to say goodbye to your nearest and dearest, get in your car to the airport and start the first day of your new life feeling clear and fresh – looking forwards instead of back.
- But before you go make sure you do a last minute check. Passports, papers, special toys or blankets, dummies, contact lenses and glasses, medicine, small children...most things can be bought at the airport or at the other end if they are forgotten, but a few things can't. Remember your list – check, check and check again.
- Finally, deep breath, in the car, wave goodbye and hope you don't have to make an embarrassing U-turn halfway down the motorway because someone's forgotten their passport.

A note on planning the move

One thing I have realised over the years is how much easier it is for all of us if my husband goes on ahead and gets things set up (phone, car, Internet connection) at the other end before we arrive. It also allows him to have his handover period with his predecessor without having to worry about settling us in to the new country. This is now possible because our children are older and the thought of flying with them alone no longer fills me with dread, but when they were younger we preferred to all travel out together. If you do like the idea of sending your partner on ahead then the last few points in the list above will be slightly different and you may need to think through the logistics differently. It's up to you whether you think the positives outweigh the negatives – but it's certainly something we'll be doing when we move to Pretoria.

What to take? What to leave? What to wish you'd never packed?

When it comes to what to take with you, everyone has his or her own opinion. So basically it's up to you and your baggage allowance. Many people start out on their first posting, young, childless and having not yet accumulated all the rubbish that you seem to gather as life goes on, with just a couple of suitcases and a carry-on bag.

Anthea, whose first overseas move was to join her French husband in Morocco, said none of her subsequent moves were as straightforward as that initial one: 'It was dead easy,' she recalled. 'I arrived with two suitcases and that was it!'

But others stuff their shipping container with every item they own, terrified to leave anything behind just in case they suddenly wish they'd brought it the moment they get to their new country. Of course, what you leave and what you do with it also depends on whether you have anywhere to store it or what your budget is for storage costs. Or whether you are willing to get rid of a lot of stuff. But my advice would still be to take more rather than less. You can always get rid of some of it the next time you move...

So what do people recommend you don't leave behind?

Many of the people I spoke to whilst researching this subject talked about things that hold memories, especially for the children – so photos, bedding, toys, all their familiar belongings.

Alex, who has lived abroad half her life, recommends a 'treasure box' for each child to keep their special items, souvenirs from their travels.

Others talk about making sure you've got anything you might need for special hobbies – Sandra, who moved from the UK to Switzerland, regrets not taking her 'craft stuff': 'I gave it away thinking I wouldn't have time for it here; how wrong was I!' she said.

And Judy, whose first posting was to Azerbaijan, regrets not taking more knitting wool.

Rachel, from New Zealand, wishes she had bought more appliances and her coffee machine, as well as more medications. She might only have been moving to France where you could reasonably assume you could get everything, but sometimes only exactly what you can get in your home country will do.

In fact, one piece of advice from Louise, currently living in Portugal, is to take what represents home with you. She says, 'If you're living in rented accommodation then having your favourite photos/pictures/bedding ornaments makes it feel like yours...and like home.' Although she also advises being a bit selective. 'We took books and have lugged many of them around since. Pick a few favourites and leave the rest behind.'

Other people speak about taking special food that you can only get at home and yes, I have been guilty of taking jars of Patak's curry pastes and Heinz Baked Beans back to the Caribbean from the UK. British tea bags are another favourite and in the days when we could use the diplomatic bag, we were known to smuggle in sausages and Cheddar cheese, as well as asking anyone visiting with similar privileges to do the same. It's amazing what you miss when you can't get it – I would have carried in fish and chips if I'd had the chance, and any Jamaican flying back to the UK after a visit home is likely to be carrying a big bag of frozen patties with them.

But Josine, who has lived in Singapore, China and Taiwan, has another piece of advice. She thinks you should take as little as possible with you to force you out in your new country to search for things that you need. Certainly, one of the things I've always enjoyed about moving to a new country is searching out items in the local shops and the sense of satisfaction when I finally found what I needed. Although, like everything, this really depends on where you are going – it's probably going to be a pretty hopeless quest to look for pork products in a Muslim country, and any clothes over a (UK) size ten are notoriously hard to find in places like Singapore.

So before you go mad and pack everything you might possibly need and a lot you almost certainly won't, it's definitely worth checking to see what you can and can't get at your destination.

If you didn't get the chance to visit before moving and weren't able to check out the shops personally, ask your partner's colleagues, check out forums and websites or anyone who might know what's worth bringing. It's also worth thinking about the cost of things at your destination; how much do items such as toys, clothes and books cost? How much is worth buying in advance? We took a year's worth of nappies to St Lucia – which might have seemed slightly OTT until you saw the extortionate price of disposables on the island. Other things we never regretted taking were lots of surge protectors, adaptors and multi-plug extension leads. Plug sockets in other countries aren't always as plentiful as you are used to.

Amanda, who has two young girls and whose husband works for a technology company, regretted getting rid of the small things – like her children's kites – that wouldn't have taken any space but meant they had to buy them all over again; particularly gutting because everything was so much more expensive.

Off you go

You've bought everything you need; you've packed your crate for the sea freight, your trunk for the airfreight, your suitcases and your carry-on bag. You've held your farewell party, given away your houseplants, sent your dog on ahead and checked and rechecked that your passports are up-to-date. You've organised your taxi to the airport, handed over the keys for your house to the estate agent and watched your tearful child say their final good-byes to their teachers and friends. Your lists are all ticked, your final preparations complete. Your new life awaits…and in the next chapter, we'll look at what happens when you first arrive in your new country, including how to cope during those early, potentially terrifying weeks.

Useful Websites to Look at While You Are Planning the Move

A comprehensive website covering all aspects of the move, including lists, lists and more lists! In fact just an all-round fabulous website: http://definingmoves.com/

UK government website detailing paperwork you may need to consider before you move: https://www.gov.uk/moving-or-retiring-abroad

Lots of pre-move info from the US State department: http://www.state.gov/m/fsi/tc/c49333.htm

Store your important documents safely if you don't want to take them with you: http://www.vitaldocuments.co.uk/

Lots of different relocation packages: http://www.relocateyourself.com/main/

Arrival and the Early Days

'We arrived on the Friday and on the Monday we took the girls to school for their first day and then my husband went off to work. Talk about feeling lonely. I hardly left the apartment for the first few weeks. I cried a lot – wanted to go home. Felt totally useless as I went from doing everything to doing nothing as we had a full time maid who took over all the chores. Gradually though I found my feet and my only regret was not making the move overseas sooner, especially when I saw how happy our children were now that we were a whole family again.' Lesley, Indonesia, Qatar, Saudi Arabia and Kenya.

'Steve and I flew back to Dubai together (he'd been in the UK for the weekend for a friend's wedding). We landed in Dubai at 6am. It was bastard hot and the taxi queue (for which read: scrum) was massive. In the taxi (by now both in a bad mood) Steve got a call from some random guy telling him that his bank had delivered him Steve's credit card in error and what should he do? Cue: massive argument with the bank who denied any liability, the weasels. By the time we reached the apartment we were both pretty stressed. The apartment was empty apart from our suitcases and some really horrible rental furniture. Steve showered and went to work, still glowering. I had been planning to go and explore, but totally lost my nerve, curled up in bed and stayed there until mid-afternoon. Not a great start!' Rachel, who subsequently moved to Hong Kong where things went a little more smoothly.

Lesley and Rachel's experiences pretty much sum up the first few days, weeks or possibly months for many trailing spouses: the overwhelming loneliness when your partner walks out the door for work, the isolation, the feeling of being a spare part.

This is normal – totally normal – and it WILL get better.

In this chapter, I will be looking at more early-days experiences, including what it's like to live in temporary accommodation, why it's a good idea not to arrive at the start of the summer holidays, how does that first day feel and where exactly do you meet people? In some cases, things will improve very rapidly. In others, you may never feel really settled. But for almost everyone I have ever met or spoken to, as well as from my own experiences, there is nothing as difficult as the early days.

In writing this book I have been struck by the similarities between moving overseas and having your first baby. One of my other jobs has been as an antenatal teacher (a good, convenient portable career option) and in our classes we discuss things like expectation versus reality, post natal depression, communication between partners and how difficult the first few weeks can be, but how generally things do start to improve once you know what you are doing.

The same could be said for moving abroad: your pre-move excitement can come crashing down the moment reality hits; the stress of the move and living in a completely new place can lead to depression as well as culture shock; you really do need to keep talking to your partner; and yes, things will get better once you've met a few people, know your way round a bit and have sorted things out such as your accommodation and transportation.

I've had many experiences of moving overseas, and each has been very different. As a child I remember the excitement, the wonder of a new place, of exploring houses and gardens, bagging rooms and discovering terrifying creatures sheltering in abandoned corners (in Venezuela, this included a whole family of cockroaches in a bedroom cupboard; in Cameroon, huge lizards the size of small dragons had us chase them through the house).

Later on I moved by myself to Jamaica; outwardly I coped but I internalized the stress to the extent that I ended up seeing a doctor with breathing problems and dizziness. The loneliness of a single-ton moving overseas should never be underestimated but at least I went into the office every day and soon found colleagues to spend evenings and weekends with. The move to Islamabad was something else altogether.

We made the massive mistake of moving in the summer holidays. Without really thinking this through, what we hadn't realised was that pretty well every other expat family was elsewhere – mostly back in Europe or wherever their home country was, escaping the cruel summer heat. And hot it certainly was – leaving the cool air-conditioned interior of our house was like stepping into the centre of one of the tandoor ovens the local Pakistanis baked their delicious breads in. It was too hot to do anything for the bulk of the day. Even taking the children swimming, had I been able to manage two on my own, was too much of a risk for their still-pale skin. There was a small play park on the diplomatic compound where we lived, but again apart from briefly in the early morning or evening, it was a no-go area unless you wanted to risk heat stroke. I was trapped – stuck indoors all day with a very bored two-year-old and a baby.

Of course, things were made worse by the fact that our heavy baggage took weeks to catch up with us – so we were reliant on the few toys we had brought in our suitcases and anything the one family left on the compound when we first arrived could lend us. All I can say is, thank goodness for Peppa Pig DVDs!

Like me, Farah, who moved to the Netherlands with her partner and three young sons, said she felt 'overwhelmed' in the first few days after arrival. 'Without toys, books or distractions, those first few days were miserable,' she said. 'We still didn't have our proper coats and hats to go outside – so I felt more than stuck and extremely resentful of (her partner's) ability to just get up in the morning and go out to work.'

But it's not just lack of toys for the children that makes the pre-heavy baggage days difficult. Warren found his and his partner's apartment in Dhaka to be depressingly drab and miserable without their own belongings. 'With no natural light, the white walls appeared slightly grey, especially with no paintings, photos, ornaments, crockery, glassware or books to brighten and warm them up,' Warren remembered. 'Such a difference when we finally had the pictures to put up on the walls!'

Sue, who has lived in Madrid and the US with her husband and boys, made the same mistake as we did by making the transition during the summer holidays. 'We actually arrived at both posts at the beginning of the summer holidays…we didn't know anyone and had lots of time on our hands but didn't know where to go,' she said. 'It would have been better to go just as school was starting so the kids don't get bored and could start making friends straight away.'

And from Emily, in Austria with her husband and young sons: 'It was the single hardest part of our time here, no question. Once we'd been here six weeks or so, once we had our permanent apartment and then when our stuff arrived from home, things got SO much easier.'

Emily's experience highlights another reason why those early days can be so difficult: temporary accommodation.

We humans like our own homes, we like to live in familiar surroundings and feel relaxed in our own space. However, when you know the place you are in is not permanent, it's very hard to relax. It's okay for a short time, when it still feels a bit like a holiday. But when days turn into weeks and even into months, you can start to get really sick of the room service club sandwiches or the soul-less rented apartment atmosphere.

Finding permanent accommodation is stressful, but it's also worth getting right. And this can take time. Time that really is not much fun for the partner left at home, as Sharon remembers from one of her postings: 'When we went to Rwanda I had been told we would be going straight into our predecessor's house – so as a result didn't bother to pack and take UAF (Unaccompanied Air Freight) believing we'd be in our house, with our baggage, in a matter of days.

'As it was, the office decided they were going to let that house go and as a result, after we arrived, I learnt we had to find a new home and would face the prospect of spending over six weeks in a hotel room. Me, in one room with no books, no English language TV, no car, no means of getting any of those things or just getting about and FOR SIX WEEKS...

'Having thought I had learnt my lesson, the next posting was Jamaica. THIS time I made sure I hired a car in the first few days and got myself mobile. Unfortunately, the office had decided to pack Mark's induction schedule with trips around the region: a two week tour of the Caribbean for one. So there I was, in a hotel room, in a strange (and dangerous) city, completely on my own this time – albeit with a car – but with nowhere to go and no one to visit. In both cases, if someone had just told us of their plans BEFORE we arrived, I could have (and would have gladly) stayed on in the UK for the extra weeks and joined Mark at a later date. But I wasn't even given that option.'

Lessons learnt here are: try and find out in advance where you will be living, but plan for all eventualities. Make sure you have as much as possible to do during the time when you will be stuck somewhere that possibly won't even be your permanent home, without most of your possessions, for what could be weeks at a time. Double, or triple this if you have children (will your early accommodation have WiFi? If not – download, download, download while you have the chance).

So you're in your temporary accommodation, with none of your worldly goods and no means of getting around. How much worse can it get? Well, for many people, the very lowest point of their early weeks, if not their entire posting, is when their partner first leaves them to go to work.

In a way, this is the whole crux of this book, its whole *raison d'etre*.

This is the point when your and your partner's lives divide or, indeed, when your old life ends and your new one begins. Up until this point, you have more or less been in it together (depending on circumstances; some partners do fly ahead leaving the packing up to their other half); it's been a shared adventure. If you're lucky and/or organised you will have arrived with some time to explore your new destination together – a week is lovely, a few days are great, even a weekend is better than nothing. But eventually the time comes when he or she puts on their work clothes, kisses you goodbye and makes their merry way off to their world of work. Leaving you on your own.

Jules, whose two children are now on their third language, described the feeling: 'On our second move, my partner went to work quite quickly. I did indeed feel abandoned and alone in a foreign country…it just gets harder every time but of course for him (her partner), he steps into work and is in a familiar situation very quickly, leaving him unable to understand why the rest of the family are floundering behind him.'

Angela, who moved to Kingston with her husband and baby daughter, also remembers the feeling of being left out: 'Although Neil was introduced to everyone, no-one seemed interested in Molly and me. There was only one other family with a young child already in post. Even though Molly and I had come out with Neil, I didn't feel as if anyone thought I might need support during those initial few weeks.'

One of the dangers in this period is that resentment will build up between you and your partner (I go into more detail about relationships in a separate chapter dedicated to the subject). He or she may not understand the strength of your feelings, especially as many people try to hide this from their other half.

Hilary, living in a rural part of Holland, said: 'I felt lost. Lonely, bored, isolated and neglected. It took him six months to ask me how I was feeling about being abroad and our marriage nearly didn't survive. I felt like a square peg in a round hole for a long time.'

You might be worried that they have enough on their plate, especially as they are likely to be starting a new job and trying to settle in with new colleagues. But your feelings matter, your happiness is absolutely paramount to this posting being a success and problems generally are made easier by sharing them.

You might not feel you want to burden your partner with your emotions but often in the very early days there just isn't anyone else to talk to. So please do talk to him or her, tell them how you are feeling and make sure they understand that you're not necessarily expecting an instant solution but hopefully you will at least get a bit more sympathy. Even when you're posted to a beautiful place like St Lucia, with its white beaches and abundant swimming pools, those early days can be very, very tough. I know because I did it – as a second posting (as the trailing spouse), I was far more ready for it than I was when we went to Islamabad; but nevertheless I still had a hard time for the first few weeks. But what got me through was knowing that it would get better – eventually.

For many, things begin to improve when you start getting to know a few people. This might happen straight away – especially if you are lucky enough to have a specific person designated to look after you on arrival, or if you have been canny and made contact with potential friends in advance of arriving (through forums, for example, or just through personal contacts). For many others though it might not happen for a good while, or it might take a long time to find anyone you really 'click' with.

I've always thought arriving in a new country is a bit like starting university. You spend your first six months or so madly making friends with anyone who will have you, and the next six months trying to shake some of them off (although I should add that I have good friends today that I met both in my first few weeks as a student and also in the very early days as an expat in various different postings). For this reason, it's no bad thing if you want to take things a little slower. I think it's important to know that you will, eventually, make friends – very good friends, probably lifelong friends (now that we can keep up with each other on Facebook or by email). If you can stand to be a bit lonely at the beginning, your patience will pay off and you will meet people in the most unexpected places. I met my best St Lucian friend at the local swimming centre where my daughter's took lessons. But most of us are naturally social creatures and you will almost certainly be looking for someone – anyone! – to talk to in your first few weeks. So where do you go?

Having children certainly helps. Many of the spouses I spoke to said their early friends were made at the school gates. Shirley, currently in Paris, explained that her first posting was made much easier by having primary-age children, 'so contacts were made in the school playground…it's much more difficult when the children are older or have left home completely'.

And Carole, whose first posting was to Japan when her daughter was still relatively young, really noticed the difference when they made their second move to Berlin, saying, 'It's much easier with young kids; when they reach the age when they go to school independently, you've few opportunities to meet school parents. I spent several days lurking around the school gates (just when Rhiannon started school at first) saying hello to anyone who passed – not one single person responded…'

Being pregnant or having a very small baby with you can be another way to strike up new friendships. I certainly remember the first conversation I had with my friend Jelena at a school new-parents evening in St Lucia was because she was so heavily pregnant she looked like she was going to go into labour at any moment (and not coping well with the extreme heat – having had my first pregnancy in Jamaica I was very sympathetic).

Belinda, who moved to the States with her German husband Rudi, found she was very unprepared for how difficult it would be to meet people locally, believing naively that a shared language (of sorts) would make it relatively easy to make friends. She said, 'In the end, I met all my friends through antenatal classes and baby groups… I think I would have really struggled if I hadn't been pregnant/had children.'

Marianne, another of my St Lucia friends, agreed that it was much easier to meet people when you have children. 'My landlady got information for me for the local baby group, which I joined straight away,' she said.

I remember my mother telling me about a woman, who herself was the mother of the girl who would become my best friend in the Philippines, accosting her in the supermarket simply because she had an English accent and a gaggle of kids following her around (me and my brothers). Similar tactics were deployed by another of my St Lucia friends, Kirsty, who set up the baby group Marianne talks about above.

But although children can help you to meet people, moving when you've just had a baby is never going to be an easy thing. The immediate post natal period can be an extremely stressful and disorientating stage of your life at the best of times, let alone with you've just upped sticks and moved half way round the globe.

Olga, who moved to the Netherlands, found things more difficult because she had a new baby: 'It was hard because I was on my own and she cried a lot. I didn't want to reach out for help because I felt I could do all of it on my own…luckily later I contacted expat organisations and found friends, but I was pretty much on my own except for two friends I found via day care and a language class.'

Others who don't, or didn't, have children talk about the special kind of isolation that comes from not having any obvious place to meet others in the same situation, especially those who can't or choose not to work. Rachel, who described her arrival in Dubai at the start of this chapter, turned up with a few friends-of-friends contacts to chase up but little else. 'Despite the massive number of expats, I found meeting like-minded people very hard,' she said. 'I think the problem was that I was in my mid-thirties, but didn't have kids and wasn't working so I didn't really have a medium through which to meet people. We did make friends but our social life was never especially large or solid. In the week, I spent most of the day alone, which I was fine with as I am a bit of a lone wolf. But some trailing spouses…found it very depressing.'

Certainly early support is so important, whether it comes from informal or formal sources. In Islamabad, we were lucky enough to have two Community Liaison Officers (CLOs) to help us in our early days, check we were okay, show us the shops, introduce us to other families.

Haylee, who was in Pakistan at the same time as us with her husband and three children, remembers how helpful this was: 'She showed me where the local shops were, gave me the names and numbers of people to call that had similar aged children. We were very well supported by her.'

By contrast when we arrived in St Lucia there was no formal support in place but luckily, as it was my second posting as a spouse and with children, I was better prepared for the isolation and loneliness of the first few weeks. But I wouldn't blame anyone for packing up and going home if they ever find themselves in a similar situation.

However for others, even without any kind of emotional or practical support, the early days can be full of exhilaration and excitement. Adele moved to Qatar with her husband and three children at the same time as his colleagues and their families. 'It was a real honeymoon period,' she recalled. 'There was a huge group of us who all arrived within weeks of each other, Brits, Aussies, Americans, Canadians, Scandis…it was so sociable, all of us there together, all basically on holiday. We just had a good time around the pool. I remember saying I don't think I could ever go back to the UK.'

Philippa, whose two young children both go to a local school where they live in France, agreed with Adele: 'The first few weeks are fantastic, a new place to explore, new people to meet and of course boxes to unpack,' she said.

And being an independent sort, who doesn't mind getting out and about on your own, also helps: 'I'm pretty self-sufficient and comfortable with my own company so have never had an issue with being by myself and getting things done,' said Evelyn who lives in Belgium but has previously lived in the US, Hong Kong, Zurich and Shanghai.

So that's how the first few weeks can be – now what to do about it?

A good start is simply to realise that, as already mentioned (but it's worth repeating), things WILL improve. It's so important to understand what is normal and what isn't. I'll cover both culture shock and depression later in the book, but many of these early feelings and emotions are simply down to the fact that you have just moved somewhere completely new, you don't have your usual support networks to rely on (let alone many of your home comforts) and you might well be having a very different experience from the one that your partner is having.

You may also be having a very different experience from the one you'd imagined you would be having, and that people back home imagine you to be having – all of which makes talking about it to anyone quite hard.

As mentioned above, bringing things to occupy yourself and your children, if you have them, is important, as is trying to do things like sorting out transportation for the first few weeks. If you don't have a car and can't use public transport, can you hire one or borrow one at first? Hiring a car might be expensive but it's better than the claustrophobia of being stranded in whatever accommodation you've found or been allocated on arrival. If possible, make a plan to do something every day – find somewhere to go, explore, check out the local markets or shops. Be a tourist for a while. Give yourself mini-tasks – finding a local bakery or butchers, or places where you can get keys cut, shoes mended, clothes dry-cleaned. If you have children and school hasn't started yet, try and set them tasks as well – learn to understand the new currency, memorise a few words of the local language, try some new food.

It can all be fairly excruciating but all you need to do here is tread water for a while and wait for things to improve. It might happen suddenly, it might creep up on you but one day, I promise, you will wake up and feel at least in some small way like you belong.

Now you've got the very early days under your belt, it's time to look at the more practical elements of setting up home in your new country. In the next chapter, I will look at some of these – including how to find the perfect living accommodation, what to do about furnishing it and the importance of being able to get around.

Some Websites to Help You Settle In During the First Few Weeks or Monthes in Your New Home

A relocation company that provides a settling-in service: http://www.iorworld.com/settling-in-services-pages-176.php

Loneliness can be a real concern, especially in the first few months. This article looks at how to overcome the effects of isolation when living overseas: http://www.expatarrivals.com/article/beating-loneliness-as-an-expat-living-abroad-or-working-overseas

I wrote an article about where to meet people and make friends when you live abroad on my own blog: http://expatpartnersurvival.com/2015/01/23/so-youre-a-fresh-expat-in-town-where-do-you-meet-new-friends/

One of the sites I list in my article is Meet-up: (http://www.meetup.com/), a website which brings up multiple possibilities for clubs and groups in your area.

Another site someone told me about is Gone Girl International: http://girlgoneinternational.com/ – although apparently it is aimed at younger, single women as the emphasis is on going out in the evenings…

Forum aimed at expat women all around the world, although with an emphasis on the Middle East: http://www.expatwoman.com/

An article about the first six months as an expat partner: http://cheeseweb.eu/2011/10/expat-trailing-spouse-the-first-six-months/

Practicalities Part One:
Accommodation, Furnishing, Transport

The early days in a new posting will probably be a bit of a blur – a mix of excitement, stress, jet lag, confusion, depression and possibly hundreds of other emotions all coming one on top of another. But in amongst this swirling mass of feeling you will still have to function, to eat, sleep, shop, look after your children and continue with the daily grind of life. To help you do this there will be a few things you need to get sorted and the next two chapters looks at some of these, what I call 'practicalities'. In the first part, this includes how you go about finding that perfect home, how to find ways to make it more perfect still by furnishing it, and how to make sure you have the means and wherewithal to get out and about independently as soon as possible. In other words – either get yourself a car or learn the local bus routes!

Accommodation: finding a house...

First and foremost you need somewhere to live. At this stage, many people will be in temporary housing. Some will be in a hotel or in someone else's house while they either look for their own home or wait for their predecessor to vacate it. Others might have moved straight into their new house and have moved on to accommodation – part 2: furnishing. But whatever your situation, and as long as you have some choice in the matter, it is very, very important to get where you are going to live as right as possible.

One of my favourite contributors to this book has been my friend Sharon, who has lived in several different countries with her

Department for International Development (DfID)-employed husband Mark. I met Sharon on their final posting (to date) in Kingston, Jamaica, where she was already an old hand at finding the best possible place to live and making it as homely as she could. Sharon wrote so eloquently about the need to be happy with where you live that I just want to reproduce her words here: 'I've written a considerable amount under this question – and it's made me realise just how important creating a *home* was to me during my time abroad. I love houses, and where I live is very important to me. I am sure I am not alone in this.

'Over the years I have seen more arguments, upsets and grievances caused by housing issues than almost anything else. And there is a simple explanation for this – the house (or rather *home*) is the centre of the trailing spouse's universe. With the other half in the office and the kids in school/nursery there is nothing else. And unhelpfully there is, I believe, a commonly held view of spouses often being overly precious or demanding about housing needs.

'In most cases this is unfair. For many spouses, the effort it takes to set up and establish a new house/home in a posting is phenomenal. They often have little choice as to what they are given and face many obstacles in trying to sort everything out: from battling random & petty rules (like the one in Jamaica where I was told by an FCO wife "only first secretaries can have pools"…despite houses with pools being within budget for lower grade staff), to security needs (where I was gleefully told that I would need a "rape door" installed in my house), to having to complete a "works request" for every niggling problem, only to then wait weeks for a response from the office with the form having just sat in the someone's in-tray until you have chased and nagged them into submission! Far from being overly demanding, spouses are often powerless.'

Sharon is spot on – getting it right at the beginning, if at all possible, is so important. First and foremost, remember that old estate agent adage: location, location, location.

Before you even start to look for your house, decide where you want to live. Think about things like schools, work commute (for your partner – but also for yourself if you are also planning to work), traffic, local facilities, the availability (or not) of public transport, where other expats live, safety and all the other things that you think are or will be important to you.

In many cases, you might already know where you are likely to live – there might just be one area for expats, you might be on a compound or you might need to live very close to the school you have chosen. But more often you will have a vast and potentially dizzying number of districts, areas, communities or localities to choose from. If in doubt, ask around – other expats are the best place to get this sort of local knowledge and if you have a friendly local expat website then certainly pose the question there.

When you have pinned down one or two areas you are interested in, visit them – at different times of the day if possible. A nice quiet road at 10am in the morning might turn into a giant traffic jam at the peak of rush hour. What you thought was going to be a ten minute drive to the office could easily turn into a gruelling hour long journey every morning.

Once you know the sort of area or areas you want to live in, you need to start thinking about your priorities. Just like buying or renting a house back in your home country, you need to weigh up size, space, number of bedrooms, storage, garden, pool (for some lucky people) and all the other important things that estate agents witter on to us about.

Our only real decision about housing when we moved to Islamabad was whether to live on or off the compound. In the end, the decision was more or less made for us – the security situation deteriorated so quickly that most families were encouraged to live in the safety of the diplomatic zone. In St Lucia, though, we had to find our own house. Not an easy task in a country where the typical abode is either a shack or a mansion. There wasn't a very large 'expat' community on the island and most of the available housing for rent were holiday villas – which weren't really furnished properly for long-term rental. On top of that, my husband's job as a liaison officer with the British Consulate meant we really needed good security. In the end we found two reasonable homes (moving from the first to the second after a year to be closer to the school and expat 'scene') which, to the untrained eye, looked like the most luxurious of holiday homes, far larger than anything we could expect to live in in the UK – but not really furnished appropriately for family living.

Many others have remarked on how much bigger their homes overseas were than those they lived in back home. The general rule of thumb seems to be the poorer or more difficult the country to live in, the bigger the expat houses. But big doesn't always mean better and sometimes what might look good on the outside can be falling apart on the inside.

Philippa, who lives in France with her two young children and whose husband works at the local airport, reported that her house was bigger than anything they had ever had before saying: '...but the electrics in the house were appalling, the light bulbs were hanging on loose wires... My husband decided he would do them himself and found condensation on the wires – arghhhh!' It is definitely worth remembering that health and safety regulations will be different in every country and very possibly not as strict as you are used to in your home country. If possible, get someone to check things like wiring and electrics before you move in, especially if you have young children.

One point that was repeatedly made to me when researching this chapter was how stressful it could be using an agent to find yourself a home. Whilst you are almost certainly going to need someone to show you around, always keep it in the back of your mind that they are not your friend, that they are there to make money from you and that they are almost certainly going to show you some entirely inappropriate homes in the hope that you will eventually break down and take anything.

Nicola, now in the Netherlands, described how they used an agent to negotiate the rent on a property they were interested in close to their son's school in Hong Kong. Having been told what the rent was by the former tenants of the apartment, they were then shocked to find it had doubled when the agent showed them around a week later. Unfortunately, by the time the landlord had contacted them directly and offered them a reasonable rent, they had already signed the lease on another property.

Hong Kong is obviously one of the harder places to find a trustworthy agent, as Rachel also had problems there: 'In Hong Kong, we didn't get the allowance as it was a local package. My husband's employer arranged an agent who was not great as he just didn't really seem to "get" expats and showed us a lot of over-priced crap.'

This was also my experience as a singleton in Jamaica where I am still haunted by some of the shiny soft furnishings I saw on my tour of 'suitable' houses when I first arrived. There is something about the Caribbean and taste that somehow doesn't quite meet...

As well as finding their home, many new expats will also find themselves in the unenviable position of having to negotiate the lease/contract and deal directly with the landlord for the duration of their stay. As civil servants we were reasonably lucky and had others do most of the hard work for us – although in St Lucia we did have to deal directly with the landlord on many matters, a situation I would rather not repeat (he was having a long-running dispute involving his terminally ill ex-wife, his new girlfriend and the short-term rental of his villa which we somehow got caught up in).

Olga, who lives with her German husband in the Netherlands, said not only did she have to negotiate on rent but they also had to do all the work themselves when they eventually bought a house: '(The landlords) wanted to raise the rent up by five per cent every year – it was too much so we bought a house. We did the negotiations ourselves, with help from in-laws and a consumer organisation. It wasn't easy because the real estate agents negotiate really hard. We're lucky to have found a nice house that fits our growing family.'

If you do find yourselves having to get into negotiation over things like rent and the finer details of your lease, it is definitely worth trying to get someone local that you trust (if you're lucky enough to have found someone so soon after arrival) to give it the once over. If you haven't got any contacts, try a forum like British Expats – you'll usually find someone with good local experience who has been around the block a few times and is happy to give out advice. In the end, though, just be very cautious and check everything at least twice as much as you would in your home country. And if possible, take Judy's advice who said that after postings in Azerbaijan, Egypt and the UAE they eventually worked out that 'choosing a "good" landlord was part of the decision process'.

But if possible try and avoid a landlord like Sandra's: 'Our landlord is okay although he does have a bee in their bonnet about the fluff in the tumble dryer. Unlike many rented apartments we are lucky enough not to share a washing machine and dryer. However from time to time it has stopped working. The landlord mentioned that the fluff had not been emptied when really it was just that I emptied it when I put the next load in. He gave me a forty five minutes lesson on how to de-fluff it as he was sure I never did it. Even supplying me with a toothbrush to clean the filter!'

That story is made slightly less surprising when you realise that it took place in Switzerland.

...and making it a home

Once you have found somewhere to live, you will need to think about furnishing it. You might be lucky and inherit a fully-furnished, even – if you're REALLY lucky – tastefully furnished, house or apartment that needs nothing more than your own finishing touches like pictures and perhaps new curtains.

On the other hand, you might need to throw everything out and start from scratch.

For many this is a dream come true – if you've got the budget, you could have a delightful few months trawling the local shops and markets for fabulous furniture. Although this isn't always as much fun as it sounds: local availability in many countries won't be anything like what you are used to at home (unless you happened to have moved to Sweden where presumably there are even more giant IKEA's than there are in the UK).

In many countries it can also be prohibitively expensive buying locally, as many items will have been imported. You might be lucky and be able to pick up some lovely handcrafted items at local markets or shops (the carved wooden items available in Pakistan were exquisite, for example), but you might be better off picking up second-hand items from leaving expats. Or take a tip out of Belinda's book, who found a good way to save money when she and her family moved to the States: 'We really appreciated all the yard sales held every weekend,' she said. 'Because we knew that we were only going to be in the USA for two years, it didn't make sense for us to buy a lot of new furniture – and in fact we managed to find most of it second-hand. Other than one trip to IKEA, which was several hours' drive away, we furnished our house almost exclusively with furniture brought at yard sales.'

Inheriting furniture from predecessors or having it supplied by your employers makes life easier in some ways, but it can be harder to personalise your home and make yourself and your family feel more settled. The Foreign Office-supplied furniture I grew up with and later re-encountered when I started work as a diplomat could best be described as 'functional'. It was always amusing to spot the identical items in someone else's home, even funnier in the days when a certain cut of fabric or size of bureau could identify someone's position in the office pecking order, as Sharon explained: 'One funny thing about Dhaka: you could tell immediately what grade a person was by their house pack. At the time, DfID came under the umbrella of FCO and as a result the rules for what you were given were VERY rigid. For example: third secretaries got teak furniture with square edges; second secretaries got teak furniture with rounded edges and first secretaries got mahogany furniture – the edges I can't recall!'

I like to think that things have changed a bit since those days – but please correct me if you know otherwise!

Transport – the importance of making sure you can get from A to B (and back again)

So the day arrives when your partner goes in to their new work place for the first time; he or she merrily waves you off and disappears down the garden path/hotel corridor with barely a backward glance, and you're on your own. Great, you think, now's the time to get out and explore, to discover all those interesting little markets or take the bored kids to one of those gorgeous parks you've been reading about in your guidebooks...but oh crap.

Your partner's just taken the car to work. You have no idea where the local bus stop is or even if there is a local bus stop, let alone whether taking the local bus is safe. You could try walking but it's about a zillion degrees out there (or alternatively it's just started to snow) and besides which without a map you might well end up in one of those 'survived for three weeks with just a chocolate bar and a bottle of contact lens solution to drink' shows. You turn around and look back at your house/flat/hotel room and suddenly it's turned into a prison.

Working out transport right from day one is one of the most important things you can do when you first arrive somewhere. Unless you're in a relatively modern city with good transport links, or where it's safe and easy to walk around, you really do need to think how you are going to get out and about if you don't want to feel completely trapped.

Even if you have access to a car, driving somewhere new is always a daunting task so you might want to practise a bit while your partner is still around. (Alternatively, the idea of trying to work out whether you're allowed to turn left on a red light, what it means when the car behind is simultaneously flashing its lights and making strange gestures out the window, and who takes priority at roundabouts with your partner next to you in the car might fill you with total horror. In which case, probably best to wait until you're on your own). You'll also want to pick a relatively quiet time to try out the car for the first time – mid-morning is a good time, after the rush hour and before things pick up again at lunchtime. It also gives you time to go home for a nice lie-down afterwards.

Once you do start driving, just accept you are going to make mistakes and you are going to get lost. It's fine, it's all part of the experience. In fact I would even say that if everything goes smoothly on your first car journey out, then you're either very lucky or you've not gone further than the end of your road. Which is fine. Baby steps and all that.

You should also try and find out as much about local drivers as possible as every country has its own foibles. Shirley has lived in both France and Texas, as well as the UK, and has found them all very different when it comes to the laws of the road: 'Driving in France is very different to the UK. I maintain that if you can drive around the Arc de Triomphe, you can drive anywhere! But driving in Texas was scary for different reasons: drivers were very unpredictable and were often doing other things while driving. Apart from the obvious using mobile phones etc., we saw people with books or newspapers propped up on the steering wheel, people shaving and even people putting on makeup while they drove.'

As well as working out how to drive a new car, where to go and how to get home again (landmarks are good – it's particularly useful if there is a large mountain or range of mountains in close proximity to your new home, like we had in Islamabad: as long as you're driving away from and not towards the large mountain you know you're at least going in the right direction), you need to know where to get petrol; whether the car takes petrol or diesel; how to pay for the petrol; how to get help if you break down; and what, where and how to park. This last is particularly important in countries where you don't want to have to walk too far in unfamiliar territory – security should always be your first priority when you are new somewhere and yet to have a feel for when an area is safe or not (see next chapter for more on security).

The other thing to remember about driving in your new country is that you are going to have to learn a whole new set of skills. I'll never forget the time my brakes totally stopped working after driving through a foot of flood water in Caracas (where I learned to drive as a teenager) and not realising I was meant to pump the brakes to get the water out. This was a long time ago so perhaps cars are made better these days, but you will almost certainly have to work out how to deal with a whole new range of road hazards – from pot holes the size of small countries, to different systems for pedestrian crossings.

Even if your posting is to my home country, the UK, there will be some things you'll need to get used to as Viktor's Kazakhstani wife Olga found out. 'In England I bought only one car because my wife refused to drive there,' he explained. 'She said that there are too many narrow roads and everybody drives on the wrong side of the road...'

Ask around before you set out for the first time – is there any particular road rule or tip that you need to know before you find yourself driving the wrong way up a dual carriageway (yup, I did that – again, in Caracas) or parking on a road that's just been closed for a state occasion (not me this time).

You also need to be ready for the other road users: some countries have unexpectedly hostile drivers, as Carole found in Germany – a country where you wouldn't expect to find yourself having to deal with road hogs on a regular basis. 'The drivers were arrogant and aggressive,' she said. 'Berlin also discourages car use so there are very few car parks which means everyone parks on the edge of the road, even on junctions.' And in Qatar, Lesley, who has also had to learn to negotiate the roads in Indonesia and Kenya, found that 'the roads were manic and the local drivers worse than manic...although the good thing about the roads in Qatar is that there are masses of roundabouts and lots of points of interest so it's very hard to get lost'.

In some countries though, it's not other car drivers that are the problem – as Nicola found in the Netherlands, where dealing with cyclists was the biggest problem. However, she found the best solution was the good old adage if you can't beat 'em, join 'em and started cycling again for the first time in twenty years.

Judging local conditions also helped Nicola in the States, where she was at first shocked, then eventually relieved when they were allocated a 'huge gas guzzler' SUV on arrival: 'Both my partner and I agreed we'd swap it for a European sedan once we got settled in our new location. However, we never did as we discovered how awful some American drivers were and that they often were in big/bigger SUVs, too, so realised we were safer in our tank. This was a surprise as we'd moved there from the Netherlands where we'd become conscious of less is more and green/eco values, using the bicycles instead of the car. Yet in the States we held onto the big car for safety and had to use it to go anywhere as walking in thirty-forty degree heat was not possible.'

Which all goes to prove that it's not worth reaching any conclusions or making any judgements until you actually get to your new home and check out the local situation for yourself.

As well as a car, some people might also need to use a driver for various reasons. Whether this is because you live in a country where you're not allowed to drive (special mention to Saudi Arabia here), or whether it's a necessity for safety reasons or just because parking is a nightmare and having someone else to back into the tiny spaces available is a lot easier, it will help you get out and about with relative ease.

In some countries, having a driver can really make the difference between getting out and meeting people and staying locked up in your prison of a house, so don't ever think it's an unnecessary luxury. Unless it *is* an unnecessary luxury. But whatever, you are allowed the odd luxury when you've just moved thousands of miles from your family and friends, you don't know how to use the gas hob in your kitchen and you've recently discovered a small army of ants carrying away the last of your favourite biscuits brought specially from home…

If you don't have access to a car or you don't want/need one, your next question is how are you going to get around. Public transport can be an excellent option in many countries, especially in Europe.

K moved to Switzerland with her husband and seven year old son and said they didn't even need a car at first as the public transport system ran, typically for the Swiss, 'like clockwork'. Katrina, who has lived in various places in Europe, believes that using public transport or walking helped her to integrate more easily: 'You actually become more a part of your local community if you walk everywhere,' she said.

Of course in some cities (and I would include London in this) having a car just doesn't make financial sense. Rachel, who had got used to having a vehicle in Dubai where 'cars were cheap as chips and petrol practically free' made do with using taxis, buses and the MTR (Mass Transit Railway – the local railway system) for the first six months when they moved to Hong Kong. 'Cars are pretty pricey here, as is petrol and parking, so it usually makes financial sense to just use taxis,' she said. 'If you have a car, it's purely for convenience. You can't justify it financially.' And in the States, Jac and her husband used public transport for most of the time, but hired a car whenever they needed one for longer journeys.

I'll give the last word on getting around to Philippa, whose description of their lifestyle in France sums up some of the reasons why so many people dream of moving abroad: 'We are very lucky, we lived within walking distance of the town centre, the shops, and the local parks. We were able to walk everywhere and it helped us very quickly learn where everything was. It also got us on the bikes and helped kicked off a healthier lifestyle, which we had hoped for. There were times when I wanted to go further from home or more times when it was raining where a car would have been lovely, but I know I feel that if we had a car from the beginning we would not walk as much as we do now. We would have become dependent on the car.'

By this point, you're hopefully beginning to feel a little more settled. The importance of having somewhere to call home cannot be underestimated. In the next chapter, we'll look at some more of those all-important practical elements to your new life, including why the simple act of shopping can suddenly take on a life of its own, how learning the local language – even if it's just a few words – can help get you places, and how important it is to know how to keep yourself and your family safe.

Websites that Can Help You with Some of the Practicalities of Settling In:

The IOR relocation company whose settling-in service is listed in the chapter above, which can also help you with your home-finding: http://www.iorworld.com/home-finding-pages-539.php

A house-hunting guide aimed specifically at expat parents: House-hunting for expat parents: http://www.womenshealthbag.com/house-hunting-guide-for-expat-parents/

House-hunting in Singapore (there are a number of similar guides for some of the more popular expat destinations like Hong Kong and Dubai): http://www.singaporeexpats.com/guides-for-expats/house-hunt-guide.htm

A house-hunting guides for expats by a couple of expats: http://thosedamamericans.com/2013/01/23/an-expatriate-guide-international-house-hunting/

Your expat home is what you make of it – an excellent article describing what it's really like to move in to a home abroad: http://www.telegraph.co.uk/expat/expatlife/9397794/Your-expat-home-is-what-you-make-of-it.html

Some advice from the UK government about driving abroad, including information about what kind of license you will need and where: https://www.gov.uk/driving-abroad

Driving tips for different countries from the AA (Automobile Association): http://www.theaa.com/motoring_advice/overseas/countrybycountry.html

Practicalities Part Two: Shopping, Making Yourself Understood (or Not) and Keeping Safe

It's easy, in the planning stages of your posting, to dream about the good times. The beach barbecues. The safaris. Sundowners on the balcony. Sadly, we all know that whilst hopefully you will eventually experience these highs, living overseas doesn't mean you can escape completely from the more mundane side of life. In this chapter I explore some more of these practical elements, and show you how important it is to try and get these things right from the start. This includes that exciting expat pastime of matching supper ingredients to available foodstuff in the local supermarkets; getting your head – and your tongue – around the local lingo; and making sure that above all else you understand how to keep everyone safe.

Shop 'til you drop

One of the first things many new expats will do, perhaps even on the very first day they arrive, is to check out the local shops. After all, we need to eat, drink, change nappies, spray cockroaches, find warmer clothes than we brought (who knew it could get to -5 degrees in South Africa...) and all the other myriad of things that we luckily have shops for.

Of course you might not have transport to do such a thing (see previous chapter), in which case you're going to have to hope someone has taken pity and already stocked your fridge with milk and left you some coffee for the morning. But hopefully within a day or two of arriving, you will get the chance to go on that first shopping adventure. It's always fun to see what the next few years has in store (geddit?) for you.

In many countries, of course, things won't be that different from what you are used to at home. Again and again while researching this, the words Marks and Spencers – a well known British store for those of you not from the UK – cropped up: Qatar, Singapore, Hong Kong, Saudi Arabia. In fact, you can now buy your standard M&S knickers in fifty one different locations around the world (outside of the UK). Debenhams, Next, H&M, Boots (yes, more well-known British shops) are all names that can also be found in exotic locations worldwide. You'll also find many other global companies, like French supermarket giant Carrefour, in worldwide locations. Many of these shops won't be exactly what you're used to at home and their stock will certainly be more limited (don't expect the sandwich/crisp/drink meal deal that both M&S and Boots offer in the UK, for example). But nevertheless they will offer some of the comforts of home and certainly might take the edge off that first bout of homesickness when you arrive.

Another way of getting your home staples is through the new(ish) networks of Brit stores which seem to be becoming ever more prevalent around the world (or their online equivalent). This isn't just a British phenomenon of course – in the UK our high streets are now full of Polish shops and the supermarkets have aisles packed with goods from Jamaica, Russia, India. But the one downside to these shops is the price. K, for example, was delighted to find her local Brit shop in Switzerland stocked salt and vinegar Walkers crisps – until she worked out how much it would cost her: 'They were fifteen Swiss francs for six packets – it worked out at more than £1 a packet,' she said. 'At the time, they were about 30p for a packet in the UK!' For some people, a small price to pay for a treat from home. But for many this will remain just that: the occasional treat.

However, while more and more global names may be popping up all over the place, most expats will still have to rely on local stores for most of their day-to-day shopping. And as this isn't likely to be exactly what you are used to at home, it is certainly worth finding out what is and isn't available before you arrive – particularly in the case of things like nappies and formula, medicines etc.

Everyone will have different ideas about what they do and don't want to take with them. For many, there will always be a list of items they will miss from home – and may initially pack into their luggage when they first travel. For many Brits, the list will almost inevitably include decent chocolate, tea bags, Marmite, Heinz baked beans and Walkers crisps. But it's amazing what you can get used to doing without after a while, as Nicola, who initially found shopping in the Netherlands more of a shock than you might expect, said: 'We had a list of two sides of A4 paper of what we'd ask family and friends visiting from the UK to bring us...by the time we left seven years later, we'd got it down to three items.'

And Sandra, in Switzerland, added: 'At least once a year we drive home with a huge list of things we cannot get here, one year bringing back seventy two tins of baked beans! Although I have to say our shopping list has changed somewhat as the girls got older – we now buy shampoo, shower gel and other cleaning products. Tea bags are still a must though.'

Based on the number of times it was mentioned in my research, one things many of us Brits don't seem to be able to do without is pork and there are of course a few countries around the world where it is impossible to buy it. In Saudi Arabia, according to Lesley, this led to desperate measures: 'Pork is prohibited, but if you live in Al Khobar then you can cross the causeway into Bahrain and enjoy a cooked breakfast with all the pork you can eat,' she said. 'Many expats also buy pork from the shops in Bahrain and have it wrapped in plain brown paper and marked as "chicken", "veal" or "beef" and then bring it back across the causeway. This is done at your own risk as customs crossing the border is very tight.' Now I love a good sausage, but I'm not sure this is a risk worth taking. I can also assure you, speaking from experience, that pork products, as well as other things you can't get overseas, taste all the better for not having had them for a while once you do get back to your home country.

It's true that inevitably there will be things that you miss, but one of the fun things about living overseas is trying out new things.

Katrina, who has lived in several European countries, said: 'I find that I gradually stop missing the things that I liked from a place, and adopt new "favourites" from each place I live in. Austrian Mannerschnitzel, Swiss fondue cheese, Italian saffron powder and Arborio rice, Greek yoghurt... I am sure that Pepparkakor will be something I feel nostalgic about when I leave Sweden.'

Having read this sentence I decided to Google both Mannerschnitzel and Pepparkakor, curious as to what these unusual dishes were. Pepparkakor are apparently the gingery biscuits served around Christmas time, which I remember from my own childhood in the Philippines, where we had Swedish friends. Mannerschnitzel however appears to be a recipe involving cannibalism. I think we'll leave that one there (and can only hope she meant Wieiner Schnitzel – breaded veal – or Manner Schnitten, which are some sort of chocolate wafers).

Anyway, whether there are things you miss but can't get, don't miss but can get or new things you have yet to try, you'll need to get some supplies in or you and your family are going to get hungry. If you're lucky and someone's shown you where the local shops are, you can trip off down there (making sure you check the opening days and times before you go – many people have been disappointed to find that other countries don't have the same 24/7 opening policies that we have become used to in the UK) and pick up some groceries. If you're not sure where the best place to start is, you will inevitably find yourself buying food at the closest shop you come to which later on you find has highly inflated prices and a poor range...but if that's true, at least you'll have bought some basics.

Shopping in a new country can be great fun. I love perusing the aisles of countries I visit, even when on holiday, just to see what you can get that's different from home. Sometimes it's tempting to buy something just to find out what on Earth it is – although this invariably doesn't really work out. (Grass jelly juice, anyone? I discovered this very odd concoction in Hong Kong and wished I hadn't). However the time will come, sooner or later – depending on the variety of food available locally – when the novelty starts to wear a bit thin and you start to wish you could recognise a few more brands and that there was more than one type of potato available.

It's interesting how a supermarket, which at first glance seems stuffed to the rafters with food, can quickly start to drive you crazy trying to find exactly the right ingredients to make a carefully planned menu, or has everything you need except one, vital thing. This can lead to one common expat phenomenon: supermarket-hopping.

To be an effective supermarket hopper all you have to do is visit more than one store, often three or four, in any one trip in order to buy everything on your list. Whereas in the UK we are used to being able to get everything we want in a single place, it is frustrating how often you'll find your favoured shop has everything you need except something really simple – such as yoghurt, or minced beef. Things get even more complicated when you've got a particular recipe in mind before you set off and then can't find that last darn ingredient without which the whole thing won't work but you've bought everything else now and what the hell else are you going to do with lemongrass, cream, rosemary and pistachios?

You might be better off doing what Rachel found was the best way to deal with this on her postings in Dubai and Hong Kong: 'If you have a recipe, you often have to go to two or three supermarkets before you can gather absolutely everything you need together – e.g. you go to supermarket one and they have smoked salmon but not crème fraiche, supermarket two is the other way round and neither have capers, so you have to go to supermarket three. Hence, I tend to go to the supermarket, find what they have and eat it, rather than the other way round.'

Of course for some people, shop-hopping isn't a problem, as long as you have the time.

Shirley loved the French way of buying in individual shops: 'Boulangerie, patisserie, boucherie etc. It takes a lot longer but it is worth it,' she said.

And in Islamabad I found using the small shops selling just fruit and veg or just meat was a great way to interact with the locals, as you would have to ask them for help rather than just picking goods up anonymously as you do in a supermarket.

Local markets are often the best place to get the best produce – as long as you know what you are looking for and aren't afraid of checking quality before buying. It may also be worth, if you are able to, taking along a local when you first start shopping this way as they will help ensure you don't get ripped off. Or at least try and find out what the local prices are. Although it's also worth accepting that you might always pay more than a local, which is usually fine as more often than not your family income will be way above theirs.

One of the other things many people encounter is only being able to buy fresh fruit and vegetables that are in season at that particular time. We're not used to this in the rich, privileged countries of the West – where green beans are flown in from Kenya, cherries from Spain, avocados from Israel and all year round now we can have pretty well any fresh produce that our heart desires.

We came across this in Pakistan, where we happened to be during mango season. Apricot season was just coming in towards the end of our stay there, but most of the time it was mangoes. Lots and lots of mangoes – many, many different varieties (who knew there were so many!), ripe ones, over-ripe ones, under-ripe ones...there certainly was no shortage of mangoes. But could you get a banana? No – well, not one in any decent condition – didn't we know it wasn't banana season? I guess a lot of this had to do with the cost of internal transportation but coming from a country where we were used to being able to offer our children a huge variety of choice, this was quite frustrating. You do get quite imaginative with a mango though.

It's all relative, however, and worth keeping in perspective. On the days when you find you can't get exactly the sort of pickled onions you had your heart set on, remember Sharon's experiences: 'Because of the sort of postings we've had (mainly what are deemed "hard" postings) we got used to NOT being able to get things. In Rwanda, for example, there used to be great excitement if it was discovered one shop had had a delivery of CHEESE! A small expatriate stampede ensued...actually I say small, but you can't have that many four wheel drives arrive at a store and it go unnoticed!'

Other than food, the sort of things people often have difficulty buying overseas include toys, clothes and general household goods. The Internet has transformed the way we shop and this extends now to living overseas. But it can also be an expensive business, so again might be one you want to keep for special occasions and treats/emergencies.

There are many different worldwide companies that offer shipping services for goods bought overseas and it is usually best to rely on local knowledge for which ones to use. Ask around when you arrive or on websites for expats.

With toys, depending where you are moving to, you might find you want to bring as much with you as possible (and think ahead to upcoming birthdays etc.) as safety standards vary across different countries. If you aren't able to do this, and can't buy more on trips outside of that country, ask others when you arrive for reputable retailers.

With clothes, the biggest problem is often size – as Carole, whose first posting with her husband and daughter was to Japan, explained: 'No way could I buy clothes there – I'm six foot tall and have enough problems in the UK. And as for shoes, I went into a shoe shop in Tokyo and when I told them my shoe size I was directed to the men's department!'

This can be a problem across south east and east Asia for both men and women, so unless you are particularly petite, you might want to make sure you bring enough with you and/or rely on shopping trips to other countries and the Internet. What is considered 'fashion' can also be an issue for some: the obsession that much of the world still seems to have with big shoulders and sequins never ceases to amaze me; although I am sure to many of our fellow citizens around the globe our love of the dire 'onesie' probably puts us beyond scrutiny.

As for other goods, household items, DVDs and electronics etc., again the availability, not to mention the quality, will vary wildly depending on which country you are in. Piracy is huge in some places and in Pakistan it was totally accepted and above board and everyone joined in. These days with downloads so readily available most of these businesses are probably closing down but it's a shame. I'll miss the movie suddenly cutting out half way through or being in a totally different language from the one we were expecting. Ah the good old days!

Another area you may need to think about in advance is what is coyly known as 'feminine products' in most stores – for example, tampons or sanitary towels/liners. It can be hard to get tampons in many countries, and those that do sell them may not stock the particular type you are used to or have been using. It can be hard to find out what is sold in your country of destination before you arrive and it might be the sort of thing you feel awkward about asking someone on an Internet forum. As so often, Google is your friend here – in just a couple of minutes I have found out that you can get tampons in Dubai (but that they might be in the baby section), that you might have to ask for them in the Philippines as they may be hidden away somewhere out of sight, and that it may be hard to buy anything but a local brand in China which 'smell funny' and are a bit heavy on the bleach. If in any doubt, take a good few months worth with you and re-stock at every opportunity.

Finally, on the subject of shopping, there are some countries where you really are going to strike lucky. I don't mean those that you might expect – reports on both Germany, the Netherlands and (small town) Florida were that the shops were dull and full of nothing tempting – but Lesley's description of Jakarta in Indonesia makes it the gold standard of shopping experiences: 'In Jakarta we were lucky enough to have M&S (with a small food department) and Next. The big department stores had a wonderful array of clothes, electrical goods, kids wear, toys but most of all shoes. The shoes were out of this world and at a very reasonable price. The malls also had the full range of designer stores (and of course Starbucks coffee). The local shops were on the roadsides or tucked away down side streets and were like Aladdin Caves. You could have virtually anything made – clothes, shoes, furniture, towels (with your name woven into them). The furniture was fantastic and so cheap compared to what you would buy in the UK.'

Learning the lingo

Most of my contributors to this project, when asked about learning the local language of their new country, were in agreement that generally it helped your overall happiness and acceptance of your situation if you could make yourself understood by the locals.

The feeling of isolation of being a new expat in a strange country can be massively increased if you can't interact with those around you, or if you find yourself left out of conversations because they are going on in a language you don't know. As Sharon put it of her experience: 'There is always a feeling of separation when you can't speak the local language. However, the most alienated I felt was when I was working in an office in Rwanda. All my colleagues were Rwandan, and male, and would often talk in Kinyarwandan, which effectively excluded me from the conversation. I did not stay long in that job because of it!'

The reality though is hard – many of us who speak English as our first language really struggle with new languages; language teaching in most of our schools (in the UK) is not fit for purpose and we're lucky if we head off for our first overseas posting with more than a smattering of schoolgirl/boy French. And then when we do arrive, things aren't made any easier by people's insistence in speaking English to us – usually because, rightly or wrongly (usually the first), their English is going to be better than your Dutch/German/Mandarin/Swahili. In some ways, although it's tougher at the start, you are better off in a country where very few people speak any English at all, as then you will be forced to learn the local language.

Katrina, who has had to try and pick up a variety of European languages in her different postings, spoke about her experience: 'The better you know a language, the easier time you will have, but learning a new language is challenging, time-consuming and frustrating. It takes time before you truly communicate with people – but if you have the social opportunities to interact you not only have the motivation but also the opportunity to practice and improve.'

Josine, who has lived in Singapore, China and Taiwan, said she found learning the local language the best way to get to know people who weren't expats: 'The only problem is you have to invest a lot of time in it, but I was happy I did so that I could participate in a local orchestra and had a lot of local friends, got to know a lot of the inside and culture of the countries that you otherwise won't see.'

Even learning just a few words can help – as all children are taught, 'please' and 'thank you' go a long way, and it's amazing how much better a positive reaction to a carefully learnt phrase can make you feel when you're having a particularly lonely or isolated day.

But how and where can you learn more than just the basics?

Some people are lucky and will have language lessons offered to them in advance of leaving their home country through their partner's employers. If you are able to do these, then there is absolutely no harm in doing so – although you might want to top them up when you arrive in post and find that local dialect/nuances mean you're still left scratching your head (or buying totally inappropriate things because you had no idea what the shop keeper was telling you).

Otherwise it's generally fairly easy to find local language lessons and many see this as a good way to get to know some friends at the start of their postings. There's nothing like feeling you're back at university by hanging out with your language school-mates! Other options include online or 'bought in' packaged lessons by companies like Rosetta Stone – although in my experience, you're more likely to stick with it if you are being taught by an actual living and breathing person.

Once you do arrive in your new country, the next challenge is trying to get people to speak to you in the language you're trying to learn. In Holland, Hilary found this particularly annoying: 'The worst thing about being here is not having the opportunity to use the Dutch that I do know...as soon as I open my mouth and speak Dutch, I'm responded to in English. And then in the next breath, I'm told I should learn to speak Dutch. Really?'

One solution to this is to try and practise with other non-native speakers: you might find them slightly more forgiving of your attempts – and you might also find you understand each other better as they are unlikely to speak as quickly as a local.

Nicola, who also struggled with the English/Dutch thing in Holland, said: 'Try to make friends with neighbours who are willing to help you learn and use the language. I found having chats with my elderly non-Dutch neighbours was easier than speaking with native Dutch speakers to start, as the neighbours were more willing to allow my trial and error and to work out what I was trying to say.'

Another way to get round the language barrier is to use your children (if you have any of course. Otherwise, you could always try borrowing a couple from a friend or neighbour). For whatever reason, children always pick up languages much quicker than adults and within about ten minutes of your arrival they will no doubt be chattering away with the little boy across the street in the local lingo, while you wave your arms in the air and shout three vaguely French/Hebrew/Swahili words very loudly as you try to ask the taxi driver to help you unload your bags. Don't be ashamed, just roll with it. Your children will also probably get language lessons at school so it won't be long before they'll be able to do all your translations for you – at the shops, the bank, the gynaecologist...okay maybe not the last one. Let's hope you get a gynaecologist who speaks adequate English.

Some people might think they're lucky; they're going to a country where English is the first language and they'll be able to communicate well from the start. They then get a shock when they realise how different English can be in different countries. I really struggled in Jamaica as I had no idea that the patois they used was English at all! Even in America, the local lingo can cause a shock – as Jenny found: 'It's strange speaking the same language but having such different idioms. In some ways it would be easier to speak in a completely new language!'

Don't worry, though, whether you arrive fluent in the local language or only pick up a word or two during your entire posting, there's always the global language of body language. If all else fails, shrug your shoulders and smile. Hopefully someone will take pity on you.

Keeping Safe

A case study: South Africa

Carole moved to South Africa with her husband and daughter following a posting in Germany. Here she reports on the differences in personal security they found in their new destination:

> 'Whilst all too aware of the many crime issues in South Africa prior to moving, I expected certain security measures to be in place. I was right: the houses are surrounded by high walls topped with metal spikes and electric fences. Security grills cover all the windows and doors and we were told to keep them shut and locked at all times.

'I should think that if we had arrived from somewhere like the UK this would have been a massive shock to the system. As it was, we arrived from Berlin, where our house was surrounded by a metal security fence (for reasons unknown). There it was just a massive inconvenience as I would have to go outside to the gate whenever someone rang the doorbell – the intercom didn't work and I couldn't see who was there. So the actual fencing here in South Africa wasn't a big deal – just the reasons for it.

'More of a concern is the "safe area" within the house – a solid door with many locks and bolts which closes off part of the house and is to be used in case of a home invasion; a chilling prospect. Burglars here *want* you to be at home so you can give them access to valuables.

'We were given a brief briefing on arrival: how to work the alarm, and advice such as, "get 'smash and grab' film put on the car windows", "watch out for car-jackers", "don't walk anywhere", and "don't go out after dark". As "after dark" is any time after 6pm this would be incredibly limiting so, on further advice from people who have successfully lived here for a while, we ignored that bit.

'A couple of months after our arrival we were obliged to attend an official security course. Presented by a local consultant, we were given crime statistics (scary) and advice on how to deal with life in South Africa (empowering).

'The course was terrifying and encouraging at the same time. Terrifying to hear which horrific crimes occur, how often they happen and the fact that a life is worthless and taken easily. Encouragement and empowerment came with being given practical methods to avoid incidents and even what to do in the case of being the victim. I sincerely hope I never, ever have to use what I learned, but it's good to be prepared.

'We left the course a little more paranoid, a lot more realistic, yet still happy to be living in this beautiful, fascinating country.'

This section could be a chapter in its own right, but I want to try and keep this distinct from the really big incidents which cause serious concern such as terrorist bombings or natural catastrophes which I will look at in a later chapter ('If It All Goes Wrong'). Instead, this part of the practicalities chapter tries to cover the sort of issues that might concern you and your personal safety wherever you go in the world – although invariably there is an emphasis on the postings where serious crime is more of a problem, as these are the countries where you will obviously need to be extra vigilant.

It goes without saying, although I will say it, that the priority for both you and your family when you first arrive somewhere is your personal safety. This will obviously mean very different things depending where you are – but whether it's Kingston, Kigali or Kentucky, there are some sensible precautions that you can take right from day one.

For starters, know your new city (town, area, wherever you are living). Most places will have some 'no-go' areas – even if these are just temporary 'no-go' until you know your way around a bit and can understand the culture better. If you are in a country with a particularly high crime rate (South Africa, Jamaica, Mexico – you get the idea), you will hopefully be offered some sort of safety briefing by your partner's employees. Take heed and follow their advice – again, at least until you have a better idea of how things work in your new country. If there is no such safety advice offered, tap into the local expat network ASAP and try and find out which areas are considered okay and which are not. All of this advice is doubled for night-time and also if you are going anywhere on your own.

In many countries these days, you will have bars on your windows, panic rooms or parts of the houses that can be locked off from the rest, gated and guarded communities and more. This can all seem quite alarming if you're not used to it, but it soon becomes part of life. A sad, inevitable part of life because these precautions are there as a daily reminder of how harsh life can be for many of the other residents of the city you live in. And necessary as these precautions might be, they'll also set you apart from the local community, add to the 'them and us' feeling that you will inevitably find if you move to many parts of the developing world (or even many parts of the so-called developed world these days). But if you do have things like internal gates or bars on your windows, use them. They are there for a purpose – even if that sole purpose is just to make you feel safer and help you sleep at night. Which isn't a bad reason to have them!

Another point about barred windows is knowing what to do in case of a fire – and in particular, making sure the children know. How would they get out of their windows, if they needed to? And if your house is more than a single-storey, do you need a ladder or some other way to exit safely? If necessary, you could have a 'dry run' to go through exactly who would do what. This would work for something like a fire-scenario, but also for other scenarios – like what to do if someone breaks into the house when you are in. I clearly remember being told in Lagos to just pretend you are asleep if you think a stranger is in your house.

There are other fairly simple precautions you should take, especially when new to a country. If you are out and about, don't wear flashy jewellery or walk around with your expensive new iPhone on display. Don't carry large amounts of cash, although do carry some money that you can offer a mugger. Be very careful getting cash out of a machine – look around before you do so, check if you are being watched, if in doubt, go elsewhere. If you're going out at night in your car, work out where you are going to park in advance so you don't end up wandering around in an area you don't know. If you feel it is necessary, tell someone where you are going and call when you get there/get home to tell them you are safe.

There are also some sensible precautions you can take when driving, especially if you are driving away from built-up areas and you are on your own. Be very careful about stopping if someone tries to wave you down – although this is a difficult one as you wouldn't want to ignore someone in genuine distress. If in doubt, stop further along the road and call the police or an ambulance. Try not to stop anywhere too remote if you are on your own, including an isolated petrol station (although better to stop for petrol than run out of petrol). In many countries, driving is particularly hazardous because of the appalling way people drive. Don't do anything silly, stay away from trouble, don't think you can drink and drive just because there are no breathalysers in that particular country and whatever you do, don't go native and start overtaking on corners!

Some of the other pieces of advice given to me by contributors includes:

- Be particularly careful around certain events or dates. For example, especially during local elections (could be a day to stay at home altogether in some countries) or on the anniversary of a particular event. Josine explained that in Greece she didn't venture out at all on November 17 – the anniversary of the eponymous terrorist group's first attack on the CIA and a day that, at least during the time she lived in Athens, was likely to lead to violent demonstrations.
- Many embassies, high commissions or consulates now have an excellent travel advice system, which you can access via email alerts, twitter or, in a crisis, via a text service. Sign up to these as soon as you can.
- Keep an eye on the local newspapers/TV news for updates to things like local lockdowns, gangland shootings that might have a knock-on effect etc.
- Make sure you always have good communication networks with the school in case there is a problem – even

if it is something as simple as the fact that you are going to be late to pick them up because of road closures.

- Be prepared for frequent power cuts in many countries. Get in batteries, torches etc. and know where the generator is and how to turn it on if you have one!
- If you've got a safe in the house, use it. As well as the obvious things like money, jewellery etc., keep things like passports and other important papers locked up.
- Consider getting a dog, especially if your partner is going to be away a lot and you'll be in your house on your own. It can provide comfort as well as a good alert system.
- Be more alert and more aware if you stand out. Being blond, for example, might gain you more attention than you wish in some countries. Blending in as much as possible, e.g. with clothing, is the most sensible option. This is especially true in Muslim countries where you will need to find out in advance what is and isn't acceptable clothing to wear out and about. This will be different in every country – in Pakistan for example I was fine so long as my shoulders and upper arms were covered, and I wore a skirt or shorts/trousers that went below the knees; in Saudi, women are expected to be covered up much more.
- Be aware of local customs and laws. Especially on some of the serious things like drugs. Well, don't get involved with illegal drugs at all – but in some countries it's even against the law to import certain seemingly innocuous medicines like nasal sprays.

For more detailed and specific advice on safety, the FCO's Travel Advice pages contain very specific and up-to-date advice on every country in the world, which should be heeded and in particular followed if it advises not to travel somewhere as your insurance might be invalidated: https://www.gov.uk/foreign-travel-advice.

Now that we've covered much of the practicalities of your first few weeks or months as an expat, it's time to look at what else can help ease you into your new life. And in the next chapter, I consider what some people consider one of the most daunting aspects of living overseas: hiring domestic staff.

Some More Websites to Help You in the Early Days:

A great (and very funny) blog post about bringing tampon supplies into your host country: http://kirstyriceonline.com/2011/02/the-traveling-tampon.html

UK Government advice for travel to every country in the world, including latest threats: https://www.gov.uk/foreign-travel-advice

And the US State department equivalent: http://travel.state.gov/content/passports/english/alertswarnings.html

And from Australia: http://www.smartraveller.gov.au/

UK Foreign Office website that provides general advice for travelling abroad: https://www.gov.uk/knowbeforeyougo

Some safety and security tips for travellers and expats: http://www.expatexchange.com/article/4231/Expat-Safety-Safety--Security-Tales--Tips-for-Travelers--Expats

For some sensible advice from the Met Police in the UK about how to protect your home: http://content.met.police.uk/Site/crimepreventionbumblebee

Tips and tricks to pick up any language. Apparently. http://www.babbel.com/magazine/10-tips-from-an-expert?slc=engmag-a1-vid-bv1-tipsandtricks-ey

Domestic Staff:
Finding Them, Keeping Them and
Treating Them Like Human Beings

Although many of you will have cleaners or childminders back home, it's often not until you move to another country that domestic staff suddenly take on such significance in your life. In this chapter I look at how to find such staff, how to handle their working arrangements, what sort of problems you might encounter and most importantly, how to treat them.

A word of warning: much of the following is aimed at people moving to countries where labour is cheap and they can afford to employ domestic staff. I realise this will not include everyone. Many of you may be 'Chief Cook and Bottlewasher, CEO of The Home and have a BSc in Housekeeping' as one of my respondents described herself. If this is you I am very sorry, please feel free to ignore this entire chapter, humble apologies etc. But on the other hand if you want to find out how the other half live, do read on!

A while ago, before I started researching this book, I remember reading a thread on the parenting forum Mumsnet's Living Overseas section about whether ones' maid in Singapore should live in or live out.

It was a perfectly reasonable discussion, involving a group of mums comparing the hassle of having someone else in the apartment all the time with you against the freedom of having childcare 24/7. At least, it seemed like a perfectly reasonable discussion if you lived in Singapore, or Hong Kong or one of those other countries where having live-in domestic staff is the norm and not an unheard luxury.

It was only when some non-overseas domiciles (e.g. other Mumsnet members who did not live abroad) started taking the pee a little that the discussion showed itself for what it really was. A perfectly reasonable discussion amongst people who lived in a weird expat bubble where everything you know and have known is turned on its head, where having not one, not two but possibly three or even four members of domestic staff working for you is totally normal, and where if you're not careful you'll forget how to iron, how to cook a meal and even how to put your own children to bed. Yup, moving to many countries in the developing world can mean that you, too, can live like a Queen...and possibly turn into a lazy slattern.

But in circumstances like this, it's fine to let other people do the hard work. After all, it's probably very hot (otherwise you probably wouldn't be able to afford to pay for any more help around the house than you would in your home country – it seems to be the law that the hotter a country, the cheaper the staff), and, more importantly, you are likely to be supporting the livelihood of quite a lot of people. Hiring staff isn't the problem – it's how you treat them that matters.

I have had many discussions over the years about having people work for you in your home. Of course this is perfectly normal all over the world. I am about to hire a cleaner to work for me to clean my house for two hours a week with the hope that she'll keep the dust and dirt at bay while I get on with writing this.

But moving overseas can be a whole new ballgame when it comes to having people working for you in your home. We're not talking two hours here; we're talking two days. Or more. We're not just talking about a bit of cleaning. We're talking about having someone who will cook and clean and dust and scrub the floors and iron and make the beds and baby sit and shop and tidy. We're talking about someone else who will mow the grass and water the garden and cut back the uncontrollable jungle or collect the mangoes from the tallest trees, someone else again who will drive you around, or open the gate when you come home from driving yourself somewhere or who will stand on those same gates all night long ensuring your safety while you sleep peacefully inside. In short, we're talking about a whole army of people who you may or may not employ but who, if you do, will hopefully work their guts out often for what seems to you like a total pittance. These people are your supporters, your saviours, your guardians and very often your friends.

So what is the one thing you need to know about hiring and keeping domestic staff to work for you?

Treat these people with respect!

It is difficult having people in your house, on their knees, scrubbing the floor or up to their ears in ironing your sheets. I can't say I have ever totally enjoyed the slightly uneasy relationship between myself, their employer, and the fabulous people I have employed over the years. I know some people absolutely hate having people in their house doing their dirty work (and washing their dirty laundry). But if you think of them as you would any other employee, as an accountant or an admin assistant or a plumber or mechanic or anyone really who makes a living doing a difficult job, it helps get round some of the awkwardness. Which, incidentally, is usually your issue not theirs – they see themselves as doing an honest job to take home a wage to feed their families or pay for their children's education or ensure their safety. End of.

Of course it would be wrong of me, not to say patronising, to suggest that everyone you employ will be some sort of perfect guardian angel. Just like people everywhere, you will come across good staff and not so good staff. There will also be personality clashes, disagreements over how things are done and even (and yes I have experienced this myself) power struggles over who is the boss of the house. I'll never forget not being allowed the key into one of the cupboards in our house in St Lucia because our helper at the time wanted to control the bed linen. I'm not ashamed to say that she didn't last long in our employ and I think it is always important to make sure that you are happy with your staff because at the end of the day you are going to be seeing an awful lot of them.

One of the inspirations for writing this book was the fantastic *Diplomatic Baggage* by Brigid Keenan. My close friend Lorna gave me this book when we were posted to Islamabad, my first venture into 'trailing spouse' world as opposed to 'my very own posting, with a job title and everything' world. Brigid's description of her life in a new posting (in her case Kazakhstan) lifted me through those difficult first few weeks and, in particular, the way she spoke about how her staff were her sole companions during the early days has stuck with me ever since. Of her three staff she writes: '...they don't speak a word of English...this is a bit worrying because in the early days of these foreign postings when the telephone never rings (or if it does it's the wrong number), lonely expat wives tend to lean rather heavily on our Ninas and Iras and Yuris since they are our only contact with the rest of the human race'.

Oh, yes, I certainly recognised this. Brigid had Nina and Ira and Yuri; in Islamabad I had Ansa. My helper-come-cook-come-nanny was my lifeline when we first arrived.

It was a big post but most of the families were still away for the summer, and it was a difficult place to get out and about before you knew your way around a bit. I found Ansa when she knocked on my door one day asking for work: she was employed by one of our neighbours and colleagues but theirs was not a happy arrangement and she was looking for something else. I thought I'd give her a go and took her on. It was probably the cleverest thing I did the whole three months we managed to live there before the Marriott bombing forced us to leave the country.

Even now, years later, both my husband and I still talk of Ansa with fondness. As well as cleaning the house beautifully, she was soon legendary on the compound for her amazing curries. She was also the only person who could get our then seven-month-old baby to sleep simply by rubbing her belly (we still call this the 'Ansa rub'). And on the one night that my husband had to be away and M (the baby) was awake all night crying with a sore throat, it was Ansa who came in the next morning and sat with her and our other daughter while I finally got an hour or two's sleep, safe in the knowledge that my children were with someone I trusted. This alone was worth the wage we paid her (much of which, incidentally, paid for the education of her two daughters).

So finding the right staff is obviously an important task. There is no right or wrong way to do this, it will differ from country-to-country, and you may have your own preferred method. Some people try taking on their predecessor's workers, which is a bit of a lottery but certainly can work.

Angela, arriving in Kingston, Jamaica with her husband and baby daughter, took on Pamela from the previous family: 'We were lucky to have her. She was completely trustworthy and reliable. I do not feel we had a typical relationship as we would have long conversations, I would make lunch for her and would drop her off back at her house. I did this because I felt more comfortable treating her this way. However, when visiting Jamaican friends I could see this was not the norm, and staff were very much treated as staff. Having said that, Pamela never took advantage, kept her eye out for me and having someone I could leave my child with without worrying was invaluable.'

In contrast Sharon, who I also met in Kingston but who had previously been posted to Bangladesh, South Africa and Rwanda with her husband Mark, preferred to find her own staff. She said: 'Having done four postings, I have now come to the conclusion that inheriting your predecessors' staff is largely a bad idea. By all means recruit from within the expat circle, but taking on staff, especially when they have worked in your house before, has never worked for me. They want to carry on as they did before, and you want to make your own mark. No rights or wrongs, just a mess!'

So if you don't take on your predecessor's staff, then how do you find them?

How urgent a task this is will depend on your individual circumstances: in some cases you can take your time until you find the right person. But if, for example, you need childcare straight away or if you live in a very large house in a very hot country, you are almost certainly going to need some help as close to day one as possible.

The best thing to do is put out feelers before you arrive and, if necessary, ask if there is anyone else's helper you can hire temporarily while you find your own permanent staff. This could either be a shared arrangement or you might find you can take someone on while the person or people they normally work for are on leave or out of the country. If you are going somewhere with a large and organised expat community this should be relatively straightforward. However, many of you will not be in this situation and will have to find ways of finding your own staff.

In some countries this will be surprisingly easy, as the day you rock up to your new home you'll find potential employees knocking on the door looking for work. How they know you're there and you're new I have no idea but somehow on the 'expat workers network' the message will go out there's a newbie in town and there they'll be.

Of course taking on any old Tom, Dick or Harry that turns up on your doorstep is always going to be a risk and if possible word-of-mouth recommendations are usually going to work better. So even if they do turn up unannounced do at least ask for references and if possible ask around the other local expats. You might find that the reason they are looking for work is because they have just been sacked for stealing. Or for being an atrocious cook. Or whatever.

When it comes to looking for someone to nanny or babysit for you, personal recommendations and/or references are absolutely essential. Most workers will know this, and will present you with said references when asked. It is extremely important that you follow these up – especially if you won't have much time to spend with the nanny/baby sitter before you have to leave the children on their own with her (e.g. if you are starting a job).

In some countries there is an established route to finding the right staff – for example in Hong Kong there is a 'HK Helpers' group on Facebook where people recommend helpers who are looking for work, according to Rachel who had a live-in helper when she lived there. In other countries you might find your land-lord or landlady can recommend someone. Or you may be able to advertise for them in local newspapers or newsletters.

But however you find your helpers/gardeners/cooks/nannies etc. it is important to make sure you draw up some sort of contract with them and that you both understand what is required. This will differ from country-to-country and individual-to-individual but a short list of the sort of things you might want to consider includes:

- Which days will they work and what will their hours be?
- Will they have a key to let themselves in, or will you or someone else always be at home when they are there? If you do give them a key, do you want to use a different lock on the day they are not there, for security reasons?
- What exactly is required of them – will you leave them a daily list of tasks? Or let them get on with their jobs – e.g. trusting them to know what needs doing on which day?
- How much will they be paid – and will this be hourly/daily/weekly or monthly?
- When will they get paid and how – e.g. in cash (most normal in my experience), cheque, straight into a bank account?
- Will they get a bonus – e.g. at Christmas – and if so how much will this be and when will it be paid?
- Will they be expected or required to do any overtime – e.g. if they are a nanny will they also be contracted to babysit some evenings; or if they work in the house will you expect them to help out at parties etc.? If so, is this included in their wages or will you pay them extra? And will the hourly rate be different or the same as their daytime rate?

- If you are employing a driver what will happen if you or your partner takes him (or her) away on overnight journeys? E.g. will they stay in the same hotel/eat with you etc.?
- What will you do about meals if they are working through a mealtime? Will you provide lunch or expect them to bring their own in?
- Will you provide a uniform? This doesn't have to be an old-fashioned, starched maid's outfit; for some staff, having something to change into and out of each day will save them ruining their own clothes.

This list is in no way exhaustive but if you are employing staff for the first time it can be a scary prospect – if possible find out what other people pay their staff and if they have contracts you can use. It's usually easier all round if everyone has similar terms and conditions, but don't feel you can't pay your helpers a bit more than other people if you feel they deserve it (especially after they have been with you for a while). If you need more help in finding out what you should be paying your staff, some countries have formal websites that can help – for example in Hong Kong there is a page on hiring domestic workers on the very useful and full of good information Gov.hk website and on the South Africa info website there is a page called You and Your Domestic/Madam. I list these websites below but if in doubt, you can always ask on your local expat forum, or quiz your predecessor, neighbour, local busybody…you know the drill by now!

It's also helpful to have a probationary period – if you feel it's not working out it's easier to let someone go this way than if you give them the impression that they have been taken on permanently. I say easier – it's still not easy, whether you have employed them for one week, one month or one year. I speak from experience of trying to sack the helper in St Lucia who wouldn't let me have the key to the linen cupboard. As well as thinking she was the boss of the house, I also found her quite terrifying and spent my days hidden away in a local café, while the girls were at school rather than being in the house with her. Eventually I realised how ridiculous this was but it took months to pluck up the courage to tell her I no longer required her services.

If you do find yourself in this situation, the easiest way is to treat it as you would any other staff member in a normal place of employment – give them warnings and tell them that if x, y or z doesn't happen (or happens again) then you won't be able to keep them on. This is much harder if it simply is a clash of personalities, in which case you might need to make up a few reasons.

In some circumstances, there will be no question about it and you will just need to sack them: stealing, for example, needs no warning (although here is a whole new debate: in very poor countries where your staff might have a lot of people relying on their pitiful wage, how wrong is it to take a small amount of money they find lying around in your bedroom? Of course stealing is always wrong but you could have a long discussion about ethics and morals around this. It's probably best just to not leave anything of any value lying around if you can help it).

So now you've hired your hopefully reliable member of staff. The next question many people will be asking themselves, especially if this is the first time they have done this, is how to treat them? By this I mean are they your friends or are they your staff?

Again, if in doubt, think back to bosses you might have had in jobs in the past. Hopefully a decent boss will treat you with friendliness and respect. But there is always going to be a slight difference between them and another colleague at the same level as you. After all, who wants to be best mates with someone they might have to discipline or, even worse, sack?

Many people find getting this right at the start can be difficult. But it probably is better to try and get it right from the beginning – you don't want to make them think you are their best friend but then find you have to start cooling off a bit if they start to take advantage.

Nicola (in Holland with husband and son) said her only advice on staff was to 'start off as a "manager" and not a friend, make sure you have a set of no go's and be clear and demonstrate how you want things'.

Kathleen, who has employed cleaners in Kuwait, Algeria, Qatar and France, said she was always friendly and polite – but they weren't her companions.

Marianne, who has lived on several Caribbean islands including St Lucia and Barbados, agreed saying: 'I found it hard to not be friends with my cleaner or help as I wasn't used to it. But try hard not to be mates and keep it professional.'

On the other side, there are people who believe that anyone who works in your home (especially if they are looking after your children) should be treated like family. 'You need to trust them, you have to leave your children with them and you have to rely on their loyalty,' said Viktor, who hired a Filipino maid in Saudi Arabia. 'You should build strong relations with them in the same way as you would with other family members.'

Katrina, who hired a local woman to help clean their house when they lived in Italy, said: 'She and her family became our extended family there. I figure if you meet Mary Poppins, welcome her into your life!'

Of course it doesn't have to be all or nothing and most people will still want to pass some pleasant time with their staff even if they don't become bosom buddies. Judy sat and drank tea, as well as learnt Russian, with her cleaner in Azerbaijan. And when I lived in Kingston, I found out more about what life was like for the ordinary Jamaican from my helper Anne-Marie than I did from any of my highbrow contacts made through my job at the British High Commission.

I would love to now give you a list of all the potential problems, issues and pitfalls you could expect when hiring domestic staff abroad. Unfortunately, this would be impossible as given how many different countries/cultures/personalities/nationalities/tribes etc. there are in the world, each of which brings their own particular issues with them, this book is not long enough to cover even half the challenges you might find yourself facing. However, from personal experience and from those of others who have contributed to this book, here are a few to be aware of:

- Poaching. A big no in many expat communities: don't poach your neighbour's staff. This is usually done by offering more money and in my experience it usually seems to be particularly good cooks who are offered the most generous bribes to move employers. In particular, it's massively unfair to poach nannies – especially if someone else's child has become used to that particular carer. By all means though, borrow or share staff.

- You might find yourself having to act as an intermediary in arguments or even physical fights between your staff. You might also find yourself more involved in their personal lives than you may wish. This happened to my own mother, Rowena, during their posting to Yaounde: 'There could be lots of aggravations - sorting out quarrels between the staff in Cameroon and lending money and sorting out personal problems e.g. the cook worrying about his son, thrown into jail in Chad for deflowering a virgin... Staff do seem to loom large in postings!'

- Let go. By this, I mean don't try and control everything your staff do. You might want everything 'just so', but telling them exactly how to do it can lead to disaster, as Warren, who accompanied his wife Jacqui to Bangladesh, explained: 'If you tell them exactly what you want and how you do it, they will do their best, but you cannot be too exacting. What works in the UK does not necessarily go in Dhaka. For example, if you insist on beef for dinner, your cook/bearer will buy and serve beef, and it might well be awful. But if you allow him the leeway to choose or listen to advice about what is in season, what is good that is available in the market, meals will be better...if your staff are experienced, better leave them get on with it, adapt yourself a bit but give them some feedback. Life will be different, but better for it.'

- Warren also had some advice about the next point, which is language problems. If you and your staff do not share a common language, you are going to have to find a way round this (dictionaries, sign language, Google translate). However, even if you do apparently speak the same language, local patois, slang or even just accent can cause quite a few problems. Warren explained: 'Our only real problem with staff is that our driver's English is not great. Although we are able to understand each other, we do need to check his understanding now and again. During handover, our predecessor gave him his car key and asked him to take it to our apartment. He meant the car, to pick us up. Instead, the driver turned up with the key, leaving the car behind...'

- Often you will be asked to lend money to your staff, or to give them an advance on wages. This is fine, especially as you might be the only place they can go to for a loan for something such as school fees, but it's best to keep an accurate and official record. It's also important to ensure you have a proper system for them to pay you back e.g. taking a little off their wages every month. It saves any stress and embarrassment between you if you can make it into a 'business' transaction. If it is easier, you could offer to advance their Christmas bonus or similar.

- If you have children, try not to let them boss the staff around. They really need to learn to respect them and the best way for them to do this is by following your example. It's also a good idea not to let the maids do all the clearing up for the children – at some point they will be leaving their expat bubble and will need to learn to make their own beds and clean up their own toys. Instruct your staff to leave things in their rooms or playrooms and get the children to tidy up as often as possible. Of course, if you have a teenager who leaves cockroach-attracting pizza crusts under the bed this might not be such a good idea. But you get my drift.

Employing domestic staff can be a tricky business, for them as well as for you, but most of all it is a privilege. I still miss the man who came in twice a week to do our ironing in Islamabad. I've been out of expat-land for a few years, and apart from the above-mentioned cleaner, we're now having to cope with doing all our own washing, cooking, shopping, mopping, childcare and gardening. Of course it's a lot easier doing all this in a country where the temperatures don't have you sitting sweating in a sticky heap in the corner, desperately trying to catch the slightest whiff of breeze from the torpid sponge of a day outside. But there are plenty of times when I'd move back to Islamabad just to have someone iron our sheets.

With staff in place – if you need them – you've crossed one of the biggest hurdles for many expats. Hopefully, your relationship with them will be long, fruitful and stress-free – leaving you the time, and energy, to concentrate on the next step in your expat journey. In the following chapter I start to look at settling in, and how to ensure you begin to find yourself some sort of a social life in your new home.

Some Useful Websites to Help You Find Domestic Staff

Information about hiring staff in Indonesia; some of these tips could be used whichever country you are in:
http://www.expat.or.id/info/hiringhouseholdstaff.html

And hiring someone in Dubai:
http://www.expatarrivals.com/article/hiring-a-maid-in-dubai

And India: http://www.expatarrivals.com/india/delhi/domestic-help-in-delhi

And Singapore:
http://www.expatfocus.com/c/aid=938/articles/singapore/employ ing-a-maid-in-singapore/

Hong Kong:
http://www.gov.hk/en/residents/employment/recruitment/foreig ndomestichelper.htm

And South Africa:
http://www.southafrica.info/services/rights/domesticrights.htm# .VL-Z0S5JSdM

What's it like to have a live-in housemaid?
http://my.telegraph.co.uk/expat/annabelkantaria/10149874/whats -it-like-to-have-a-live-in-housemaid/#more-10149874

Settling In, Finding Things to Do, Protecting Your Sanity

By this point, hopefully, you will be starting to feel a bit more settled. You'll have found somewhere to live, be driving like a local and know where to buy your food, cleaning products and other essential items. You'll be starting to find your way around, probably have got lost a few times but crucially found your way home again. So what now?

I've already touched on making friends in an earlier chapter, but now I want to look at making more permanent connections, hopefully meeting people you really click with and who you can imagine sticking with for a while. I also want to talk about how you occupy yourself, especially if you're not going to be working (again, that'll come later), and what to do if you really can't find enough to fulfil you. Finally, I'll be sharing some of the great tips on how to keep yourself sane during your posting as suggested by some of my fabulous and fabulously experienced contributors.

Connecting

For many people, making superficial friends is relatively easy. It's the real friends, the ones whose shoulders you can cry on when the going gets too tough, who will be there for you when your partner has disappeared on yet another two week trip out of the country, who you can trust to pick your children up from school and who you hope you'll still be in touch with years down the line, they are the tough ones to meet.

I will admit that most of my advice is based on that given to me by female partners so I do realise there is a bit of a female-centric bias to it. However, guys, if you're reading this and shaking your head at why women have to moan so much and can't just get on with it, I apologise. Please have a look at the chapter later in the book 'When You Don't Quite Fit In' and if you still can't find what you're looking for please get in touch by email or via my website (you can find out how at the front of the book) and let me know!

So, many of you will probably have met other expats pretty quickly – a topic already dealt with in the 'Arrival and the Early Days' chapter. Some of those expats, of course, might very well go on to be the sort of friends we're talking about (the lasting ones rather than the 'they'll-do-for-now' ones). But often the secret to real friendships is that it takes time because it's shared experiences that bind people.

This is of course true wherever you live – for example, many people make close friendships when they first have children, as they share the life-changing experiences of having a baby with a group of other parents. You've got to have those experiences before people are going to become real friends because only then can you start to forge that closeness you get by having been through something with someone else. As Colleen, previously in Canada but now in the Netherlands, explained, 'You have to build up memories with people and share things in order to make friends. I find it relatively easy on one level, but initially miss the depth of connection that you have with old friends.'

But of course in order to have those experiences with people you've got to meet them in the first place. We've already spoken about where to meet them – e.g. through the school, expat groups, colleagues, language courses, church – all the usual places. But there's also the unusual places, because it's hard to predict where – and when – you are going to meet the person or hopefully people who are going to become your proper friends.

The advice that most people gave me was just to grit your teeth and get on with it. It's no fun socialising with people you don't know well – no one particularly likes the meaningless small talk you have to make at the beginning when you're first getting to know someone.

But, as Dawn, who has moved to Chiang Mai in Thailand with her husband, advised: 'Don't wait for others to make the first move towards you even if you're an expat newbie. Put yourself out there! Seek to be an encouragement to others even if you're the new one and they've been the expat for a while.' Despite her advice, Dawn also recognised that sometimes it's better to acknowledge that it's okay NOT having friends for a while: 'We are slowly finding people we click with a bit more. However, we are trying to be patient with that process as there is plenty for us to learn as a family and as individuals, during a time that feels a bit lonelier...enjoy the additional time with your family and be okay with a bit of loneliness – I think that in most circumstances, the relationships will come (right? Or so I've been told!).'

One person who thought she could do without friends but then realised differently was Olga, who, in the Netherlands, 'thought that I didn't need friends and was very happy on my own. Until a "well-meaning" woman called the police on me because my girl had a tantrum. I then contacted expat organisations and made friends very quickly'.

Olga went on to make more friends through those expat organisations but had less luck with the local Dutch people, who she found were 'usually busy with their own lives'.

This is one of the problems with moving abroad. You might be keen to meet the locals but, unfortunately, they are usually not so keen to meet you. Not because there is anything wrong with you in particular, but rather because, for starters they don't need new friends, and besides which you're unlikely to be around for long so why should they invest their time in you?

In fact, rather than being amazed by not being able to make friends with locals when I was living abroad, I was more astonished that I made any at all. In St Lucia, I had a few local friends but almost without exception they had some form of 'overseas' link themselves. Liz, who was the friend I met at my daughter's swimming class that I mentioned in the Chapter Three: Arrival and the Early Days, was half British and has many friends and relatives in the UK. Others were married to expats.

The one exception was Shakima, whose daughter took my eldest daughter under her wing at school. Shakima had a totally different upbringing and background to me, she was about half my age and in any other time and place our paths would never have crossed. But I valued that friendship because it gave me an insight into the local culture, it helped me feel closer to the island and although I knew it was unlikely we would ever be lifetime buddies, for a short while it helped me feel just a little bit like I belonged.

However, for me, Shakima *was* the exception rather than the rule and I think most people do find that their closest friends tend to be other expats, whether from their own country or from other countries (it's interesting which nations you are drawn to; as a Brit I have often found it easy to make friends with Scandinavians, Germans and New Zealanders).

It's important to feel fine about this – leave behind any preconceived ideas you may have of only mingling with the locals and just be happy with the friends you make, wherever they are from.

Hilde, who has travelled extensively in Africa, Asia, Central America and Europe and is now living in Bangladesh with her husband and daughter, has made local friends during her overseas postings but finds that sometimes 'for a good talk I really need another expat who can understand me better, or who shares a similar culture'.

Louise recalled how she 'tried to go down the Spanish route and avoid expat clubs' in Madrid, but after nine months gave in, joined an expat club and made some friends.

Of course everyone is different and while, on the whole, most people I have been in touch with during the course of researching this book found it hard to make friends with local people, there were definitely a few who find it easier to blend in.

'Because we live among the locals, we use public transportation and so we meet people at bus stops, in cafes, by just walking about,' said Florence, who has lived in Panama and Mexico and is now in Scotland. 'We haven't really sought out expats to be friends.'

This probably depends as much on the country you are in as anything, but even within the same country you can have a very different experience. Belinda, in one part of the States, reported that 'almost all my friends were locals, or at least American; I found most people were very open to getting to know new people. I very rarely met other expats/non-Americans'.

But over in Florida, Penny found it 'impossible to meet people unless you were a member of a church. There were many, many churches and everybody went. I was amazed at this, even though I went to American schools as a child and thought I knew them. American expats are nothing like those that live in the US'.

And Apple would agree – she has lived all over the world, travelling since 1958, and said, 'The hardest places are often the most surprising – for example USA and Scotland, where getting to know "locals" is difficult – I have enough friends and family already kind of scenario.'

Another problem you might find with trying to make local friends is cultural barriers. Certainly in Pakistan it was hard to meet Pakistani women, and in Qatar Adele said she found that the locals made no efforts at all, saying: 'The men can't speak to women, and many of the women don't speak English.' Others reported a similar story in UAE and Egypt.

Occupying yourself

Whether you've made friends or not – or even, in fact, to help you make them – you'll need to find some way to occupy yourself.

This is an incredibly difficult subject to cover as everyone is so different when it comes to how to pass your time as a 'trailing spouse' or 'accompanying partner'. Even the two different terms suggest very different views on the role of the non-working partner in this situation. The 'trailing' word is hated by many as it suggests someone sort of pathetically following after the successful worker, limply hanging around in the margins, just sort of being there while your spouse works on his or her brilliant career.

This of course is not the truth at all for so many of you – some of you will be working yourself, or you'll be looking after children. But for many of you, there will be that slightly empty feeling, a yawning gap opening up ahead of you. Whether you see that gap as one to be feared or one to be filled is up to you.

Perhaps in the end it comes down to mind set as much as anything – if you look at this time as an opportunity rather than a problem, if you think of things to do that you would never have had the chance to try in your busy life back home (if you had a busy life back home, of course), you might find you end up with your life going off in directions you would previously never have planned.

For many this means being creative through, for example, blogging or perhaps other forms of writing. For others it can mean starting a small business or volunteering, learning the local language or studying. In my parents' day, being the spouse in itself could be the full-time job; certainly the life of an Ambassador's wife was almost as busy as that of the Ambassador (and, in many ways, just as important).

My mother recalls her life in Cameroon:

'After nearly thirty years of following my husband round the world and struggling to find a role for myself in each new post, being the wife of the British ambassador in a West African country was a completely different experience.

'Even before we left the UK I found myself included in many of the briefings and on arrival I instantly had a role, whether I liked it or not, as "the Ambassador's wife". For a start, we were straight away welcomed into the local ambassadorial circles and quickly found ourselves getting to know the other "HE's" and spouses so making friends was easy, probably helped by the fact it was not a country with a huge diplomatic corps.

'My role also meant I was able to accompany my husband on his visits to far flung parts of the country and to the other three countries he covered. Generally a "delegation" was expected and, being a very small embassy, I was pressed into service to be that "delegation". This led to some fascinating experiences from discussing the use of English words in the local language with the President of Equatorial Guinea, to joining in the dancing with the local chiefs' wives.

'I soon found that my rusty French was not up to diplomatic dinner conversation and joined an Alliance Francaise class which consisted of a wonderful cross section of classmates from Liberian refugees to New Zealand aid workers. My language skills increased rapidly as I found myself immersed in local politics and read the papers and watched TV to glean useful information to stimulate conversation at dinner parties where my place at the table, often next to a leading politician or businessman, gave me the opportunities to quiz their views and pass on any information gained.

'There was also, of course, a "residence" to run (twenty years ago it was simply expected that this would be done by the Ambassador's partner) and a role in keeping an eye on the British community. This involved anything from taking in a young British medical student, taken ill while on work experience in a local hospital, to running a monthly lunch for any British women who would appreciate an occasional chat with fellow expatriates. This seemed to be appreciated and those who turned up ranged from nuns to croupiers from the local casino! My time as an ambassadorial spouse was an unreal four years but great fun.'

Of course, not all of us get to be the wife of an ambassador. But whatever you choose to do, it is important to find something meaningful, or at least fun. I have seen a number of relationships fall apart because the non-working partner failed to do this and in the end couldn't find enough reason to stay. However much you love your partner, however much you wanted him or her to take this job, to have this opportunity, you do need to also remember your own needs.

When I was growing up as a 'Third Culture Kid' (TCK – the generally accepted term for someone who moves between countries – or cultures – in their childhood; as an adult, they become known as an ATCK – Adult Third Culture Kid), I remember the dreaded thing for expat wives to end up doing was playing bridge. It was almost like it was shorthand for 'bored out of her brain and just biding time until her life could start again'. It also, sadly, probably involved drinking too much alcohol.

Hopefully, these days are in the past – although if you Google 'expat wife' and 'alcohol' you get plenty of debate on the subject. But don't totally dismiss playing bridge or its modern day equivalents like scrap booking or card making groups, book clubs, activities like cultural groups or exercise classes. All of these, although they might not totally fulfil you, can help you survive until you find the thing that does. They can also be a great way to network and very often that is the key to finding your thing.

Here are some other examples of what people have found to do:

- 'Reading groups, quilting, language learning, prayer groups... I've often found groups of women gathering and engaging in these activities. It is a low pressure and fun way to meet new people.' *Richelle, mother of eight, has lived in Bangladesh, Canada and Niger.*
- 'I'm pretty good at filling my time one way or another. Setting up the ExpatChild website was one of my projects.' *Carole, mum of one, creator of expatchild.com.*

- 'I listened to others and I read the local paper to practice learning the language. It was in the local paper that I read of a charity that was looking for volunteers and that seemed like a good fit for my values. So I focussed on learning the language and then volunteering.' *Colleen, the Netherlands.*

- 'In Dubai I took up Tai Chi which I really enjoyed – at last a sport where I didn't have to sweat! Seriously though I found there was more to it than I expected and it was quite challenging.' *Judy, who moved to Azerbijan with her husband and son. She later moved to UAE and Egypt before relocating to Canada where she started volunteering as a director of social media for Families in Global Transition (http://www.figt.org/). She also now works in real estate.*

- 'I started a blog and spend a lot of my time writing and thinking about new posts, I don't "fill in" time. I am an introvert and love being by myself. Otherwise I do chores, cook or read.' *Olga, who also found work as a trainer of intercultural communication.*

- 'I went for a masters degree (distance based) and I am now studying to become a certified health coach. I would like to start an online practice and organise local activities related to health and happiness. I am also thinking of writing a book and I want to plan our next move…I don't need to fill in time. I enjoy my life abroad. It's often lonely and not always easy but if I had to choose again I would do the same.' *Hilde, newly arrived in Bangladesh.*

- 'I worked, but I also found there was much to do in the social/charity area that helped me to meet other women. Orphanages, volunteering to teach in local schools, gender entrepreneur workshops for local women and more.' *Jonelle, Baku, Azerbaijan.*

- 'Find a volunteer opportunity and it's amazing how many doors open.' *Apple, 11 countries since 1958.*

- 'I organised kid's playgroups and put together dance classes. I also looked for training courses e.g. in children's yoga, and have really enjoyed that.' *Monica, living in Bangkok with her husband and two children.*
- 'I blog, read, cook and plan to work on my masters degree. Those are my preferences.' *Tara, Al Khobar, Saudi Arabia.*
- 'In Singapore, I studied Mandarin, explored the island, went out with friends, volunteered in the kids' classrooms, sat on a couple of PTA committees. I didn't have a maid, so I also cooked, cleaned, shopped, and took care of my children.' *Maria, Singapore and Bordeaux.*
- 'I never get bored. In Dubai, I did three creative writing courses online via Gotham Writers Institute. I practiced Bikram yoga three times a week, I went to boot camp three times a week, went to the gym three times a week, and got the mother of all suntans whilst reading by the pool. I also volunteered as an accountant and admin person for a small local NGO run by a German doctor, which took up about a day a week on average. In Hong Kong, I joined a writing group, played tennis in a midweek league, went to the gym, had long boozy lunches (pre-pregnancy) and long teetotal lunches (when pregnant). I hiked a fair bit, too.' *Rachel, married to an investment banker, two young children, Dubai and Hong Kong.*

Looking back at these answers – which are just a selection of the ones I was sent – I am amazed at the creativity of partners thrust into the expat world, sometimes with little or no resources to help them find their way. In the end, almost everyone finds something to do with themselves. However, I did get quite a few replies that stated that yes, they were bored, including Hilary in the Netherlands who said she wasn't working and was 'bored beyond belief' and Nicola M, also in the Netherlands, who found things definitely improved when she found a job/role for herself.

When things really aren't working out

Of course everyone is likely to have a period, or periods, of restlessness. But what happens if you can't get past this, if you really cannot find enough to do to stop you going totally stir crazy?

You might enjoy the novelty of free time for a while, especially if you have come from a busy life back home, and even more so if you are in a country where sun bathing and pool parties are the norm. But this novelty very soon wears off and if you find yourself sitting around twiddling your thumbs every day, you're quickly going to descend into a very unhappy place. I will look at culture shock and depression in the next chapter, and relationships in the one after, but I just wanted to touch here on the fact that sometimes it really won't work out for you and in these cases it really is worth taking a long hard look at whether it's worth carrying on.

First of all, realise this: it is not your fault!

Even if you were fully behind the decision to move, even if you went into it with your eyes totally open, you've read all about expat life, you know what to expect. Even if all these things are true, you can still be unhappy – to the point of either needing, in one way or another, to get out.

For some this will mean both you and your partner (and children if you have any) leaving the posting. Sometimes this is inevitable. You didn't plan it this way, but it isn't fair on anyone – and it certainly isn't good for your relationship – if you're unreasonably unhappy. Another option is for you to go home and for your partner to commute – sometimes this is workable, sometimes it isn't, and a whole other book could be written around this very subject.

Finally, probably the least palatable suggestion of all but sadly one that is more common than people realise, is that you and your partner separate. I'm going to cover this in more detail in the chapter on relationships, but it's worth talking about the possibility of separation here as well.

Hopefully this will be absolutely the last option for you, especially if you have children. I am not a trained health professional or counsellor so can't give you proper advice, but if this does look like a possibility I would urge you to seek counselling or other help as soon as possible. The longer you leave it, the worse it is likely to be. And as any move, let alone an overseas move, can already put a huge strain on relationships, it's not surprising how quickly things can deteriorate when one (or both) partners are not happy in their new home. Which is one of the reasons for writing this book – to try and help ensure you don't get to this point in the first place.

In my research, I did ask whether people had ever thought about leaving a posting, or had actually left, because of being unhappy or bored. I got a mixed bag of responses.

Of those who answered this question, a slightly higher number of people (thirteen to ten) said they had never really thought of leaving a posting because of their own unhappiness (possibly because they were never really unhappy), that they were in this thing together. But others had considered it – either because of their own feelings or for other reasons. A few actually had left, although in most circumstances they had either left as a family or the working partner had managed to arrange it so they could continue the job by commuting. Others left for different reasons – health, work or schooling issues.

Unfortunately, a few also told me that their relationships broke down or was in the middle of breaking down, although of course it's hard to know whether this would have happened anyway. There is no easy solution to this but the main thing is to remember to go easy on yourselves and to realise that sometimes it is better to let go than to keep on both being unhappy.

Tips on surviving

So how can you best help yourself get through those times when you do just want to pack it all in and head home? There may well be a few times like this – not necessarily only at the beginning, you might find the entirety of your posting is full of ups and downs. One of the most important things for you to do is to understand culture shock and how this can affect you – and I will tackle that in the next chapter.

But here are some other tips from our experts to help you get through the difficult days:

- Holding your expectations with an 'open hand and a predetermined commitment to be flexible' as well as sticking it out a bit longer even when that felt impossible helped Richelle get through the hard times. She said: 'Trying new things that I might never have considered when I was back home in the States was also a profitable endeavour.'
- Say YES to everything you are invited to. Even if you really, really don't want to go. You can always leave if you hate it.
- 'Know what your values are, what is important to you, and find ways to express them through the various activities you do,' suggested Colleen. 'Look for things that allow you to express as many of them as possible to achieve a sense of balance in your life.'
- Judy's advice was don't turn your nose up at expat groups, or assume they are snobby or boring. 'I found that this was very rare and that these groups are a great first step in a new country. You don't have to make them a permanent part of your life, but connecting with women who can help you navigate the small day-to-day challenges and empathise with your situation – as only another expat can – will help you get established quickly.'
- Be a bit sneaky about telling people how long you plan to be somewhere, was Hilary's advice. 'When a trailing spouse says to you "how long are you here for?" it's actually their way of asking you "are you someone that I can be bothered to put the time and the effort in to get to

know and build a relationship with or are you just going to bugger off in six months".'

- Stay true to yourself, according to Olga in the Netherlands. 'If you're an extrovert, you'll find it easy to find new friends from different backgrounds. If you're an introvert, however, you may have less relationships, but make deeper connections. Also, try to balance meeting people from your own culture, other expats and locals.'

- 'Talk about it. Seek help. Know that you are not alone and that it is normal. Do not just complain, judge or blame, surround yourself with people who can help you see what is good. Do not just copy others – you are an individual and what works for you may not work for someone else,' advises Hilde, who is studying to become a certified health coach and wants to offer her services online on a website called Take Your Health to New Horizons: https://www.facebook.com/TakeYourHealth.ToNewHoriz ons?ref=br_tf.

- The Internet is a great tool, and a great way to find out about your new country, make connections etc. But it is a double-edged sword and certainly no substitute for real life interaction. Once you've made your connections online, go out and meet them in the flesh.

- Be open to new things. This is your chance to try something completely different and if it doesn't work out it doesn't matter. At least you've had the courage to try!

- 'Don't set expectations that making close friends will be really easy – it may take time and often that comes from left field. Just get involved and find people to share your experiences with. Don't try to ignore the expats – they can be painful but also a huge source of understanding and support. At the same time look for opportunities to make friends with people from the host nation – make an effort and expect that it will take a while. They are protective of

themselves as they often see expats come and go,' says
Louise, who has lived in Spain and Portugal.

- 'GET OUT OF YOUR HOUSE!' Is the very definite advice
  from Naomi, who has lived in India and Singapore. 'You
  accomplish nothing but breed more loneliness when you
  don't leave your house.'
- Try not to spend your whole time complaining about
  your new country. Try and understand and accept the
  differences, especially in a place where there is so little
  commonality between your new country and your old
  that it is pointless to compare the two. Embrace the
  newness!
- 'Go out with a smile on your face,' advises Nicola, who
  left the Netherlands to return home to the UK. 'Have a
  personal card with your address and contact details on. It
  sounds a little forward but someone will find this more
  easily than a little slip of paper and is more likely to give
  you a call or drop you an email.'

Once you've got your social life sorted, you might think it's all an
easy ride from here. Unfortunately, sometimes it has to get harder
before it can get easier and in the next chapter we look at one of the
main culprits for this: culture shock, and then what happens if the
initial shock leads ultimately to depression.

Some Websites to Help You Settle In:

Find friends and groups for a whole range of interests – a great
way to meet locals as well as fellow-expats:
http://www.meetup.com/

Internations – a site that promises to connect global minds in 390
cities around the world: http://www.internations.org/

A Small World calls itself a 'private international lifestyle club' which perhaps isn't as scary as it sounds: https://www.asmallworld.com/

Expat Blog is another website that allows you to connect with other people in your area: http://www.expat-blog.com/

There are more than 11,000 members of Gone Girl International, a website aimed at women 'living, working, loving, studying and travelling abroad': http://girlgoneinternational.com/

Apparently, us unsociable Brits are particularly bad at making friends with the locals: http://www.telegraph.co.uk/expat/11193034/Unsociable-British-expats-fail-to-make-local-friends.html

Culture Shock.
And What if Shock Turns into Depression

Everyone's heard of culture shock, but how many people really understand it? How many realise what an impact it can have on their lives, and how many people would actually recognise it in themselves or others they live with? In this chapter I take you through the basics of what culture shock actually means, how to know you've got it, and how to deal with it when it hits (and it probably will). I'll also talk about what to do if culture shock turns to depression – sadly, another relatively common issue amongst expats.

Here are a few authoritative views on what constitutes culture shock:

Wikipedia says:

Culture shock is the personal disorientation a person may feel when experiencing an unfamiliar way of life due to immigration or a visit to a new country, a move between social environments, or simply travel to another type of life.

The Oxford English Dictionary calls it:

The feeling of disorientation experienced by someone when they are suddenly subjected to an unfamiliar culture, way of life, or set of attitudes.

The InterNations online community (www.internations.org) explains it like this:

> *Culture shock is a phenomenon that all types of expats experience,*
> *no matter if they work abroad for the first time or if they are*
> *veterans in the field of expat assignments. Often, it is the deeper*
> *cultural differences in mind set, customs and interpersonal*
> *interaction that trigger this phenomenon and turn cultural*
> *transition into a struggle.*

Another way of looking at culture shock is by relating it to a grief cycle, one of the most well-known of which was originally described by counsellor Elizabeth Kubler-Ross and written up in her book *On Death and Dying*. Whilst Kubler-Ross intended her cycle to be used to help with loss in the form of bereavement, the five stages – denial, anger, bargaining, depression and acceptance – are easily transferable to other forms of loss such as the loss of identity, familiarity and confidence that goes with an overseas move.

This cycle would probably be more recognisable to someone who perhaps feels the move wasn't within their control and they weren't really part of the decision, or weren't totally happy about the move. This would make them more likely to jump into denial and anger, rather than the happier, honeymoon stage of the more traditional culture shock. However, eventually they both end with the acceptance stage – although it is generally recognised that you can go back and forth between different parts of the grief cycle and skip some bits of it altogether.

I could go on looking up different interpretations of culture shock forever, but in the end I've amalgamated as many different accounts as I can find to come up with this version of how I think culture shock can best be explained: *Culture shock could be defined as disorientation on moving somewhere unfamiliar, a rollercoaster of emotions. It is said to have four phases and each phase is described differently by different people but generally speaking they are: wonder/honeymoon, negotiation, adjustment and acceptance. You can move between the four phases in order or back and forth between them; you might skip some of the phases or not experience any of them.*

I then started asking people whether they thought they had experienced culture shock and – perhaps unsurprisingly – almost, without fail, everyone I asked said that yes, they thought they had. And those that dealt with it best did appear to be those who had some understanding of what they were going through. So it really is a good idea to read up on this before you move, or during the early weeks in your new life.

One of the most interesting aspects about culture shock is that it can affect you in whichever part of the world you move to.

When I was a lot younger, I spent six months living in New Zealand. The people of that beautiful country were lovely, easy going, fairly similar to us. Or so I thought. After not very long it really felt like I started to hate them. All of them! And their bank system! I hated the way you had to sign five different forms before you could open an account! And the way they crossed the road! And that you couldn't buy the right kind of Marmite!

Of course, these weren't true feelings; these were all just feelings as a result of one of the phases of culture shock, probably the 'negotiation' phase. Eventually I got through that phase and reached the acceptance stage, which was pretty good going within the six months that I lived there. In the end, I absolutely loved New Zealand and would live there permanently in a heartbeat – if it wasn't quite so far away from home.

I think it probably took longer in St Lucia. I know we definitely went through the honeymoon phase when we first arrived and enjoyed the beaches and the pool, exploring the different hotels where we could go for lunch and taking trips down to the all-inclusive resort on the south coast. I know there was then a long, difficult phase when I really did find a lot of things frustrating – despite the fact that I'd lived in the Caribbean before and should have known what to expect. I hated the heat and the traffic and the lack of variety in the shops and the weird school parades where we had to dress our children up as lawyers and police officers and watch them sing songs about daisies in the local Creole language. At least I think that was what they were singing about – I've never really got to the bottom of some of the odder St Lucian traditions.

During this phase we made the difficult decision to return home to the UK before the end of our posting, mostly because of schooling issues. But by the time we left, around sixteen months after arriving, I think I was moving closer to the acceptance stage and probably would have enjoyed the second half of the posting more than the first. This shows that, although we personally made the right decision in coming home when we did, it is probably always worth thinking about the culture shock cycle before making any really rash decisions.

Asked how long it took to feel comfortable, most people said it was usually around the six month mark, although many said this was when they were just starting to feel settled and in fact it wasn't until they had been there for a year when they really felt happy.

You are likely to go through the hardest part of your posting from a couple of months after arrival until around about six-nine months. From then on, don't expect it to be all plain sailing – as sometimes something small like a close friend leaving or a visit home can set off another bout of anger/hostility. But you should at least find it easier to bounce back. If you don't, it might be worth thinking about whether you might be suffering from depression (see below).

Many of my survey respondents described their experiences of culture shock to me.

Jonelle, who lived and worked in Baku, Azerbaijan for ten years, said: 'The first year was discovery of all things new (honeymoon); second year negotiation – I got hit by every local to borrow money, find a job for son/daughter/sister etc. Third year I adjusted and became more involved with expats, charity work, softball, new restaurant/social hangouts and withdrew from the local friends/clingers. Fourth year I got divorced, which was another year of adjustment. Fifth year I took a new job and was elevated on the social scale – which helped with the acceptance. Sixth to ninth year were acceptance, so pretty straightforward. But coming back to the US, post 9/11, was a roller coaster of confusion...' She then goes on to describe how she went through the whole culture shock cycle once again on her return home – something many people don't anticipate and something I will talk about in a later chapter on repatriation.

Louise, who lived in Spain and Portugal, said she didn't consciously think of it as culture shock at the time and that 'looking back I think it was part of a transition process'. But she went on to add: 'Honeymoon I can definitely relate to – excitement and fun of the first few months of exploration and newness. Adjustment yes, finding a way to make it work. Annoyance at the host culture – yes to a certain extent but that's something that continues for me, it all becomes more and more familiar but then things pop up which really gets to me at times.'

Nicola, who moved first to Ireland and later to the Netherlands, said that the worst culture shock she had was moving to Ireland, 'a culture so like my own, that I knew from childhood, but that is actually very different'. She also said that her shock was made worse because she was making the adjustment from being a 'career girl' to being a new parent – as she put it: 'mind blower'.

I have already mentioned that I think the adjustments you have to make on moving overseas have many similarities to those that you have to make when you become a parent for the first time, and in fact the emotions that go with these – including depression – are also very similar. Olga, who lives in the Netherlands and combined moving with becoming a first-time parent said: 'I tend to think that culture shock is less about experiencing different cultures, more about personal development and change – all important changes bring with them a sense of loss, questioning your identity and renegotiating it again. But for me, the biggest shock came with having a child.'

So to do them both at the same time is a double whammy, and if you do find yourself in this situation – whether you move just before or just after having the baby, be even more kind to yourself, look out for the signs of depression and seek help sooner rather than later (I say a bit more about post-natal depression in Chapter Sixteen, which looks at health).

But if you think your emotions are just the normal, common or garden culture shock, how do you deal with it? After all, no one wants to go around cursing every local and damning him or her for the way they run their wretched country. Or at least, no one wants to carry on doing this once you've got it out of your system.

Most people's advice is to deal with it by knowing that it's a totally normal part of the re-location experience and that it will come...and then it will go. It might come again, but then hopefully it will also go again.

Dawn, who lives with her children and husband in Chiang Mai, Thailand, certainly found this. She did say that because she had never experienced culture shock before, nothing about her experience felt 'normal', but she also found it helpful to be reassured by other expats: 'Ask others who are a step ahead of you in the transition what they did to cope well, to transition well,' she recommended. 'I did this and was really thankful to hear from other women who have done or are doing it!'

As well as this, she explained how she had found other ways to deal with what she described as her 'struggle': 'Multiple times when the stress mounts and I feel as if I'm about to snap, where even the easiest things seem incredibly difficult, I deal with it through my faith – I feel God has "called" us here right now so I spend time revisiting that fact and pray a lot,' she said. As well as prayer, she also found escaping from it all by going off on a motorcycle ride helped when things got very tough and added: 'Although I don't deny the fact that I am struggling, when this happens I also often try to think about how I can serve or help someone else because focusing on others can stop the spiralling thoughts of struggle.'

Colleen, in the Netherlands, said that not just recognising that you are going through culture shock, but also a full understanding of all the different elements of it was helpful to her: 'I often wasn't aware at the time exactly where I was in the phases of it. There are times when I think I've gotten there and then discover new levels of negotiation, adjustment and acceptance that I have not yet got to. Sometimes I become aware after the fact that I need to do better at negotiation in order for adjustment and acceptance to go better. If I push the negotiation away then I miss some important steps towards healthy adjustment.'

Other people's advice about dealing with transition shock is far simpler. Judy believed that she suffered quite severely with it in Azerbaijan, although didn't know it at the time. She said it got easier with subsequent locations and she dealt with it by 'just getting on with life. I knew instinctively that meeting people and making friends helped immensely. Also having a routine, something to do each day, even if it was just a domestic chore at first'.

Jenny, who moved to Australia, said she dealt with it through 'endurance, talking to fellow expats, going home... I didn't understand it at the time but familiarised myself with the expat curve a few years ago and it all made sense'.

Maria, an American who has lived in France, Taiwan, Eritrea, Italy, Kosovo, Guinea, Sierra Leone, Cameroon, Bangladesh, Vietnam and Qatar (phew!), said that she 'had done this so many times, I just sort of roll through it'. She also added that it is different managing it with a family as you are also responsible for 'several kids who are all going through it at different rates, in different ways'.

Perhaps that's the answer – if you're worrying about your children, you're probably not going to spend too much time worrying about yourself.

When culture shock turns to depression

Although just knowing that what you are going through is normal can often help you get through the early days, for some people things get worse rather than better. It's hard to know when you will reach the end of one 'stage' and progress to an easier time –

some people never do, and of course some will bounce back and forth between stages for their entire posting. But it is important to try and recognise the signs of depression and when your mood is more than just general pissed-off 'expatitis'.

Depression is one of those subjects that don't get talked about enough. Because of this, it's hard to find people who will admit to having been depressed – especially when they were meant to be having the 'time of their lives' in a new country overseas. But several people did tell me they had fought depression whilst they had lived as expats, including one (anonymous) respondent, who said she was depressed for many years, and described it as 'low grade but very hard to shift, as it is hard to find the energy to find friends and make a new start in a new place when you are battling depression'.

She said she saw therapists in different places, and 'eventually ended up on anti-depressants but hated it'. 'It turned me into someone even I didn't recognise!' she went on to say. 'I stopped that and just kept on trying to be positive and at least keep the family together. Very hard work.'

Another anonymous respondent said that she was fairly severely affected by depression due to a combination of moving, having a baby and being involved in a bad car crash all within a few months of each other. 'I had counselling for three months but found it didn't help at the time as needed,' she said. 'I then went to a coach and felt I got to move on quicker. Looking back eleven years on – I wish I'd asked my mother to come and stay for a while at that time but I didn't realise I needed that family support and just got on as best I could.'

It is also fairly common for your partner to become depressed and this is something else you might want to look out for. Even though on the face of it life may be easier for them – after all, they're the ones with a job and structured life to get on with – one of the main causes of depression is change and they will be going through as much change as you will be (and their depression might in fact be directly related to the change in their work circumstances).

Catherine, who lives in the Netherlands with her family including two young sons says she believes her husband did become quite depressed even if she herself didn't even feel the effects of culture shock. 'He became quite stressed/depressed about his job - felt he was at a dead end career-wise (it's a small company),' she said. 'But when he applied for jobs in London, he realised that life there would be far less enjoyable. Once we decided to put down roots it became much easier.'

If you are worried that either you or your partner might be depressed, talk to each other. Be as honest as possible. Signs of depression include things such as:

- finding everything too much of an effort;
- crying a lot;
- losing your temper easily; and
- sleeping a lot or not being able to sleep at all.

In fact, there are plenty of symptoms but many of these individually are normal when you are going through something so stressful as an overseas move. What you need to look out for is how many symptoms you have and how long they go on for.

One way to help you to do this is to keep a 'mood diary'. This can be something as simple as writing down a number from one to ten at the same time every day, and then seeing if that number consistently goes up, down or stays the same. There are also several websites or apps that can help you, for example Mood Panda at http://www.moodpanda.com/. If after a given time (perhaps a few weeks) your mood seems to be staying the same or going downhill it may be worth considering that you may be depressed and that you should seek out help.

And yet another sobering thing I think I should mention here...

Alcoholism is another problem not often talked about, but sadly very common amongst the expat population. It's not hard to see why – as well as all the emotional reasons for drinking (see above –

isolation, stress, loneliness), expat life is usually a lot more sociable than your normal life back home. And alcohol is often cheaper and more plentiful. Even if you live in a country where alcohol is, on paper, forbidden, expats do seem to find a way to make sure it's available – even if it means brewing it themselves.

Just like depression, alcoholism is something that can creep up on you. It is also something you need to get help for. I am not going to bang on about it too much but I think it's worth being aware that it can be a problem for expats, and that if you think this is some-thing that is or might affect you – get help.

Hopefully this chapter won't have brought you down too much. It's important to recognise and acknowledge that living life as a trailing spouse will have its difficult moments as well as, hopefully, the good times. But whilst we're thinking of some of the harder aspects of overseas life I want to tackle another of those difficult topics: your relationship. So in the next chapter I look at the impor-tant dynamics between you and your partner, how the move might affect you (for better and for worse) and if things aren't going well, what you can do about it.

Websites to Look at to Help You Deal with Culture Shock and Depression

An article about the term 'culture shock' and where it originated from: http://www.telegraph.co.uk/expat/expatlife/8105279/Culture-shock-a-very-modern-phrase.html

Lots more tips and help to make your expat experience a better one: http://www.globalcoachcenter.com/

Top tips on moving from 'isolation to social connection': http://expatcounselingandcoaching.com/expat-psychology-moving-from-isolation-to-social-connection/

Online counselling specialising in expats:
http://www.expatnest.com/

Alcoholics Anonymous – find a group near you, wherever you are in the world: http://www.aa.org/

An article about the particular challenges faced by expat women: http://www.escapefromamerica.com/2011/11/challenges-faced-by-expat-women-2/

CHAPTER NINE

You, Your Partner, Your Relationship: What Doesn't Break You Makes You Stronger.

I've already touched briefly on some of the issues around your relationship with the person who will, in all probability, be the most significant other in your life for the foreseeable future. No, not your cleaner, your partner! But in the course of writing this book, just when I thought I was finished, I realised that I hadn't really done this subject justice. Maybe because it's a difficult subject to tackle, maybe because it was only by writing the guide to start with that I saw what huge pressure your relationship is almost certainly going to come under. Whatever the reasons, I knew it needed a section all to itself. So in this chapter I look at what sort of affect (positive as well as negative) an overseas move might have on your partnership, how it may manifest itself and, if necessary, what you can do to help make things better.

Let's start with the good news, which is that it's certainly not all bad news. Of all the people I asked the specific question what did moving overseas do to their relationship, the most common answer was that it made it stronger. I wanted to get a range of answers and experiences, and certainly not everyone had only a positive tale to tell (see below for a different set of responses). But on the whole, most people felt that one thing to come out of the move to another country was that it brought them and their spouse closer together.

123

This was something that some said was particularly true in the early days, as they and their partner went through the excitement of discovering their new home together.

Keri, who had young children when she and her partner moved abroad, certainly found this, and said: 'We were both making a new start and needing to make new friends, so it was almost an ideal opportunity for us to grow into our new family and new home together.'

Judy agreed the early stages were a time when the family grew closer, saying: 'Particularly on our first posting, where there was huge culture shock, our nuclear family became a refuge of "normalcy".'

And Curtis, who moved to the tiny island of Mayotte off the coast of east Africa, said he and his wife found there were 'so many new things to discover and discuss' that the move did bring them together.

But even later on, after you've been through the early, honeymoon stage and settled into your new home and new routine, many still find the experience of being an expat has nothing but a positive effect on their relationship. Yuliya told me very touchingly: 'All the moving around definitely brought us closer together. Even if there were occasional problems, by solving them we grew stronger. He's my best friend now.'

Liz said: 'I would say it brought us closer together, as in a way it was just the two of us when we first arrived as we didn't know anyone else. We spend more time together now that I don't have a job and tend to socialise together more too as we have made friends as a couple rather than separately through work.'

Julia added: 'Having spent the last twenty eight years abroad has really brought us closer together since we had to rely on each other without the support of extended family. Each new assignment was an adventure and created shared memories.'

And from Christy: 'There are experiences as an expat living abroad that no one other than your spouse understands. You go through the highs and lows together. The laughter, the tears, the absurd situations. This has only strengthened our relationship.'

Another aspect that was mentioned when discussing relationships was that it doesn't just bring you closer as a couple, but as a family unit. Certainly some of my strongest memories as a child is of the many inventive games I played with my brothers because we were in remote places with no-one else to play with and nothing much to occupy us. Now as a mother myself, whenever we go away, even on holidays, I notice the children play together better. I like to think that travelling does bring you closer as a family – but sadly I also think there is a flip side to this in that it may drive you apart later on, as you rarely all end up living in the same area.

But back to your main relationship, and although there are luckily many positive stories about expat life and what it does to you as a couple, there are of course also a few cautionary tales.

Before I discuss some of these, however, it is important to point out that some people did say to me it was often hard to distinguish what was caused by moving around and being an expat and what would have happened in a relationship anyway. Let's face it, being in a long-term partnership isn't always easy, whatever your circumstances. Who is to say that staying in the same home for your entire married life wouldn't have driven you apart with boredom, or the frustrations and resentment of missed opportunities turn you against each other? We'll never know what our other life would have been like, so if you do find yourself having a difficult time with your partner it is worth realising you can't always blame it on the life you have chosen. As seasoned expat Apple Gidley, author of a book called *Expat Life Slice by Slice*, said: 'If a couple is compatible, have the same ethos and actually like each other, it really shouldn't matter where one lives.'

Having said all that, there are, without a doubt, certain pressures that you will face – both as an expat and also as a 'trailing spouse' that will have the potential to harm your relationship. If you want a quick reference as to what those pressures will be, there's a very easy way to do it: look at the chapter titles in this book. In other words, pretty much everything you go through has the potential to cause a rift in your relationship. The stresses of the move itself, your isolation and loneliness at the start, all the confusion of trying to find your way round your new home, worry about safety and security issues, fears about the children, not being able to find a job, giving up your identity as someone with a career back home, an unforeseen emergency…there will be a lot of things that you will have to deal with that you wouldn't have if you hadn't moved abroad, and all of these things are potential pressure points. However, dealing with difficult issues doesn't necessarily have to be a negative thing. Like those people quoted above who said being an expat brought them closer to their partner rather than drove them apart, you could find that seeking a solution to the problems is a way to strengthen rather than weaken your partnership.

Of course none of this helps if this isn't what happens – and one point that was made to me many times was that you really do need to consider whether a move is the right thing to do if your relationship isn't strong enough to withstand some of these extra pressures you will come under. 'I think that if there were problems to begin with then this would exacerbate them. Moving anywhere is very stressful, and if you move abroad it can be a lot worse,' Liz said.

'Make sure your relationship is STRONG. Both spouses have to be able to be independent. If one spouse's happiness is wrapped up in the other one, it will be very difficult. If there are problems in the relationship, a move will shine a spotlight on them,' added a contributor who wanted to remain anonymous. And Margaret told me: 'If your relationship has any weaknesses, (moving abroad) will make or break it quicker.'

But strong or not, and sometimes we won't actually know how strong that relationship is until it's properly tested, many, many couples will face some pretty tough times when they move to a new country, away from their usual support networks and the routine and comforts of a home they both knew. It's a difficult subject to talk about but I did have some very honest answers to my questions, not surprisingly from people who wished to remain anonymous. This included from one who said moving to another country put a strain on their relationship to the point of fights, blaming, guilt, depression and eventually an 'increased and very unhealthy use of alcohol'.

Another respondent told me that their relationship had broken down and she had returned to the UK after her husband went into denial and refused to recognise there were any problems in their relationship.

Anecdotally, another respondent told me that they saw 'plenty of marriages fall apart when overseas, mostly where there wasn't a shared goal in being there... Definitely harder doing something like that than just staying "at home".'

Certainly this chimes with some of the things I have observed while living and working overseas. In one posting in particular, I saw a lot of marriages break down – as well as a fair amount of alcohol use and abuse amongst the accompanying partners. This was particularly true of those partners who weren't working (with no prospect of this changing) and didn't have children – the situation in which I think it is often hardest to settle into a new life. There are those particularly resilient people who will be fine, whatever the situation. But for many partners finding themselves in this situation, it's no surprise that they start to take things out on their spouses.

So what can you do to try and ensure you don't get to this point? The one piece of advice that rang out loud and clear was that good old chestnut – talk.

We are probably all aware how important communication is in any relationship, whether an expat or not. But when you are about to leave your life as you know it hundreds or potentially thousands of miles behind you and start anew in a completely alien place, you definitely need to get used to discussing things with your other half. And preferably before you even take the decision to go. 'Make sure the decision to go is a mutual one,' said Keri.

Couples need to be 'really honest and open in communication with each other', suggests Christy.

One contributor advocated doing more than just talking, but spending as much time together as possible: 'We talk about everything – the good, the bad, what we like/don't like, how we're adjusting. We're intentional on spending time together to touch base. We're having more dates here than in the US (only about 1 or 2 a month, but just a dinner out can be enough). We're taking bike rides on the weekend, going into the city for events, just any chance to spend time together. I believe we have an exceptionally strong relationship (we've been together 25 years, married for 23) and have definitely grown with every move.'

As well as communicating generally about problems or unhappiness when they arise, it's also worth having a conversation about what you, the accompanying partner, is going to do when you arrive in your new home. This might not be something either of you know for sure yet, but their expectations and your expectations about what your life will be like might be very different. This is especially true if you are giving up work. It's probably a good idea to make sure in advance that your partner doesn't expect you to suddenly turn into a 1950s housewife (or indeed househusband – although I don't think there were many of them around in the 50s). It might not yet be clear to you exactly HOW you are going to spend your time – but filling your days with the drudgery of housework is not a route to happiness (unless you like doing housework. In which case fair do's to you. And can you come round to clean my carpets please?)

Hopefully (referring to the chapters on socialising, finding things to do and work) you will eventually find something or more than one thing that at least goes part of the way to fulfilling you in your new life. Just make sure that while you are waiting for this to happen, you don't create unrealistic expectations of what your partner can expect from you. In other words, whatever you do, do NOT meet them at the end of every working day with a martini in hand.

For many couples, communicating openly and honestly about your fears, your problems, your unhappiness or anything else that might be affecting your relationship, will be enough. There will be ups and downs in any partnership, but as long as you recognise and discuss this with each other, then hopefully you will be able to get through the difficult times.

However, there are many, many more couples for whom this isn't enough. Problems can go a lot deeper than just the day-to-day issues of living in a new country and sometimes you need some outside help.

Counselling is something that many people still shy away from – at least in British society where it is still considered a bit odd-ball to want to talk about yourself and your relationship to a stranger. But it is slowly becoming more accepted that the best way to save a partnership is often to fix it before it's too broke. Certainly, this is something that many expats realise only too late – several of those who responded to this particular set of questions said they wished they had considered counselling a lot earlier in their expat life. 'We did seek counselling much later in our marriage, and it was not that useful,' said 'L'.

'I wished we had done it earlier when the problems were less ingrained.' And Maria added that they hadn't sought counselling but was 'starting to feel like maybe we ought to have, but feeling it's a bit late now'.

Julia Simens is a long-term expat but also a counsellor who specialises in expat counselling. She said she often tells families that to seek out counselling is a 'positive way to grow', and added by saying: 'I wish more global families would benefit from seeking a professional counsellor.'

It's certainly helpful to know that there are counsellors out there with not only the expat experience to understand better your particular issues and concerns, but also the technical ability to do so – some offer counselling by Skype or email, for example. Although this isn't always a perfect solution, it can work better that trying to seek someone out locally who won't necessarily understand your needs – as one of the anonymous respondents to questions about their relationship said: 'We did seek counselling, with our local GP. No expat experience or specialism so it was of limited use.'

Another piece of advice is to be careful about where you move to – if this is within your control at all. Moves are difficult wherever you go, but to plunge straight into a culture so different from your own that you feel like you've landed on a different planet will be harder – and place more strain on your relationship – than one to a relatively familiar country. As another of my (anonymous) contributors said: 'I will say that this move was relatively easy in the big scheme of things – USA to Australia. I imagine the more different the new country, the more difficult the transition could be. We've had no language barriers or any huge cultural differences. The move was arranged for work, so there is no financial hit we're taking which I'm sure helps with our adjustment/satisfaction. We keep talking about how we won the "relocation lottery" getting sent to Australia for four years.' I will add though that sometimes the proper 'hardship' posts are ultimately easier for the partners, as the expat community is a closer one, and people tend to look out for each other.

Finally on the subject of how to help make sure the move doesn't wreck your relationship is the piece of advice that I would give to any of my friends, wherever they are in the world (home or away) – talk to others in the same boat. As much as I hope your partner would be the type to open up and communicate, let's face it – this doesn't always happen. Or their intentions might be good to start with, but if they are not a natural 'talker', they might let things slip a bit once you are established in your new home.

So what's the next best thing to talking with your partner? Talking with your friends! The saying 'a problem shared is a problem halved' is a bit trite, but it is true that sometimes all you need to feel better about things is to get it off your chest. I recently followed a thread on an expat forum where one 'trailing spouse' posted how unhappy she was, another sympathised, a third said she felt the same, then someone suggested meeting for coffee, another said she would happily host – and within a couple of days, all these unhappy expats were arranging to meet up and (hopefully) talk in person about what it was that were making them so unhappy. It helped that they were all in the same country/region, but even if you can't find any 'real-life' friends close to where you live to talk to, there's always the Internet. Post as yourself or post anonymously, hopefully you will find someone who is either in the same position as you or has been through it at some point in their lives – and will give you the virtual 'hug' that you need. Or if not a 'hug' then perhaps some damn good advice.

Of course, sadly, not all relationships will make it through an international move (or maybe they will make it through one or two, but not move after move). What happens then? It's important to know in advance if possible what you would do if your partnership did break down while you were overseas. What are your legal rights? Where would you live? If you have children, what are your partner's financial obligations to them – and would it be affected by where you live. Would you return home, would you ALL return home? What legal access rights would the partner who doesn't keep the children have? If they remained overseas, where and how would they see the children?

These are all questions I can't answer for you – but that you need to at least consider, even if you think you have a solid relationship. Many partnerships break down but the couple remain friends, which is easiest all round (especially if there are children involved). However this isn't always the case so it's worth thinking through which issues may be made more complicated by you being overseas.

One of these things is something that I learned about first hand when I lived in one of the countries we have been posted to. Without going into detail to protect the anonymity of the people involved, I helped a mother leave the country with her two children to escape from an emotionally abusive husband. There is nothing to say that anyone is more likely to become either physically or emotionally more abusive because they have moved away from their home country. But if this is something that happens, and you have children, you need to be aware that taking children between some countries without the consent of both parents has become a lot harder in recent years because of new regulations around child abduction. I've put some links up at the bottom of this chapter to look at – this is particularly important if you move to certain countries (in particular those which have not signed the Hague Convention) and if your partner is a different nationality to yourself.

This advice is of course only for the extreme cases, and hopefully not something you will be affected by. But if you think you are at risk from any of these issues, then please seek legal advice.

On a lighter note, and going back to the questions I asked people about their expat relationships, I was impressed by the amount of good, sage advice I was given. In order to do them justice, I reproduce below some of their best tips:

- If your relationship has any big weakness it will make or break it quicker. Remember there are two people in a relationship not just you.
- Be honest with each other. Be supportive and non-judgmental and communicate. Allow the emotions to surface and then work through them together, knowing you're not the first nor the last to experience this. You are both in this journey together – let it bring you closer.
- Don't go as a way of trying to improve your relationship – if it's not good already, the stress of the transitions etc. could well finish it off. Be willing to invest even more in your relationship, especially if you're not both going with a common vision (e.g. only one partner working).
- I could not have made a decision to move overseas for forever. This was a 4 year assignment we chose to accept. When the time comes for the next one, we'll decide then what type of move we're ready for.

- Relationships are particularly tested when the transferring partner has to travel a lot, or take a short term assignment alone (we experienced both). It depends very much on the family, but for us this was FAR harder than us all staying together, no matter what the circumstances. However I know for some families this is a workable solution. Sending organisations need to know that there is no 'one size fits all' answer when it comes to expat assignments.
- My husband and I have always had a One Year Rule – that is, we commit to a new place for a year. No matter how bad it is, no one can say they want to leave before a year is up (health or personal safety would be the only exceptions). At the end of the year, if either is still unhappy, they have the right to initiate the process of the next move. Neither of us has ever had to exercise the 'get out of jail card' at the end of the year.
- It's hard but totally worth doing. The golden rule is to make sure you are straight with each other, open and honest about the good as well as the bad.
- Do your homework. Be open and honest with each other about what opportunities there will be for work, socialising, following interests/hobbies etc. Acknowledge the difficulties and put in place strategies for dealing with them. Make time for each other.
- I would recommend to use your words wisely – you could say something harsh, when you are stressed after the move or tired adjusting, but those words would stick at the back of the mind of your partner and make your life harder later on. Stick together and work as a team!
- Be open and honest about issues immediately. Letting things fester only makes them worse.
- Talk about concerns before you go so the door is open to keep talking about them later. Communication is key.

Finally, one story left to share. The most interesting response I had to my questions about your relationship came from a contributor I shall call Rita, who told me that expat life actually saved her marriage. A few people told me that they felt their problems have been perhaps ignored or shoved under the carpet due to the changes they have made, but Rita's story was a positive one. 'We were about to separate before we left the UK, flat had been rented, children told that Mummy and Daddy weren't happy and would be spending some time apart,' she said. 'Then he came back and said he had this opportunity of a new job in Switzerland and could we all go. We talked, a lot, but we both thought it was worth doing it together, last chance saloon. I could always come back with the children if it didn't work.

'Six months on it has worked and has brought us back together. The experience has made us talk to each other. It has made us rely on each other in a different way. It has turned us into a team and whilst we still have some problems we are working on, we are stronger and have gone through the experience together.'

Which just goes to show – sometimes moving overseas can actually save a marriage.

Now that we have covered relationships, hopefully you will have a better idea of some of the possible problems you might face as a couple and what can be done to help tackle any issues. You should also have come away knowing that moving abroad as a couple definitely doesn't have to be a negative thing – and that many of those couples come out much stronger than before they left their home country behind. But of course many of you won't just have your partner to think about, you'll also be thinking of others in the family. In the next three chapters we start to look at one of the other main worries facing many expat partners – their children, and how to help them make the transition to living in a new country as easy and stress-free as possible.

Websites to Help You with Any Potential Relationship Issues

An article in the Telegraph about what you need to know about international divorce: http://www.telegraph.co.uk/expat/before-you-go/10084787/International-divorce-know-before-you-go.html#disqus_thread

Reunite is the International Child Abduction charity: http://www.reunite.org/

Information from the UK Foreign Office about child abduction: https://www.gov.uk/government/publications/international-parental-child-abduction

Expat counselling service (based in New Delhi but works world-wide over Skype): http://www.expatcounselingandcoaching.com/

Article about counselling miserable expats, and how much work there is out there in this area: http://www.telegraph.co.uk/expat/expatlife/10693045/Counselling-miserable-expats-can-be-a-full-time-job.html

More online counselling: http://ukonlinecounselling.com/whatioffer/life-as-an-expat

Article about expat relationships from an expat website: http://www.expatinfodesk.com/expat-guide/moving-with-your-partner/staying-strong-as-a-couple/

Article about the importance of saving your expat relationship – before it's too late: http://expatriateconnection.com/expat-relationship-balance-save-late/

Children – Your Third Culture Kids, Your Little Global Nomads

This topic is such a large one that I really won't be able to do much more than skim the surface of it. To do it proper justice would be a book in itself – and in fact there are already books, as well as excellent websites and many, many blogs on the topic of expat parenting. Some of these I list at the end of the chapter – but in the meantime I hope to give you a bit of food for thought at least, to help you think and plan ahead and hopefully to make the transition to your family's new life a slightly less painful one.

I tackle this enormous subject over four chapters. The first one will look at the general topic of children, preparing them for the move, what might – or might not – affect them the most and how others have found it. As each different stage of childhood has such wildly different needs, I divide this chapter up into age groups.

The fourth of the kid-related chapters will cover childcare and schooling – often one of the first things you need to think about before accepting a post or at the very least before arriving in your new country if you have children of that age.

And in between the two, I'm throwing into the mix some real life stories from children who have lived abroad themselves – known in the expat culture as Third Culture Kids (or TCKs), and also from a couple of grown-up former expat children (including my own story), known as Adult TCKs (i.e. ATCKs). Hopefully some of these stories will help reassure anyone who is worried about taking their children away from home into the unknown.

But let's go back to the beginning, when you first start to think about how you're going to prepare your beloved offspring for the challenges ahead.

Many of you contemplating an overseas move will probably at some point already have thrown your hands up in the air and cried, 'But what about the children?' Not all of you, of course. Some of you might not have children. Some of you may have grown up children – I realise they're still your babies, but their needs aren't quite the same as the rugrats. And some of you might not actually think the needs of your children are that great – in which case, well done, you have passed one of life's parenting tests – you will not let your kids dictate your life (goes off to change pink cup for blue cup on the demand of youngest daughter. Sighs).

However, if you do have children under the age of somewhere around the 18-25 mark (older than that and they really are adults – aren't they?), and in particular if you will be taking them with you, then you really do need to think about them and how they might be affected by the move.

Overall, it's hard to be too prescriptive with advice on this topic as every child is an individual. What works for one won't necessarily work for another – not even siblings. I often hear of one child who takes to the expat lifestyle like the proverbial duck to water, whilst their brother or sister really struggles.

As an example of this, I had friends who took two children to a French-speaking Caribbean island. Their daughter chose to stay on the island to complete all her schooling (and apparently to settle into the social life without too many problems), whilst their son opted to return home to board at a school in the UK. And as Richelle, who has to claim major expat mum expert status for taking her eight children to various countries including Bangladesh, Thailand and Niger, told me: 'A lot depends on expectations, age, memories, circumstances. I wish it were more formulaic because then all you would have to do is plug in the right variables and it would work each time for each kid.'

The very early years – from newborns to toddlers

General agreement is that the younger a child is, the easier it is to move them overseas. They won't yet have formed the same sort of bonds to friends or places that older ones will have, and if they haven't started school this whole worrying aspect of moving will pass you by completely.

Our youngest daughter was only seven-months-old when we moved to Pakistan and for her, as long as we were around, she had no idea she had actually moved. Of course there were a lot of changes and adjustments for her to make – from the outside temperature suddenly being several million times hotter than she was used to, to the strange food we started to try to feed her (that would be mango then as we were there in mango season – see Chapter Five). But at her age, there were lots of new things in her life every day anyway – the first time she went for a walk in the snow would have been just as alien an experience for her as the first time she went on a plane or swam in an outdoor pool.

Babies are amazingly adjustable and as long as you know you can meet all their everyday needs in your new country (e.g. buy nappies, find food they will eat, make sure you know where to access decent healthcare etc.) then you probably don't need to worry too much about them at this age. As Richelle, my expert mum (see I told you she knows here stuff!) said: 'The easiest age is before they are old enough to recognise the world around them is really changing...which means in the first three months.'

Toddlers present their own challenges – but to be fair, they are challenging whether you live in Tunbridge Wells, Toronto or Timbuktu. However one of the issues you might need to consider at this age is language development.

Nicola took her son to the Netherlands when he was sixteen-months-old and said it did affect his language skills: 'He developed his own language between the age of two and three – a mix of English and Dutch,' she said. Her son went to a Dutch-language preschool and as they wanted him to go on to a Dutch-speaking school persevered with this, rather than helping to learn English at the same time. She said they regretted this later as they felt they hindered, rather than helped, his language development.

Despite this warning, many bilingual families I have met do seem to have had success in helping their children learn two languages at the same time – one at school, one at home, or one parent speaking one language, the other another. The brain at this age is an amazing thing – don't underestimate the ability of a small child to pick up more than one language at the same time. Instead, embrace it and if possible continue with it if/when you move on to another location.

Otherwise, the lives of toddlers still tend to centre on the immediate family, so, as long as you are still around, the rest of the world doesn't matter too much.

The possible exception to this might be the loss of the close relationships with extended family such as grandparents and cousins, aunts and uncles. However, Skype and other 'face-time' communications methods really are an amazing thing – if you keep up regular contact, your child will probably retain close links with family members in another country.

You will also probably find that longer periods together during holidays will add to this closeness. I remember having a very special relationship with my granny even though we lived in the Philippines for four years from when I turned four until I was eight years old – and there was certainly nothing like Skype in those days. I think it mainly came down to the fact that she was able to stay with us for a long period of time and vice versa when we returned to the UK on holiday.

The other possible issue to be aware of with taking very young children aboard is that they might not remember or have any attachment to their home country, which might not be an immediate problem, but may have an impact on their future.

There is a lot of research currently being done on third culture kids and the effect living overseas has on them. Although everyone has individual experiences and copes differently, one thing I have noticed is that those who move when they are very young often have more problems with identity when they are older. I think it is important that a child knows where they are from and understands their home culture (or cultures if they come from parents with different nationalities).

If this is the case with you and your child or children, there are things you can do:

- take them home for holidays as much as possible, and while you are there explore your home country with them;
- take them to places that you loved as a child and introduce them to the wonder of their own land;
- watch films and TV shows from your own country;
- help them 'get' the humour or the topical jokes;
- make sure you celebrate your home country's big festive occasions even if it is not celebrated in the country where you are living; and
- talk about 'home' with them; help them understand there is a place where they belong and where one day you and they will almost certainly return.

In terms of preparing children of this age for a move, the key is to not tell them too far in advance. Just like any major change in their lives (such as a new baby in the family or starting school), there is no point in worrying them months before the event.

Closer to the time, start to casually mention the move and then introduce them to your new location through photographs or videos if possible – it will help them if they can visualise where they are headed. Be excited about it around them (even if internally you are quaking in your boots). Talk about the adventure of the plane trip or journey to get there, discuss things like what sort of animals they might encounter, or how different the weather might be. Things they can understand at their level.

There's also little point in explaining why you are moving beyond 'for daddy/mummy's job' – that'll probably be enough for them. Have you ever noticed how children of this age seem to have very little interest in what you or your partner does when they're not in the immediate vicinity? I think as soon as you're out of the house, very young children have so little concept of what you are actually doing that trying to explain in great detail about a new job or whatever it is that is taking you abroad would almost certainly go straight over their heads.

Pre-teen, school-age children

As your children grow older and understand more about what is happening to them, moving will throw up a whole new set of challenges. For a start, what do you do if they don't want to go?

I asked people whether they included their offspring in the decision to move overseas and found that many 'involved' them but didn't let them have the final say. Others said that they would have considered not moving if their children really weren't up for it – but luckily so far no one admitted that this had actually happened.

Richelle said that her children 'are allowed to tell us what they think and then we weigh that into our decisions – but it doesn't make/break a decision'.

Nikki, who recently moved to Singapore with her two children but who has previously lived in the US and Korea, said they brought their children along for their 'look see' and involved them in helping to choose a house and school, but that they did not have the final say on the move.

Others, however, have admitted that they would stop and reconsider if their children were really against the idea – Hilary, who lives in the Netherlands, said: 'We have regular family meetings, we discuss things with them that will directly affect them. If they said that they didn't want to go then unless it was unavoidable…we wouldn't go. They are part of the process, too. Their thoughts and feelings are just as valid as the grown-ups.'

My research suggested that the best way to tackle this is to ensure they know from as early a stage as possible that this is happening and that's that – but then let them be a big part of the decisions about the actual move. However, it is undoubtedly extremely difficult if you feel you are uprooting your child from a happy life to take them into the unknown without their approval.

Many people expressed relief that so far their children hadn't been against the idea of a move, including those who were already overseas and were moving to another country. In this latter case, it is often easier for the children, as by now they are living in an expat environment where their friends are also up and moving on every few years.

Once you get used to the idea, it's easier to accept that your turn will come sooner or later. In fact, for many it really is something to look forward to: 'I must admit, my boys have always been quite excited about the next posting, it's always such a new adventure, and the saying goes: grass is always greener' is how Liz, recently moved to Beijing with three boys, explained it.

Once you arrive in your new home, the challenge is to help your children settle in, at the same time as you are battling your own relocation demons.

Hopefully having children to concentrate on will help take your mind off your own issues – although it won't help if you've arrived in a Middle Eastern posting in the middle of the summer to find all the other families won't be back until school starts again, it's so hot outside you can't leave the house during daylight hours and the only toy you've brought with you has run out of batteries and you have no idea where to find a shop to buy new ones...in other words, do a bit of homework, be prepared, and don't – whatever you do – move in the middle of the summer holidays if you have school aged kids! And bring plenty of batteries/a charger/the right plug or an adapter for that one toy that's going to keep your child sane until they start school and can make some new friends.

Another tip to help them settle quickly is to organise their bed-room to be as similar to the one back home as possible. If you can, bring their bed linen from home with you on the plane, pictures, favourite teddies, even things like fairy-lights. This way, at least their room will feel immediately familiar to them – so important in those first few days and weeks.

Things will almost certainly get easier once school starts and you all begin to get into some sort of routine. But the question of boredom may well rear its ugly head again as soon as another long holiday rolls around – the three (sometimes four) month long school summer holidays some countries impose on their poor parents can only be the brainchild of some particularly sadistic leader.

If you're lucky, you'll get a nice holiday back home during this time – although beware that different countries have their long holidays at different times so when your children are on their break, you might find it's the middle of a very dreary winter back home. You might also use this opportunity to explore some of the country you have been sent to, or to neighbouring countries – one of the most exciting things about moving to Pakistan was the thought that we could reach some of those dream destinations that were too far for us from the UK, such as Thailand and Malaysia; whilst in St Lucia, we made regular visits to Florida.

But you will almost certainly still have weeks, if not months, to fill and how on earth do you do this without going totally stark staring mad from the constant and incessant whines of 'I'm booooooored', 'what can I doooooooo?'

As Olga, in the Netherlands, said: 'Holidays are hard because nobody is available, everybody has gone to their home country or on vacation…it is the start of the summer and already I see my children grumpy and bored.'

I remember the long summers in the Philippines as a child, in the days when we only flew back to the UK every other year. It was the rainy season and of course we had no Internet, DVDs, tablets, Gameboys or any of the other modern day preoccupations of small children. In fact, apart from one glorious year when my parents borrowed a television to watch the Olympics, we didn't even have a TV – so we wouldn't have been able to watch the satellite channels even if they had existed back then. How my poor mum (my dad being at work, of course) didn't completely lose her mind trying to keep us occupied I don't know – although I do remember a lot of swimming, tree climbing and getting into scrapes in neighbours' gardens.

Yup, kids today – don't know they're born. However, that's not going to help you when you've put the eighth DVD of the day on, the kids have declared they're sick of watching TV and it's only 9.30am…

Just like so much of the business of moving abroad, preparation is the key. Try and find something for the children to do every day – even if it is just a play date or a visit to the pizza shop or a local playground. If you live somewhere with summer camps/sports clubs, use them (and of course if you are working you will no doubt have had to arrange all of this in advance). Take advantage of the local facilities – it's amazing how many TCKs are phenomenal swimmers thanks to early years in the pool.

You might also find there are other local sports/activities that you wouldn't have access to back home, or perhaps wouldn't be able to afford. Find other families in the same boat as you and do child swaps. Take the children out on that same boat if you have to…anyway, you get my drift.

If you're lucky and you have more than one child and they get on with each other, let them do just that – get on with it. Siblings can become incredibly close through the shared experience of overseas life, especially one with less of the modern-day distractions of life in the developed world. The more siblings there are, the more likely they are to be able to entertain themselves, as Richelle explains: 'My kids are flexible and are close knit as a sibling group…they are also self entertaining and occupied. I love to play with them, but I've never been the one to find things for them to do.'

Teenagers and beyond

Just like it does in 'normal' life, things get harder as your TCKs hormones start to explode. My own children are still very young, so this is a slightly unknown area for me – although I can still remember being a teenager when my parents moved to Venezuela, leaving me behind at boarding school. I can't say it was a happy or an easy time – certainly, the whole identity who-am-I, where-do-I-belong thing caused me endless hours of angst, scribbling into my teenage-girl diary. And certainly feedback from those parents that I spoke to reveals that the hardest adjustment for any of their children or at any point in their life is amongst their teenagers.

Recently, a post on the website Expat Child about self-harming by expat kids caused a huge outpouring of emotions, stories, anecdotes…from adults who had been TCKs, from counsellors and psychologists, from the children themselves (you can read the post here: http://expatchild.com/tck-problems/).

Self-harming is of course a way of expressing distress, frustration, sadness…all those emotions that typical teenagers could be feeling anyway, but which may be exacerbated by your lifestyle. I am sure there are also other ways that teen TCKs express their feelings, maybe going 'in' to themselves, or drinking too much for example. It's hard to find research on the subject, but anecdotally this is a problem. It is also a problem that is made no easier by the distance between you and your child at this age, whether that be a physical distance (if they are at school in another country) or the more usual emotional distance as they start to find their own path in life.

Of course many, many expat children are absolutely fine – they take the moves in their stride, or they deal with it in their own ways. A lot of how your child will react to these big changes will depend on how old they are when you move, what their lives are like at the time, where you move to, what sort of person they are – there are as many different scenarios as there are children.

But it is certainly worth being aware of the affect your peripatetic life may well have on your offspring. And making sure you follow a few simple suggestions – like talking to them, talking to others, seeking help if necessary.

As different people deal with their children's issues in different ways, so will the children themselves.

Nikki, in Singapore, said her teenage daughter was very unhappy and really missed her old friends but 'a visit back home helped her, as did social networking'. The daughter of another of my respondents was on anti-depressants for a year to cope and 'escaped' back home to Scotland as soon as she was old enough for university.

On the other hand, Olga sees the positive side of having older children in that you can speak and explain things to them; discuss things like identity issues, culture and the benefits of being an expat. And Richelle explained that although her children had had what she described as 'periods of sadness, but not depression' she has dealt with it by asking for 'permission to cry and mourn with them and then (at different times) asked them to help me count my blessings...walking through those sad seasons with them has worked for our family'.

As a family you need to navigate your own path through what could potentially be a very difficult time. But overall, it is better to be aware in advance what might be coming than left totally in the dark.

So that's the advice for you, the support to help you guide your child through this tricky transition period. But what about the children themselves – how do they feel about all of this? We can assume we know what they're going through, what they're thinking, but do we really? In the next chapter I let them be heard.

Websites and Articles to Help You Help Your Children with the Transition:

A great resource for parents. I would definitely recommend a good browse of the Your Expat Child website: http://expatchild.com/

Another good website for parents moving abroad, with an emphasis on multilingual parenting: http://www.europeanmama.com/

Lots of articles and information from the people at Families in Global Transition: http://figt.org/free_articles_and_information

A blogger reviews, chapter by chapter a book about bringing up 'global nomads': http://lauradcampbell.wordpress.com/2013/03/30/unrooted-childhoods-a-chapter-by-chapter-review/

A 'humorous guide for parents with teenagers moving country' (lol): http://expatriateconnection.com/the-lol-guide-for-parents-with-teenagers-moving-country/

Coaching for parents with an emphasis on moving overseas: http://www.familymatterscoaching.com/purposeful

One mother's journey raising third culture kids: http://raisingtcks.com/

Support for expat students and third culture kids: http://seachangementoring.com/

Blog about travelling with children: http://www.motherofalltrips.com/

Innovative new app to help children stay in touch with their (hopefully tech-savvy) grandparents: http://www.gingersnapadventures.com/join?at=custodian&l=gc

Article about being a Third Culture Kid:
http://myinternationaladventure.com/11/being-a-third-culture-kid/

Coaching for 'internationally living families':
http://www.utesexpatlounge.com/

A website for parents about travelling and living overseas with children: http://babyglobetrotters.net/

The Child's Viewpoint

So often, we forget that our children will have a completely different view of overseas life than we will. The things we worry about, for them as well as for ourselves, will not be the same as the things they worry about. Our concerns will not be theirs.

So to try and see things from their perspective, I asked a few children who had moved with their families overseas what it had been like for them. Unsurprisingly, their answers were as interesting, as honest and as diverse as those of their parents. And all of them, in their own way, showed a wisdom beyond their years:

Valentina

Age 17, nearly 18; has lived in Italy, Switzerland, New York and moving to the UK. Has one sibling, six years younger.

What have you enjoyed most about moving or living overseas? Do you have any favourite experiences to share?
Generally speaking, it has been an indescribable learning experience that I wouldn't change for the world. It's hard to pick one single moment so I am going to say two. Firstly, I have had the fortune of calling more than one place home and having more than one family. I am soon going to be leaving for university and my immediate family will be an eight hour flight away; however I estimate I have more than fifteen different places to go and people who can host me near where I will be going to university.

I consider myself particularly lucky to be blessed with these people, with this secondary family spread around the world.

Secondly, I have thoroughly enjoyed being exposed to so many different cultures, all of which have affected the young woman that I am today. As a Third Culture Kid you become a sponge, you absorb all the different aspects of each environment you live in. So I am not 'from' one place but rather from an infinite amount of places because all the people I have met have given me something of theirs that I would otherwise not have had the opportunity to experience.

How different do you think your life is compared to living in your home country? What sort of differences are there?

I like to say that I have 'formed' myself in New York, meaning that I have commenced and almost completed my adolescence in this city. A city full of open mindedness and diversity. Full of culture and opportunity. In my home country there is a general close-mindedness and ignorance to concepts that are unknown, such as homosexuality, religion that is not their own, other cultures etc. I think that living away has allowed me to explore these different ways of leading life without remorse or being judged. It has given me the power to be different and happy. Living abroad has also given me the gift of independence, I have become much more reliant on myself, which can be a good or a bad thing at times.

How involved have you been in any moves that you have made as a family?

I think that the last couple of moves have been the ones in which I was most involved. By the last couple of moves, I mean when we moved from Switzerland to New York and between apartments in New York. I helped my mum pack the boxes for my room; it's become quite routine when you have to throw away as many things as possible, never knowing how much space the new place will have.

Is there anything you have found challenging or difficult? If so, how have you or your parents dealt with this?

The most difficult thing about moving from place to place, 'home' to 'home' is the fact that each home feels completely temporary. As in, my room isn't really mine. I talk to my friends whose parents are local, who painted their walls and have a ton of posters put up because wherever they'll go in the future that will always be their room. These kids get to keep their 200+ stuffed animals because it's their house, their room, their home and this is always something I've had such a hard time dealing with. Or like who have made marks on the walls with how much they've grown and every crack has a story; in my apartment the crack was there before I was. I find that keeping the room tidy and organised makes it feel like my own. Since I know where everything goes, I know it's mine (for however long it is), it has my things. I try to put up pictures, posters, mementoes. I started crying while writing this. I try to keep as many memories as I can but I need to start labelling which ones are more important than others 'cause I can't keep everything.

How have you found it when you or your friends have moved on? Do you manage to keep in touch with them? If so, how have you found is the best way to do this?

Most of the time, it depends on the friend. With social media, it's easy to keep in touch but you have to want it. My best friend and I haven't lived in the same country for the past six years. The relationship clearly has to change because you don't see each other every day and you only talk about important things. However, it's very much will power – we don't talk every day but we have two hour long Skype calls every couple of months and we'll see each other for a week and spend every moment together. The dynamic of the relationship changes but it can still be a great one. However, it's much easier to fall out of touch with people, there are time zones and new friends and new interests. It all depends on how much you want to stay friends with said person!

How have you found it fitting into new or different schools?

The first couple of months are usually the most difficult, but in my experience doing things and joining activities, in and out of school, can help create friends – who don't all have to be in the same group. I find this very important for third culture kids because it allows greater diversity between the people with whom you surround yourself.

What would you say to a child of your age who is going to be going through a similar move?

Talk about it. Keeping all feelings in is bad and it will hurt more. Find someone who is going through a similar situation and talk to them about the problems you're facing in this new place. Get busy and do many things. I joined three different acting schools and it really helped keep me busy and make friends outside of the school environment. Go out a lot and try to learn new things about the place you're living in. Talk to your parents, express your concerns, ask them when you are going back to your old home. Plan summers so that you can see your old friends. But mostly stay busy and try to remember it's supposed to be a good experience rather than a bad one.

Justine

Age 14. Has lived in South Africa, Belgium, the US and Colombia.

What have you enjoyed most about moving or living overseas? Do you have any favourite experiences to share?

Nothing. I hate moving.

How different do you think your life is compared to living in your home country? What sort of differences are there?

In the US people appreciate witty comments, sarcasm, irony and satire. In most other countries that have no idea of the humour these things contain. They are confused by them.

How involved have you been in any moves that you have made as a family?

My dad's job moves us so I have no say at all.

How have you found it when you or your friends have moved on? Do you manage to keep in touch with them? If so, how have you found is the best way to do this?

I keep in touch using SnapChat, Instagram, Facebook and Skype. It is hard when you leave good friends behind and then they move on without you. You have to kind of insert yourself into their lives again when you visit home.

How have you found it fitting in to new or different schools?

It's tough making new friends from different cultures. Especially when there is a language barrier, and even though you all may speak English during lessons they revert to their home language during breaks and then you have no idea what they are saying. They tend to talk to each other and you are left out, not under-standing.

What would you say to a child your age who is going through a similar move?

Hang in there. I know it's hard. Join clubs, do sports. Keep trying. Good luck.

Thea

Age 14. Has lived in England, Germany, South Africa and Belgium. Has one younger sister.

What have you enjoyed most about moving or living overseas? Do you have any favourite experiences to share?

I like that I get to see different places in the world and experience different cultures.

How different do you think your life is compared to living in your home country? What sort of differences are there?

Living abroad is difficult because you have to learn to converse in other languages, whereas in the UK I can speak English to everyone. My life is very different abroad because my friends I have there are within the expat circle. In the UK I could be friends with anyone because there would be no language barrier.

How involved have you been in any moves that you have made as a family?

I haven't been involved in past moves as I was too young to be of any real help. I would have just got in the way.

How have you found it when you or your friends have moved on? Do you manage to keep in touch with them? If so, how have you found is the best way to do this?

I try to keep in touch with friends but after a while you drift apart. The best way to keep in touch for me is Facebook or Snapchat.

How have you found it fitting into new or different schools?

I find it slightly difficult because I know that I'm not going to be there forever so I struggle to find motive. I do normally find friends but it takes a while.

What would you say to a child your age who is going through a similar move?

That they should keep in touch with their old friends, start new activities so that you can find friends and meet people. You should also try to learn the local language, in my opinion.

Polly

Age 13. Has lived in England, Germany, South Africa and Belgium. Has one older sister.

What have you enjoyed most about moving or living overseas? Do you have any favourite experiences to share?

I have loved being able to meet new friends and learn about all the different cultures. Learning languages is a lot easier in the country they speak it in. I took part in a bilingual class for two years and did half my lessons in French. That is probably my favourite experience.

How different do you think your life is compared to living in your home country? What sort of differences are there?

I think I wouldn't have had as many opportunities in my home country as I have had abroad. It's a lot easier to learn other languages and it's always really nice to be able to go home in the holidays. In expat life you have at least two homes, the one where you live and the one in your home country – which might be your grandparents' house.

How involved have you been in any moves that you have made as a family?

I haven't been very involved in the moves as I was always a bit young to be able to help. I will be able to help now, though, for the next move. Hopefully.

How have you found it when you or your friends have moved on? Do you manage to keep in touch with them? If so, how have you found is the best way to do this?

I hate leaving or saying goodbye to my friends. It's always really hard and I always try my best to stay in touch. However, sometimes it's difficult, especially when I live in Europe and one of my friend's lives in Australia. The best ways to stay in touch are probably Skype/FaceTime, iMessage and Facebook, if your friends have it.

How have you found it fitting into new or different schools?

I'm quite loud, talkative and outgoing so I find fitting into new schools reasonably easy. The hardest part of changing schools for me is leaving and saying goodbye rather than saying hello. I feel I can just start afresh at a new school.

What would you say to a child your age who is going through a similar move?
I would tell them to look forward to it and consider it an adventure. When you first start it can be a bit hard but you make new friends really quickly and you'll really enjoy it. I would say be positive and just enjoy it!

Sarah

Age 11, lived in Doha, Qatar and Shenzhen, China. Has one sibling, aged 8.

What have you enjoyed most about moving or living overseas? Do you have any favourite experiences to share?
I loved getting to experience all the different cultures and moving/living overseas; getting to go on vacation to many places I wouldn't normally go.

How different do you think your life is compared to living in your home country? What sort of differences are there?
I have to deal with the long airplane ride and at school a lot of different people from different countries who have different backgrounds. I love learning about everything!

How involved have you been in any moves that you have made as a family?
I helped as much as I could and we all tried to make the best of it.

Is there anything you have found challenging or difficult? If so, how have you or your parents dealt with this?
Just moving and being sad about leaving what was my home.

How have you found it when you or your friends have moved on? Do you manage to keep in touch with them? If so, how have you found is the best way to do this?
Yes, I have. I use email, Skype, I-message, Viber…and calling, texting.

How have you found it fitting into new or different schools?
It is hard at first but very soon you will feel like you have been there forever.

What would you say to a child your age who is going through a similar move?
Just remember, wherever you are, you are always you.

Tom

Age 10. Has lived in Bangladesh, Iran, Kenya. Has one brother.

What have you enjoyed most about moving or living overseas? Do you have any favourite experiences to share?
Getting to see new places. My favourite experience is the new friends I've made.

How different do you think your life is compared to living in your home country? What sort of differences are there?
Languages and the different, fun things we do in the different schools.

How involved have you been in any moves that you have made as a family?
Being told about some of the places we might be going.

Is there anything you have found challenging or difficult? If so, how have you or your parents dealt with this?
Leaving the schools and friends I have. [I have dealt with it by] sometimes talking on Skype with old friends, emailing them.

How have you found it when you or your friends have moved on? Do you manage to keep in touch with them? If so, how have you found is the best way to do this?
I keep in touch with some of them by email and Skype, but it's hard.

How have you found it fitting into new or different schools?
Not that hard.

What would you say to a child your age who is going through a similar move?
Even though you are leaving your friends, it doesn't mean you are never going to see them again. One of my old friends said to me 'see you in the future!'

Toby

Age 10, nearly 11. Has lived in Ireland, the Netherlands, USA and the Netherlands again. 'I now live in UK with my mum and my dad works away – he is in Singapore now and I would like to live there.'

What have you enjoyed most about moving/living overseas? Do you have one favourite experience to share?
I was born overseas so it's always been normal to me. Now I live in the UK, I miss my family being together as my dad stayed working abroad. In California I loved that we had a swimming pool at our house to use when I wanted to.

How different do you think your life is or was compared to living in your home country? What sort of differences are there?
I don't really know as this is the first time I've lived in the UK in my life. I miss my Dutch home and school friends at the international school, but otherwise my life is the same I think.

Have you ever had any say in where your parents move? If not how does this make you feel?

I was too little to say anything about moving from Ireland where I was born to the Netherlands and again when we went to USA. I was 8 when we moved back to the UK. My parents told me that's what they wanted to do and I didn't mind.

Is there anything you have found challenging or difficult? If so how have you or your parents dealt with this?

When I was at international school, my friends were always leaving. I missed my friends from this school as I'd been with them from four years old to nearly nine, when I moved to UK. Making new friends hasn't been easy.

How have you found it when you or your friends have moved on? Do you manage to keep in touch with them? If so, what have you found is the best way to do this?

I have a best friend who is still in the Netherlands – we Skype each other every now and then and see each other when I go to the Netherlands or she comes to UK. My mum keeps in contact with some of the mums of my friends via Facebook, so I know what my friends are doing, too.

How have you found it fitting in to new or different schools?

It was okay. Making friends is hard as a lot of the boys know each other a long time and it's strange to have friends who are girls in the UK, yet I'm friendly with the girls, too. In school some of the lessons are different but it's been okay.

What would you say to a child your age who is going to be going through a similar move?

Just have fun.

CHAPTER TWELVE

The Adult TCK's View

And what of these children years later? How will they remember their childhood? How will they be affected by moving on every few years, leaving friends behind, being schooled in different systems and living in different cultures? Below are two stories – the first is from my school friend, Penny, who lived in Indonesia when she was young. I've left it fairly unedited because I think her enthusiasm for her former life just shines through in her words.

The other is my own account, written originally as a blog for the Your Expat Child website – partly as a way to reassure parents considering taking their child abroad that usually us TCKs turn out okay in the end.

Penny's story

Background

My name is Penny Knight. My parents met in the Sudan in 1958 and married in 1962. My two elder brothers were born there, in 1964 and 1966, I think. My younger brother (Andrew) died at two weeks. My mother began haemorrhaging at seven months, and no airline would fly her home. He was born healthy at about 32 weeks, but there were no incubators and he succumbed to a chest infection. I don't think she has ever really recovered. Anyway, those were the pitfalls of living in a remote country in the 1960s. I was born in England in 1967, fat and healthy. My mother had travelled home early on in the pregnancy just in case.

My first two years were spent in the Sudan, until all the British were kicked out after Independence. We were under house arrest for two days – the soldiers and their guns and grenades were a great source of interest for my elder brother, Christopher. I have no memories of this period. We had a pet Hunter's Gazelle called Mandy who used to chase my brother around in the garden and play ball with him. We had twenty four rabbits. We swam in swimming pools and in the Red Sea: an idyllic existence for parents and kids. We lived in Khartoum and Omdurman and Port Sudan. My father spent seventeen years there and yet has never been back. Andrew is buried in the cemetery in Khartoum.

In 1970/71 we moved to Lagos, Nigeria. My earliest memories from this time are random: being very ill with dysentery and seeing Jesus, our servant who came with us from the Sudan, come into the bedroom with an enormous pile of white ladybird underwear he had washed that day – I had failed to make it to the loo that many times.

At the end of 1972 we moved to Medan, Sumatra, Indonesia. In 1978 we moved to Jakarta, and in 1984 we moved to Ujung Pandang, Sulawesi, Indonesia. My parents finally left in 1987, when my father retired. I went to school there until autumn 1980, when I went to boarding school in England. My childhood there was idyllic. I hated returning to the UK to go to school.

What are your memories of living as a 'Third Culture Kid' like? Are they predominantly happy? Sad? Describe any particularly strong memories you have.

My memories of living as a 'Third Culture Kid' are fantastic. The things that stick in a child's brain are quite interesting – a bus so overfull that it is leaning heavily to one side with men on the roof, hanging off the door (age three, Nigeria); my brother's birthday party when a film was ordered and set up, big screen and all. The only TV we had was *Skippy the Bush Kangaroo* on a Sunday, so a whole film was just fantastic, and we ate sausages and baked beans – no idea how my mum got hold of them; going to the doctor every day to get tumbleflies pulled out of my scalp one by one; my mum pulling ticks out of the dog's ears and the dog crying the whole way through the ordeal; sitting on a wooden boat sinking gently in the river delta, life jacket on, and friends passing by in a speed boat offering to help and my dad saying we were just fine; power cuts; the 'club' –swimming and bloody feet from broken glass; being picked up from nursery by Jesus and walking home with him assuming my parents must be dead (a green mamba had ruined mum's bridge game and its partner was being sought in the garden).

My memories of Indonesia are absolutely happy. Travelling every Saturday (it seems!) to the natural swimming pool in the rubber tree plantation – amazing. A friend of my parents dropping by on her horse at 4pm for G & T. The Dutch Missionary (Father Van Daam) coming by for old stamps and bottle tops – he built a maternity hospital and an orphanage out of it, and I once put on a show to raise money with my two friends, age eight – some particularly awful song lyrics and tuneless singing, I recall! Rabbits, guinea pigs, ducklings, terrapins, dogs, cats; you name it, we had it. Hash House Harriers – paper trails through the 'kampongs' (villages and rice paddies) with drinks and singing at the end.

Going to the airport on our bikes and going up the control tower, and yes actually talking to pilots flying in. Golf course right next to the runway, no fence, little boys on bikes on the runway, a siren was sounded if anything was coming in to land. Seeing a plane stop while taxiing to let a latecomer on! Flame trees; Hibiscus, butterflies, orangutans – visiting friends in the rain forest who worked for WWF. Lake Toba – tea plantations, Batak people who ate dogs. My parents talking to hippies living with the Bataks, unaware what lunch was (the hippies, that was).

Holidays became one long party during my teenage years – lots of jumping into swimming pools with not many clothes on. Lots of boyfriends! Days sailing, playing squash, etc. Parties too with parents and children – just as much fun. There were drivers to take you round and about. And through it all living in a place with a vastly different flora, fauna, geography, religion and culture. I was always very aware of, and respectful of, the Indonesian culture.

You would never go into town inappropriately dressed, for example.

One summer the government was cracking down on crime in their dictatorship fashion. This involved sending masked 'vigilantes' to shoot certain criminals on sight. One afternoon I came out of the photo shop, driver said hurry up, and we sped off. I turned back and saw masked gunman getting off a motorbike right behind us...

What was school like?

I went to kindergarten in Nigeria and had a very close friendship with David from New Zealand. Apparently we held hands in playtime all the time! Between Nigeria and Medan I had a term at a school in England, where I learned to read (first term of reception). Hence when we arrived in Medan I was put in first grade of the Joint Consulate School, which was really run according to the American system. The school was a racial, national, religious melting pot and as such I had no awareness of 'difference', as everyone was different. My accent, however, did mark me out, as most people spoke English with an American accent. We had mixed races of all kinds, Nigerians, Russians, in fact most nationalities were there. These differences were not seen as issues in any way at all, it was just the way it was, if you know what I mean.

I was much younger than the other children in first grade and while academically I was able, emotionally I was a bit of a mess. However, in the long term this was great as I maintained this age advantage until I came back to the UK age 13.

By this stage I had done French up to 'O' level standard and was two years ahead in maths. In English I was also miles ahead, as in the American system a lot of emphasis was placed on grammar, which at the time was very unfashionable in the UK. I was in the 'clever' class at my first boarding school and was top of the class in English, thanks wholly to my previous education. In science, I had done 'earth science' which was advanced in weather, earthquakes, etc. I had done world history and 'central area studies' which was a sort of melting pot of culture/politics.

The transfer to all girls boarding in the UK was a real shock to the system – after all, in Jakarta you could get a smoking pass! No phone calls, no jeans, no going up the front stairs, washing all your own clothes by hand, polishing the cups, washing up on weekends, clearing tables, fines for undone buttons on uniform or holes in tights, the rules were aplenty and none of them written down.

I was constantly challenging this outdated sense of authority and consequently often being punished! Meanwhile the other girls looked to me for advice and counsel as I was seen as much more mature and worldy-wise. Despite my defiance, I also got voted on to the 'privilege list' (where you were allowed to make phone calls, or not wear uniform home) at the first opportunity, so obviously the teachers saw that I was reliable and capable. On weekends we had cooks but no washer-uppers, hence our duty, and I remember suggesting they bought some dishwashers and then they could save money on the weekday wage bill and save us from the trouble! That didn't go down well at all. I think I had to get up early and wash the kitchen floors for that one. The first half term I missed my parents somewhat, but no more so than those with parents in the UK.

After two years of single sex education I started looking at options for sixth form. One of the brochures to come my way was that of Bedales, a mixed-sex boarding school. I asked my parents if I could apply there prior to sixth form and they agreed. A trip to Debenhams ensued, coming away with a totally Lady Di outfit – frilly collar and all. Despite this I managed to gain a place and went to Bedales in January 1983.

This transition I found very difficult because I was one of only two new people that term and friendships were already firmly established. The culture of the school, however, suited me much more as it had no uniform and a much more relaxed rule system. There were many other children like myself who lived abroad and we would often find ourselves on the same planes or in the same taxis being ferried to the airport.

In hindsight, I think my varied educational experience benefitted me enormously. I ended up studying French as part of my undergraduate degree, and this must in part be thanks to my advanced level by age 13. Bahasa Indonesia was also compulsory, so I had had exposure to another language not just verbally but also in written form. My Bahasa is still lurking in the depths of my brain, much to my surprise when I visited in 2009 after a twenty three year absence.

Boarding school was a blast. I know it doesn't suit some, but really I think our parents suffered our absence more than we did. It made us more independent at a younger age, but also made me value the time that I did have at home with parents. Then when I went to university I was shocked that other students considered my background to be sheltered. I had to show them how to use the launderette, boil an egg, etc., and I wasn't homesick! They had no idea and some suffered so much they returned home and were never seen on campus again.

Do you recall how you felt about leaving Indonesia, especially about leaving friends behind?

Leaving Medan in 1978 was heart-breaking as I loved our life there. I am still in touch with my best friend from Medan. She is American and lives in Seattle. The last time I actually saw her was 2004, but physical connection is irrelevant – she is inside my brain! Leaving friends behind in Jakarta in 1984 was devastating and I still wish we had stayed in Jakarta rather than move to Ujung Pandang. I felt powerless and frustrated and angry. But it was out of my father's control; the boss dictated we move, so we moved.

I didn't like leaving school in Jakarta to go to boarding school either, but adapted very quickly. Leaving the first boarding school was very easy! I kept in touch with a few friends from my first boarding school until I was in my mid-20s. I lost touch with friends from my second boarding school when I went to university but reconnected with some of them many years later. I kept in touch with my holiday friends in Indonesia, who were all at boarding school like me, for many years and still have contact with one or two. The problem is that you all go off to different universities and jobs; some moved abroad, some married young, so there was a gradual drift apart. I wish I was still friends with them all but I allowed things to drift. I am now much more conscientious when I make friends!

How do you think being a TCK has influenced the person you are today? Do you think that you have a different outlook on life from non-TCK contemporaries?

Even as I was living through these times, I was aware of how lucky I was. I absolutely loved Indonesia and when I visited very briefly in 2008 I was shocked at how 'at home' I felt, even though so many years had passed and the country has changed so much.

For many years I felt Indonesia was more home than the UK. I was truly blessed. I would be a totally different person had I not grown up abroad, with different opinions and outlook. I am happier in my own skin, perhaps, and more able to consider change and accept it. I can never thank my parents enough for my amazing childhood experience.

Being a TCK has had a huge influence on me, not just in terms of personality but also in terms of career, by default really. I think that from a young age I had to overcome any shyness in order to cope with new people and places. I experienced other cultures and people much more disadvantaged than myself, which made me aware of how lucky I was and more appreciative of my parents and the society I was born into. Maybe it is not true of all TCKs, but I have always had a 'live and let live' attitude as a result of living in foreign countries and mixing at school with children of other races, mixed races, and other nationalities, religions and cultures.

In the workplace too I have benefited.

My 'big break' career-wise came when I joined a small US brokerage firm to help cover the Middle East client base. It came down to two candidates and I was favoured over the other one because my prospective employer felt that as I had experience of living in a

Muslim country I could appreciate and understand the clients more. Possibly total rubbish, but I wasn't complaining!

I did find that others in the office were very reluctant to deal with my clients in my absence as they felt they couldn't communicate with them as easily as I did. Perhaps a bit of lack of confidence from those who have never been outside their comfort zone and so would rather not venture out there? The contrast for me was that, yes, I too get nervous when dealing with strangers for the first time, but you take a deep breath and look them in the eye and go for it! Human beings are all very different from each other but if you accept and understand that there are differences and allow for them then the world would be a happier place. Unfortunately, too many refuse to accept others' viewpoints and that's where it all goes wrong.

Really my whole life has been influenced by where and how I grew up, just like any other person, and as that was abroad, it makes me 'other'. I am, to a certain extent, rootless. Only in the past ten years or so have I really come to feel that the UK is 'home'.

I went to India once on holiday (1994), to Kerala. I had no idea it was tropical rainforest, like Indonesia. I looked out of the window on our descent and saw red earth and rice paddies. I then disembarked, my hair frizzed up in an instant, I breathed in, and I thought 'oh my gosh, I am home'. I felt like I had been there my whole life – the climate, flora, fauna the same as Indonesia. The people and culture, of course, completely different. But I was comfortable and immediately slotted into the craziness that is India. It shocked me how strong the feeling was. It feels unnatural to have that emotional response in a country you've never visited before – but it's uncontrollable. Then when I re-visited Indonesia in 2008 I had a similar response, albeit a little more diluted. The language came flooding back to me and I spent the entire ten days boring my husband silly with memories.

So, yes, in general I believe that TCKs have a slightly different outlook on life.

Do you travel/have you lived overseas as an adult?

I have lived overseas as an adult and I have travelled a lot, but since having children this has been put on hold. I am constantly itching to travel but am unable to do so!

I would love to have the opportunity of living abroad again, preferably in South-East Asia or Africa. I spent six months in the US in 2004, a most miserable experience in small-town USA – not to be recommended. Religion dominated society there and it was a cultural desert. I then spent four years living in France from 2004-2008. I had my first child there, and it was interesting to compare childbirth there with that in the UK. France might be a mere twelve miles or so separate from the UK, but is amazing how different a culture it is.

Have your experiences of living overseas as a child affected how you have brought up your own children? Have you consciously made any decisions, like whether to move overseas with them, because of your own experiences?

I feel sad that I cannot offer my own children a similar experience. I believe that growing up exclusively in one country definitely limits one's experience and ability to adapt and understand others. I worry that they will grow up in one town with a very closed outlook on life. I want them to appreciate what's out there. I would definitely move abroad with them should the opportunity arise. They have travelled a little, mainly Europe, but I did take them to South Africa last year. What surprised me was that they seemed so incurious – no questions about why everyone there was black or why our friends had a live-in maid etc. I would have thought that there would have been some curiosity. Perhaps at seven my son was a little too young and I am being unfair! Even on a more basic level, for example seeing elephants outside the car window, they were asking when they could have ice cream – aaagghh!

My story

As you pack your child's suitcase for yet another overseas posting, start looking for a second, third or even fourth school for them and if you lay awake at night worrying about how they will fit in with a new set of friends, it might be reassuring to hear a story of how one former expat child (me!) turned out.

There have certainly been ups and downs along the way but here I am, 45 years after being born to diplomatic parents on their second overseas assignment, and I think I'm pretty much okay. Hopefully my story will help reassure you that bringing them up as third culture kids isn't going to damage them – and in many ways will give them opportunities their counterparts back home would never get.

I was born in Havana in 1968, the third child of what would eventually be four and the only girl. I have no memories of living in Cuba although often wonder whether my intense dislike of the cold stems from my birthplace. My father was a diplomat with the British Foreign Office and his wife, my mother, was herself the daughter and granddaughter of expats. We returned to the UK after Cuba but postings followed to the Philippines (a blissful place for children – I have some fabulous memories of swimming and snorkelling in clear blue waters, travelling all over the country and living a very carefree, outdoorsy life), where we attended the International School in Manila; a short-lived trip to Nigeria (we left after my father fell ill and was medi-vacced out), Venezuela and Gibraltar. I was at boarding school by the time they went to Caracas and at university during their last posting to Cameroon – so only visited rather than lived with them during this time.

One of the lasting results of my upbringing has been a wanderlust that has taken me to more corners of the world than I can remember. At first I tried holidays, then I took off for a late 'gap' year round the world at the practically elderly age of 30. But eventually I gave in to my itchy feet and joined the Foreign Office myself. Whilst I realise this sounds like quite an achievement, I do think my background helped. I would hate to think nepotism was involved but travelling and living overseas does give you a certain outlook on life and it was definitely useful when it came to my first posting to Kingston, Jamaica.

Here I met my husband and we now have two daughters. I left the FCO but his job has taken us to Islamabad (for three months, before we were evacuated) and St Lucia. Life as a 'trailing spouse' was very different from going with my own job – and certainly had its challenges. But I am so glad we gave our daughters that opportunity to live in a third culture and experience things they would never have had the chance to if we hadn't gone. We have now returned – semi-permanently – to the UK, where my children are now attending the local primary school.

So how have I 'turned out'? Well, I've had a couple of good careers, I'm married and I have two gorgeous daughters. I've had many and varied jobs, including as a journalist, diplomat, antenatal teacher and freelance writer. We have a nice house in a nice town. I see my parents regularly. Hopefully this indicates that I've turned out more or less okay. All my brothers turned out okay too, had steady relationships, and children. All three have had good jobs in law, teaching and the voluntary sector, but tragically my eldest brother Matthew died young at the age of 49 of a heart attack. Of all of us though, only I seemed to have caught the wanderlust – my youngest brother doesn't even travel out of this country and none of the others have had jobs that have taken them abroad for more than short periods.

Socially, as well, I think I'm okay. It's taken me a while and I found it hard in my twenties to connect with people who hadn't led the sort of life I had. But I think we all chill out a bit as we age and now find I can fit in almost everywhere and make friends with people from all sorts of different backgrounds, cultures and even age groups. This is probably very typical of people who travel a lot – when you find yourself in a new place, you need to fit in, not expect people to fit to you. Otherwise, I think I have a natural infinity to 'outsiders' and often find myself befriending people I think look lonely (they're probably just enjoying their own company!). I guess this stems from always feeling a little 'different' myself – one of the hardest things about having the background I did is finding other people who 'get' me.

Perhaps this is why so many former expat children do, themselves, travel. However, even now that we're settled (sort of) back in the UK, I still find ways to link up with expats – through Internet forums, Facebook where I keep in touch with so many of my friends from my Jamaica days, and most recently Twitter. I might have settled back in my home country, but in my head I think I'll always be moving on...

Although both Penny and myself have turned out okay, many TCKs and ATCKs do find life difficult thanks to their peripatetic background – and there is now increasing recognition of the particular issues someone who has grown up in more than one culture might face. There are books on the subject and more and more websites springing up to offer support (for some of these, see below). It is worth bearing this in mind – even though the vast majority of children will find the global life an advantage in the long run, for many it will cause problems in the future. Just like so many other things I've discussed, the best thing you can do is to prepare yourself for this – to follow the advice in this book and in the websites below and to ensure that when your little ones do finally grow up and fly the nest, your care for their needs as TCKs doesn't fly away with them.

Now that you know more about how your kids might turn out, it's back to the present. At this stage, there's almost certainly one thing on your mind above all else – and that's schooling. So in the next chapter I tackle this tricky topic, and look at all aspects of your children's educational needs.

Information That Might Help Adult TCKs

A website dedicated to the highs and lows of being a TCK – and the effect it can have on your romantic relationships: https://tckdating.wordpress.com/

A Facebook group for TCKs: https://www.facebook.com/groups/tckid/

Interesting research into American Adult TCKs: http://tckresearcher.net/Cottrell%20ATCK%20commitment.pdf

Look at this – a whole Meet-up group dedicated to Adult TCKs in the UK (why didn't this exist when I was growing up?): http://www.meetup.com/Adult-Third-Culture-Kids-ATCK/

A blog by the writer of a book aimed at counsellors of ATCK's, but one which all ATCK's and parents of TCK's might find useful to read: http://mangotreereflections.com/belonging-everywhere-nowhere/

Schooling

As I've already mentioned, schooling is probably one of the most pressing topics for anyone with children as they plan their overseas move. In this chapter, I look at the best way to find a school in the first place, how to help your children settle in to their new school, alternatives to traditional schooling and how to handle the different education systems. I also touch on special needs.

It is hard to think about an overseas move with school-aged children without first thinking about where they are going to be educated. Certainly this has always been at the forefront of my mind every time there's been even the hint of a possible overseas move. Hence, I know quite a lot about the uniform options and lunch menus of the expat-friendly primary schools of Bangkok – even though we never actually went there. And more recently, with our impending move to Pretoria on the horizon, there isn't much I don't know about the South African school system.

It is a huge part of your child's life, and you are going to want to get it right. But how easy is this when the schools in question are thousands of miles away and your main information is keenly gleaned from their glossy – but possibly not totally impartial – website?

Of course, there are other ways to help find the best school, and I would urge anyone looking at where to send their child or children to try and talk to as many other parents as possible before making the final choice – especially if you aren't able to visit beforehand. We'll cover these issues in this chapter, as well as looking at some of the other potential pitfalls along the expat-education route.

First, find your school...

So, you've decided to accept a posting to the Middle East – let's say Dubai. You don't know anyone there but you understand there's a pretty huge expat community so you're not too worried that you won't find a school. Putting your feet up, coffee in hand you idly type 'schools' and 'Dubai' into the search engine – and up pops 53,500,000 results (I've just tried it!) – most of which, you later discover, are already full. Right, perhaps this isn't going to be so easy after all.

Benedicte, who has lived abroad for fifteen years, latterly in India, said they found the school BEFORE accepting the move – and that making sure there was a 'great' school for her children was one of the main pre-conditions of agreeing to the posting. Others have realised, thankfully with enough notice that you really do need to get in there early if you want a place at a decent school. In some cities, expat-friendly school places just aren't keeping up with demand as the global population becomes more and more transient.

Hong Kong is one such place, where Rachel was luckily able to get her children on the school waiting lists as soon as they were born. 'It is very stressful moving to HK and needing immediate school places,' she said. 'There are simply not enough places in international schools, partly because many local people use them as well, as they don't like the local system.'

Adele found similar long waiting lists in Qatar and said that all she could do was put her three children's names down on as many lists as possible and then 'take what you can get'. I know there are similar problems in parts of South Africa (in particular, Johannesburg and Cape Town), so it's certainly worth getting on to the Internet as quickly as possible if you do even get so much as a sniff of a posting in these countries, or others like them.

So, Dubai, Hong Kong and South Africa aside, what sort of choice or choices are you likely to face when looking for a school in another country? This, of course, depends on where you are going.

Sometimes there simply isn't a choice at all – K moved to Switzerland and found you 'had to attend the school in your town/village'. Evelyn found that in Belgium 'there was only one school that was suitable for my children'. And in Singapore, Maria always knew they wanted their daughter to go to the Canadian school: 'My younger daughter was already struggling with the move, and we figured if she had teachers with familiar accents and a curriculum that was more or less the same as the one she'd just left, she'd feel more grounded and secure,' she said. She also found they had no real choice in Bordeaux – where her daughters' weren't accepted into the local schools because their French wasn't good enough, and there was only one International school option.

But if you are lucky enough to have a choice of schools, which one you finally plump for will depend on many things, including what sort of education you want for them. Would you, for example, rather they went to a local school (especially if you want them to pick up the local language), or one aimed squarely at expats? Would you even prefer them to go to a school run in another language altogether?

For parents with secondary school age children, the most important thing is likely to be the curriculum and which system they follow e.g. the British system, the American one or perhaps the International Baccalaureate. You might also want to find out more about things like their disciplining procedures, bullying policies or security. Or are you simply after the best or the best fit for your child that is available?

Once you have thought about the sort of school you want (and if you are really lucky, this might even include things like what sort of uniform they wear and what the after-school club choice is like), you can start to pinpoint one or two possibilities. This will also help you think about where you want to live – although some of you might have to do it the other way round and find the school after you know where your new accommodation is likely to be.

The most obvious way to decide on which school you finally go with is to visit them. But since this option isn't available to everyone, the next best thing is to follow the same advice as for everything else and try and talk to parents whose children are currently at the school (or have recently left). Target anyone who is there already, friends, friends-of-friends, forums, contacts through your, or your partner's, work. If you have any sort of liaison at the other end, make sure you ask them, or ask them to point you towards other parents. You can, of course, read the school's website and email the head/owners (and unfortunately some schools are run more as a business than an educational establishment) to ask questions – but you might not get an entirely unbiased view this way.

All of the above advice applies equally to whatever type of school you are looking for, including pre-schools. In fact, choosing a pre-school is probably more important than for any other age range – you really are not going to want to leave your children at that age if you are not entirely happy with the people you are leaving them with. For this reason, I would suggest you definitely visit a pre-school before signing on the dotted line (and probably handing over a substantial amount of cash), unless you know the school really is of a certain standard.

Ange told me about her experiences in Jamaica: 'I had heard about three pre-schools, mainly through mothers I had met at the playgroup. These catered for expat children as well as Jamaicans, which I felt was a good mix. When a new family arrived, we went together to look at the pre-schools. On visiting the three, there was only one that I thought had the right atmosphere, equipment and standard of care right for Molly. Although initially she was not happy to go, once settled, I was very happy with the school and Molly made friends, some of whom she is still in contact with today.'

Settling in/getting used to something a little different...

As we all know, travelling abroad is full of adventures, experiencing new things and moving way outside of your comfort zone – and schooling is certainly no exception to this. They might be speaking the same language as they do at home, they might even be following the same curriculum. But without a doubt, something – or possibly an awful lot of things – will be different to what they (or you) are used to.

Both my eldest daughter and I were slightly shocked and more than a little confused when she started at the Montessori school in St Lucia. Where were the toys? Why did they have to walk everywhere with their hands behind their backs? What was this strange Marguerite festival they were expected to celebrate where they had to come in dressed as a lawyer or a judge (you seriously couldn't make it up)?

The lunches were a total no-no for an English four-year-old more used to eating fish and chips than fish stew, so we stuck with sandwiches. The uniform was a source of huge stress – an itchy pinafore dress made out of surprisingly thick material, worn over a T-shirt plus a pair of 'modesty pants' because boys in her class were obviously quite unused to seeing a pair of girls knickers (back home in the UK, they still get undressed in front of each other for PE). Yes, her 'settling in period' was not a happy one and I still tear-up a little at the memory of her (wonderful) teacher prising her off me every morning, wailing as they led her to the back of the classroom and out of my sight.

But she settled in, she got used to the strange customs and ways of doing things. She made friends, she learnt to read and write and she even started to speak a little Creole. Altogether, she got a fantastic start in her schooling life and looking back now I couldn't have asked for more. But it certainly didn't feel like that at the time.

One of the things that many people have mentioned to me at is how much better they felt the schools were overseas than at 'home' – wherever their particular home might be. This could partially be because of the fact that they were getting a private school experience, something they probably couldn't afford back in their 'real life'. Along with the bigger house, daily maids and weekly beach trips, small class sizes and decent equipment is yet another possible perk of the expat life. Naturally, this doesn't always hold true – there are many great schools in the UK, for example, and I would still rather my children went to our local state primary than any other school in the world. But for others, a private level of education is simply out of reach unless they are expats.

Of course this is only true of certain places and for those that can afford the private schools. But even without the more obvious 'extras', you will almost certainly find the experience of mixing with children from another culture, or even multiple cultures if they are at an international school, will give your little ones a fantastic educational grounding for the rest of their lives.

One mother, Claire, who lives in Malaysia with her three children, said one of the main reasons they had moved was to give their children a 'better education'.

And as Lesley said about her experiences in Indonesia, Qatar, Saudi Arabia and Kenya: 'It's a definite advantage living overseas as the children (and parents) become more open and tolerant to other cultures and religions. It also gives them a wider understanding of things that happen around the world.'

You really can't put a price on that.

Unfortunately, not everyone has positive experiences of schools overseas and, in some cases, things are so bad it forces a move back home.

Adele, who took her three children to Qatar when her husband got a job there with the local airline, said the schools in Doha were all private and profit-making, with high fees and – in her opinion – low quality. She said there weren't enough books to allow every child to take one home to read every day, and the number of non-English speakers affected the overall dynamic and subsequently level of learning in the school. She also felt the discipline was at a lower level than she wanted for her children and concluded, saying, 'The quality of the schooling was a major factor in us leaving.'

One of the main worries parents have is whether their children will fit in to the new school and make friends, especially if they are trying to do so in a different language or a totally unfamiliar culture. For some, this is something they will struggle with, and many children opt for an alternative such as boarding school (see below) rather than stay on in an environment where they are unhappy. This is something you will need to be prepared for and it is important that you know as much as possible about what is going on with your child at school.

For many, though, language and cultural barriers will fall away very quickly – especially if they are still primary-school age. Lesley again: 'Children don't really have cultural differences – they are very resilient and take everything in their stride. A game of football or hide and seek and everyone is friends.'

Where there might be problems, however, is with the curriculum – it may take them a while to adjust to the differences from home and for the teachers to work out where to place them compared to the other children. You might also find the curriculum covers a whole new range of topics, especially in subjects such as history and geography – which isn't necessarily a bad thing, but which might take a bit of getting used to. Religion, of course, might be a whole can of worms, depending on where you live. And then there's also the worry that they might cover the same topics two or three times over every time they move. How many times can a child get excited about the Romans or Space?

All of which brings me to…

Alternatives

If you are a parent expat for long enough, you may well at some point have to start thinking about the alternatives to the local school system. This, as with everything, will depend very much on where you live. But for many people, the time when they start to think about what other school options there are is at secondary age (e.g. around 11-years-old). And for most, if the local system isn't going to work for one reason or another, there are four choices:

1. going home (or moving to a third country with a suitable school);
2. home schooling;
3. boarding school; and
4. private tutoring.

The first of these could be relatively straightforward. If you find you are at a natural break in your posting (perhaps you have been there a few years and are ready to move on) and this coincides with your child reaching secondary age, this could be a good time to consider moving home or to a country with an education system that fits your needs.

However, things could be more problematic if you haven't reached this point, or the working partner can't leave the post without losing his or her job. Many people at this stage do return home with the school age child or children, leaving their partner abroad without them. This comes with a whole range of potential complications, slightly easier if he/she doesn't live too far away and can commute home relatively frequently, but never an easy decision. For many, though, it is still the better option than the other two alternatives.

Home schooling is something many people consider as an absolute last resort. For most, the idea of not just spending every waking hour of their day with their offspring but also trying to be their full-time tutor fills them with absolute horror. However, it can work really well for both child and parent if you are the right sort of people and if there is a good home-schooling community where you live.

I was home-schooled for a very short time after we were posted to Lagos when I was twelve, too young yet for the boarding school I eventually went to but with no decent local alternative. We had the advantage that my mother was a trained teacher, but even so, my main memories are of learning maths by going shopping with her, English by writing hugely imaginative stories, biology by exploring our large garden and PE in the swimming pool. It was great fun, but it's probably a good thing it only lasted a few months, as I'm not sure my education would have ever caught up again once I got back into the UK system!

Some people certainly like the idea of home schooling, even if they haven't tried it themselves. Evelyn said she would certainly have considered it in the US as the Michigan state system was under huge pressure and the quality of education being offered was declining. However, 'we decided to stay with the school system as the home-schooling population is mainly creationist (Michigan teaches evolution)'.

Hilary, massively unhappy with the schooling options in the Netherlands (which she called a 'substandard of education') said she would have definitely done it if it hadn't been illegal there.

But equal numbers of people I asked reacted with horror at the thought of home educating their child or children. 'God, no, we'd end up hating each other!' was Carole's reaction.

And Lesley said that although she herself hadn't considered home schooling, she had friends who had done it but 'they found it hard for their children to integrate with other children as they spent most of their time with adults and had no contact with other children during the day'.

To home school you also need to know what you are doing. There are plenty of online resources out there (some of which I list at the end of this chapter) but I still can't help but think that as a parent, you must be fairly confident in your own abilities before putting your child's education in your own hands.

I am sure that if you live somewhere with a network of home schoolers, where you can help each other out with your specialities (I would be okay at teaching reading and art but would be terrified of trying to explain anything more than very basic maths to my children, for example), life might be a bit easier. But if you are an isolated home-schooler surrounded by school-educating families (or, for those of you being posted somewhere a bit more remote, surrounded by no other families at all), then things could definitely be trickier.

This might be your only option for one reason or another, so all I can do is advice you to be as prepared as you can be: read as much as possible in advance; plug into home-schooling networks at the earliest opportunity (whether online or in real-life); talk to others who have done it or are doing it; work out what you need to take with you in terms of things like books (and what you can easily buy or get sent to you at your destination); prepare your child by introducing them to other home-schooled children.

But if home schooling really isn't a viable option and you can't or don't want to move, boarding school does often end up being the best real alternative. Some prefer to put their children into a boarding school before this need arises – knowing that you might be moving somewhere without a good local school offering your preferred curriculum. It's probably better they start boarding at the same stage as others (usually 11 or 13 – but 16 is another good age to start), rather than in the middle of an important exam year or after everyone else in their year group has settled in.

I want to add a disclaimer here: I went to a boarding school in the UK from the ages of 13 until I was 17 (being summer-born, I left before I reached my 18th birthday). It was not a happy experience for me, but I know that some of my classmates had the time of their lives. I went to the same school as my brothers, which, of course, sounded like the best option and was certainly the most convenient for my parents. But looking back, I might well have been happier somewhere very different – just because one school suits one child doesn't necessarily mean it will suit them all.

Whatever happens, it's important that you both (e.g. you and your child) visit the school/schools you have in mind before making a decision. Sometimes your options might be limited by factors such as cost, and without a doubt it is better that the school is close to someone familiar to the child (grandparents, aunts or uncles, family friends etc.) who can take them out at weekends and become their guardians. But if you do have a choice or choices, choose wisely. Once your child starts it's not impossible to move them (and it is better that they do move if they are definitely unhappy) but logistically it's not an easy thing to do once you are back in your posting country.

Hopefully though, your child/children will settle in well to the boarding school life. Things are very, very different from my day. I am sure pastoral care is better than it was (at least I hope it is!) and with modern technology you can keep in much closer contact than I was able to. But it is still much easier if it is something your children choose for themselves that they want to do.

Carole, who was so horrified by the idea of home schooling, decided that the best place for her daughter as they moved from Germany to South Africa was at a boarding school in the UK. She said: 'It worked out wonderfully for us. We needed her to be up to speed with the English curriculum as we were expecting to be back there soon. Loads of research and school visits are a must, and the kids must want to go, too. Otherwise I can imagine they would feel utterly abandoned.'

Lesley's eldest daughter also made the choice to go to boarding school. She actually mentioned it when she was in year 9 (and 13 years old) but Lesley dismissed it as a 'passing fad'. It was only when her daughter was still talking about it two years later, that Lesley realised how serious she was and allowed her to start researching where she would like to go. 'She did this and chose a school…reluctantly we applied and she was accepted. It was the best thing she ever did!' Lesley explained, adding that it made her 'more independent and streetwise' and advised others thinking of doing the same thing to make sure they do plenty of research and speak to as many students and parents at the school as possible.

As for tutoring, this is something you could consider either as a stand-alone education option, or to supplement the local school system. This may be particularly useful if the system you are going into is different from the one at home (UK 'A' levels as opposed to the International Baccalaureate, for example) and you wanted to make sure your child or children was keeping up to speed with the home curriculum.

Many people will chose this option if they know they'll be repatriating after a short time (say up to two years) or if their child is at a particularly important point in their education. We ourselves are going to try using a UK tutor for our oldest daughter as she will be going to an American school, but returning to the UK system. We're using a local tutor who will work with her online (via emails and Skype), but there are more and more companies setting up to help you with tutoring and schooling over specialist websites like Tutor Me (http://www.tutorme.co.uk/) and Maths Whizz (http://www.whizz.com/).

Moving on/moving home

Although I will cover repatriation in greater detail in a later chapter, it is worth mentioning here the particular issues around moving back home or to another country when it comes to schooling. Although the initial move is always likely to be the hardest of all your moves, uprooting your children yet again can be really hard on both them and you, and moving them between school systems comes with its own problems.

For a start, the school starting age is different in many countries with children starting at any age between 3 and 6 depending on where they live. This might mean that your child has only just started 'formal' schooling (what we, in the UK, call 'reception' – the bit where they start to read and write, anyway) at an age where their contemporaries are a couple of years into their education.

Usually if this happens, you will find that even if they haven't yet 'formally' learnt the basics, they'll pick it up pretty quickly. Plus, children at this age are all so different, the teachers will be used to a vast variety of abilities. But it is something to keep an eye out for and if necessary ask the school at your overseas posting if they can go into a class early (if you think this is right for your child) if it means they will fit back in more easily at home.

In St Lucia, children were put up from pre-school to reception when they were ready for it, not by age – although most would have moved up by the age of six. On the other hand, they were taught reading and writing in pre-school if the teachers felt they had the ability. We were lucky as our daughter was keen to learn to read early so was one of those who went up to reception as she turned five – the same age as she would have moved up back in the UK. But we could easily have returned home feeling she was a year behind everyone else in her class.

Another thing to be aware of when returning home (and this is not just relevant to schools but to your children's return generally) is that they might be keen to pick up friendships where they left off but that those friends might very well have moved on.

Even if they have kept up with their friends when they have been home on holidays, it would be hard to expect a young child not to have made any new 'best friends' after their old buddy disappeared off into the sunset with barely a backward wave. It might feel to us as though we've hardly been away, but to the friends we left behind, there was a big gap that had to be filled somehow.

This, of course, is also true of adults (what d'ya mean they're not all sitting at home every night waiting for me to come back so we can continue the party?). But it will be up to you to manage this in your children – or to at least be there for them when they discover it for themselves.

Special needs

It goes without saying that if your child has special, complex or different needs, it is even more important to heed all of the above advice – in particular choosing a school, or deciding on a posting based on what schools are available.

What is available to help children with different needs varies vastly across the world and, of course, your own child's particular needs will also dictate where you can go. You know your own child or children best and will no doubt take their needs into consideration before accepting a posting, but issues to consider include:

- whether there is a school that can accommodate them and provide them with the standard of education that you would expect and accept;
- whether there are accompanying services for your child like physiotherapy, counselling and extra teaching assistance;
- what the physical environment is like – for example, if your child has restricted mobility, will they be able to get around (which, of course, is also true if you or your partner has restricted mobility); and
- what the local health services are like and can they provide the service that would be acceptable to you and your child; if necessary, how easy is it to get to a neighbouring or nearby country for better health facilities.

As well as the more obvious special needs that families will almost certainly know they will have to consider before moving overseas, there are more subtle issues that you might consider. These include things like allergies (can you be confident that the school will cater for, or even recognise, these?), learning needs such as dyslexia that may be more understood in some countries than in others, and even gifted and talented learners. Many of these issues are not necessarily deal breakers as to whether you move abroad or not – and many of them you might not find out about until your children start school – but they are all things worth considering before you take that final step.

Rachel moved to France from her home country of New Zealand with her family, which includes a daughter with Downs Syndrome. They are all at an international school in Toulouse, but the family have found things challenging due to what they feel was a lack of support at the school and are looking for an alternative. 'The main consideration in coming here was Hannah's schooling, and this is an ongoing issue,' Rachel explained. 'It has definitely made our transition to France more difficult.'

It might not be something you can be fully aware of until your children start at their new school, but make sure you plug into any special education needs networks as soon as you possibly can when you arrive. It can be a challenging road ahead, and even more so if you have a child whose needs are more complex than the norm.

Now we've dealt with the small people, it's time to consider those other loves of your life. No I don't mean your partners, I'm talking about your pets. In the next chapter, I consider all the things you may need to think about if you want to take your four-legged friends with you.

Websites and Articles to Help You with Schooling:

An article about finding British schools abroad: http://expatsincebirth.com/2014/08/22/finding-british-schools-for-your-expat-children-luke-rees/

An interactive map of British schools overseas: http://www.expatandoffshore.com/british-schools-abroad/

An article about home-schooling your children overseas: http://myinternationaladventure.com/05/homeschooling-your-children-abroad/

An article about an American family who homeschool in Belgium: http://myinternationaladventure.com/05/americans-homeschooling-in-belgium/

A UK website which offers advice and support, as well as a wealth of information, to anyone home-schooling their child, even for short periods (eg between postings): http://www.educationotherwise.net/

Relocation service that helps you find a school: http://www.iorworld.com/school-search---tours-pages-540.php

Information about international schools around the world: http://infotools.lloydsbank.com/schools/#/s/

CHAPTER FOURTEEN

Pets: Our Furry,
Feline and Feathered Friends

'The pets were more expensive to move than our plane tickets, but it didn't matter to us. They are a part of our family and they go where we go. I read stories on message boards or Facebook groups about pets that are abandoned when families move to another country and it just breaks my heart. I just can't comprehend it. Yes it is expensive, but when you adopt a pet into your family it is supposed to be for life.' Jen, an American who has lived in China and Qatar and taken her black Labrador and cat with her.

I have to admit, including a short chapter on pets was a bit of an after-thought for me. It's not something that I first considered as I planned this book. Children, yes, lots on children – telling them, preparing them, settling them…but then it occurred to me that to some people, their pets ARE their kids. And I realised I couldn't ignore them. So in this chapter we consider what sort of documentation you might need in order to take your pet with you, how to help them settle in when they arrive, and how to tackle the thorny subject of leaving them behind when you move on.

I think one of the reasons I didn't include pets in my original plan is that they have never been a big part of any of my moves. Which is strange when you consider how many pets we owned as children: cats, rabbits, guinea pigs, mice, rats, hamsters, gerbils, fish of all different descriptions, ferrets, terrapins, even a couple of chickens (which turned from cute little yellow fluff balls sold to us outside the International School in Manila, into vicious cockerels who chased us round our garden) and non-egg-laying quails.

But for all the animals we kept as pets, I don't recall ever taking any from one country to another, which is probably because we never had dogs. Cats are easier to leave behind, and I fear the rabbit we left in the Philippines got turned into stew. Dogs, though, are often part of the family – and for some, leaving a dog behind would be not that far off leaving one of the kids. Actually, I expect there are a few parents out there for whom leaving one of the children would actually be preferable to leaving behind the family dog, but we won't go into that here...

These days, things are a lot simpler than they used to be. Back in the day, we were always put off by the idea of long stays in quarantine, which seemed so cruel for a family pet, especially when you heard tales of animals dying during their six months enforced imprisonment. But now with microchips and pet pass-ports, it's a lot more straightforward taking a pet from one country to another – although, of course, some countries are easier than others.

So the first thing to do before you decide whether to take your pet or not is to have a look and see which countries are 'listed' and which are not. In most cases, I suspect we're talking dogs – cats just don't seem to love us or care about us or let's face it, notice us, in quite the same way as dogs. We're pretty replaceable for cats – as long as someone's feeding them and giving them the occasional tickle behind the ears, they're usually happy (although they'll want you to think otherwise).

If you're considering taking any other pets, unless it's a simple move to a neighbouring country with no controls, I would think very carefully. If it's the goldfish or your child's pet stick insects you're wondering about, I'm not sure you're quite ready for that overseas move just yet...

You can find which countries are listed on the GOV.UK website under Taking Your Pet Abroad (link below), or if you are not in the UK, your local equivalent. Moving between EU or non-EU listed countries (which includes much of the Caribbean, Australia, New Zealand, Canada and the US, as well as others), things should be relatively simple as long as your pet has all the required documentation (microchip, rabies vaccination, pet passport, tapeworm certificate for dogs). You should be aware, though, that you need to use an authorised carrier and approved route – all details of these routes and carriers from and to the UK can also be found on the GOV.UK website. The US also has similar information on its State Department website (see below).

If you are going to a non-listed country, it's not just taking your pet into that country that you need to think about: you will need to make sure you can meet all the requirements if you want to bring it home again. And this may involve a long quarantine stay – the costs of which you will have to meet yourselves.

As well as the headache of all the paperwork involved in the move itself (not to mention the cost), you then have to deal with the hassle of settling your pet into their new home. Of course many pets (stick insects, for example) won't even notice they are somewhere different – especially if the weather in the new country is similar to the one you've just come from. But in other cases, it may take a while for an animal to settle in - just like it does for the rest of us.

As well as the temperature (which could be a real issue for an over-furry cat or a dog bred for colder climes suddenly finding itself living in a roasting heat), smells, food, other animals – lots of things will be different for our pets which we might not have even considered. So don't be surprised if they go off their meals for a while, or seem a bit down. And if you are moving between time zones, don't forget that pets can get jet lag, too.

Another thing to consider before you move and decide to take your pet(s) with you, is where you will be living at the other end.

At home you might have been in a roomy house with a huge garden, or close by parks with lots of walking opportunity. Suddenly you might find your new accommodation is a small apartment on the 28th floor of a block in the middle of a busy city. Not much good for anything but the smallest or calmest of dogs, and no good at all for any cat that is used to having a cat-flap exit into the world outside.

Hopefully you will know well in advance where you will be living, or even have some choice in the matter, so can include the needs of your pets along with the needs of the rest of your family when you make that choice. And (despite what I said earlier in the chapter about pets being like children to some people), it's worth thinking very carefully about whether to take your pet at all if you don't know exactly where you will be accommodated at the other end.

Carole took her cats from the UK to Japan, where they acquired a dog. The dog then came with them and one of the cats (the other having died in Japan) to Germany and, on to South Africa. She said there was 'rigid paperwork and bureaucracy' but they have never had to worry about quarantine. 'We wouldn't have gone if quarantine was mandatory,' she said. 'I also couldn't leave a pet behind.' Overall, she has found the cat has adjusted easier to the moves than her dog. 'The cat takes it all in his stride,' she said. 'The dog is not keen, and gets anxious.'

Jen found both her pets, a cat and a dog, adjusted well to their moves to China and Qatar, although the cat 'had a little trouble with time change – both trips we heard some meowing at strange times until he got his days and nights figured out. But don't we all have a bit of trouble with that?' The dog, Bridgette, enjoyed their move to China where they moved into an apartment complex with 'beautiful gardens and a boardwalk right next to the China sea, lots of areas for her to explore and lots of other dogs around for her to socialise with'. She was, however, puzzled by the elevator for the first few days. Their move to Qatar was slightly more difficult as 'it is so hot, and mostly just sand and dust' but as an 'older' dog she needed less exercise and they were able to get away with a combination of their small, fenced in garden and the beach for her walks.

Some people chose to use a company – described by Jen as a 'professional pet shipper' – to help move their pets. There are a number of these sorts of companies around and although they can be expensive, they can also make things a lot easier for you. Jen explained: 'It eased my mind, especially in China where it was essential to have someone that speaks the language and can ease frustrations.'

On the other hand, another (anonymous) respondent who took two cats to China, the US and the UK (which included a stay of six months in quarantine in the UK) said they did not have a good experience with one of these type of companies: 'It's franchised, and the level of service differs greatly from country to country,' she said. So, like with almost everything linked to an overseas move, ask around and try and get personal recommendations if possible.

Finally, you should anticipate that you may well have to leave a pet behind at some point – sometimes it's just a kinder thing to do all round. This could be hard for your children if you have them, so get them ready for this possibility from the start. If they know the pets are not coming with them when they leave, it'll make the parting that much easier. And if you're prepared to get a new pet when you arrive in your new destination, you'll probably find that the old one is pretty quickly forgotten. I have found that, when it comes to pets, children are fairly fickle creatures!

For the last few chapters, we've been concentrating on the needs of others – in particular, those of your children and your pets. In the next chapter we get back to the important person in all of this – which is you. And we get a bit more serious, as we take a look at the world of work – or how to occupy yourself if getting a paid job just isn't an option.

Useful Websites and Articles to Help You Move Your Pet Abroad:

UK Government advice on taking your pet abroad:
https://www.gov.uk/take-pet-abroad/overview

And from the US Government:
http://www.state.gov/m/fsi/tc/c10442.htm

The Wall Street Journal's expat site's pets hall of fame:
http://blogs.wsj.com/expat/tag/expet-hall-of-fame/

A blog about a diplomatic dog:
https://diplomaticdog.wordpress.com/

Pets are people too – especially when you are moving…:
http://figt.org/pets_people/

The World of Work

In this chapter, I take a long, cold look at the options open to you if you wish to find a job when you're living overseas. I start with what the barriers are to getting that job in the first place, including the difficulty of needing a working visa or permit before you can even start; go on to look at what sort of work you could actually do and what you might be able to do to prepare for finding a job before you leave; look at some of the other options to a traditional job including unpaid or voluntary work; cover some of the problems you might encounter in the workplace – relating back to the chapter on culture shock; and finally discuss briefly the long-term effect this move might have on your career (both the negative and the positive).

'I have been lucky in that I have always managed to find some sort of work in all my posts. I did not know I was going to be able to work before any posting – and it would have made things easier if I had, but I realise this would be difficult. All my jobs have been within the Embassy as then I avoided the need for a work visa. Most of the work has been part-time, fairly basic clerical work and poorly paid. But having something to get up for in the mornings, and give me purpose has been a lifesaver at times. Without work I don't think I would have stayed in a couple of the posts (Rwanda & Jamaica) as there was little else to do.' Sharon, posted to several countries with her partner Mark, now settled in the south of England with their daughter.

'I found work as the CLO (Community Liaison Officer), and later as the PA to the Defence Attache, at the British High Commission in Kingston – a massive departure from my normal job as I am a marine biologist by profession. Immerse yourself into the local and expat crowds. "Work" comes in many forms and you cannot be too choosy! If I had insisted in staying in science I would not have worked, but because I was flexible it worked out okay for me. You must remain open to all sorts of opportunities, and be prepared for a lot of change.' Nicola, who found her first role after being approached by a management officer in a bar after Hurricane Ivan struck Jamaica.

'I went to Singapore with no plans to work. At that point I'd been a stay-at-home mom for about six years, and I expected that to continue. After two years, though, I started to get a little bored. (I don't play tennis, I don't like spas, and I don't like shopping.) I got a part-time job in the communications department of one of the international schools. It was easy to get a permit; I just needed a letter from my employer. I didn't find [the job] easy, mostly because I'd been out of the workforce so long and I couldn't seem to change my mind-set to working mom. Also, the job was not what was advertised, and so I was bored there, too! It was quite interesting though, being one of two non-local employees in the office. I learned a lot about Singaporean culture from my time there.' Maria, Singapore 2002 – 2005 and Bordeaux 2005 – 2007.

In the mad, bad twenty-first century world we live in, where it's normal to have a mortgage as large as a planet and supermarket bills that have you hyperventilating at the check-out, it's usual that most adults do something to earn their living. Even those who aren't actively making money – stay-at-home parents or full-time carers, for example – have some major occupation that takes up most of their time. And for this reason, work defines us.

The first question you get asked when you meet someone new is: 'What do you do?' When we describe ourselves, many of us will start with our profession or our occupation. We often spend more hours with our colleagues than with any other person in our lives (yes, okay, I know many people spend just as much time with their kids, but considering how many of my former colleagues behaved like my kids, sometimes I get my lines a little blurred). But for many – possibly most – of you, that is all about to end.

Reading this back, I realise how doom-laden that opening paragraph sounds. Many of you will of course find work when you move abroad; you might already have something lined up before you get there. Others prefer not to work, to use this time to concentrate on something else in their lives – their family, their creative side or even their suntan. And there is absolutely nothing wrong with that if those things can fulfil you, or at least occupy you until it's time to move on.

But what about those who are giving up an interesting job, a good salary, a pension – all for what? Sitting at home staring at four walls while your helper cleans under your feet? Meeting the other Ladies Who Lunch (or perhaps Dads who Dine) for coffee and cake every second Monday? Mah-jong and bridge afternoons? Well, perhaps. But let's look at what you can do to ensure that doesn't happen or, at the very least, to prepare you for the possibility that it might.

Barriers to work

I found that most people who I spoke to in the course of researching this chapter did want to work. And along the way, most of them did end up doing something – whether paid or voluntary. But many of them also found at least one, and sometimes several, barriers in their road to a fulfilling career/pocket-money occupation (delete as necessary).

One of the first barriers many will find when they think about finding work in another country is difficulties in obtaining work visas or permits. For some, this is only something they'll find out after, in the early whirlwind of excitement, they've already accepted the posting. It might even be something they only realise isn't as straightforward as they thought it would be after arriving in the new country.

Even at this stage, the reality is hard to understand – how many of us think giving up work for a few years will be fun, will give us time to finally write that novel or learn to speak the local language? Well yes, to some extent. But when the reality of a long, lonely day with nothing to fill it finally hits home, many regret that decision made in those early heady days when all they could see ahead was excitement and shared adventure.

For Liz, the reality of her new non-working life was obvious from the start: 'It was written clearly in my husband's work contracts that I was NOT allowed to work in Israel and China,' she recalled. She was able to take on unpaid voluntary work, but her advice? 'Read your husband's work contract before you move!'

Obtaining a work visa can also be an issue – Elizabeth lived in Saudi Arabia where there were crackdowns on anyone flaunting the 'no visa, no work' rules; and Hilde found that in Zambia they were only allowed one work permit per family, so, not being the main bread-winner, her options were very limited.

For Adele, a GP, insurance was the problem: 'I was not going to work without insurance because if anyone makes a complaint you would lose your work permit, lose your exit permit, and be stuck in the country until it was resolved. And, as with driving, if a Qatari makes a complaint – even with no proven basis – the charge will be followed through. It's their word against yours, and their word counts for more! They are used to getting their way, and if you don't comply, you could get into trouble.'

If getting a visa or a work permit is not a possibility for you, there are some options for getting round this requirement. Some people manage to work from home or work remotely for a company in another country. Belinda knew that she wouldn't be allowed to work in the USA on her visa, but did do some free-lance translation work for the company her husband worked for (which was based in Austria). 'I'd heard that as long as I didn't work for an American company and wasn't paid in dollars, there shouldn't be a problem,' she said. 'Although I must admit that I didn't look into it in any more detail!'

But if you are lucky enough to have a visa that allows you to work, or if you fight through the local bureaucracy and manage to win yourself a coveted work permit, or even if you live in a country that allows you to work freely (for example, the EU for British nationals), you may find there are still plenty more hurdles to get over before landing your dream job.

For many people, just like for so many of us at home, one of the main problems is simply lack of options. But why this is a more of issue when you are overseas is due to a few factors that you will need to consider. This could include because they require you to speak the local language (which may not be a problem if you spent the first half of your posting exploring your creative side and learning the local lingo – see above). Or you might think you know enough of the local language to get a job, only to find that when they say fluent, they really do mean just that. Or the hours might not suit you – even though this can be a problem wherever you live, it's a lot harder if you don't have the back up of family or local friends and you can't get trustworthy childcare. Or they might require a local reference – pretty difficult when you've only just moved to the country.

Another issue that comes up a lot is that of finding a promising job – only to realise that the (local) weekly wages are the equivalent of your daily coffee bill back home, and you're only allowed two weeks leave a year.

If you are in a position to negotiate this (for example, having more, unpaid time off), it may still be worth doing the job for low wages to keep your skills up to date, to get you 'into the workplace' and therefore more open to other opportunities, and to stop yourself going insane. It's just hard when you're having a bad day not to walk out knowing that your earnings will not be missed.

What to do?

So you've got your visa/permit, you're happy in the local lingo, you've booked the child-minder, worked out how much money you'll need to earn to make it worthwhile going out to work at all...but what are you actually going to do? And will it be a continuation of your career back home, or are you about to venture into something completely new?

The responses I got to this question when I asked around were about as varied and interesting as the people I was asking, and the countries they lived in. From working in schools to teaching English as a foreign language, coaching to consultancy work, the solutions people had found to finding work were admirably creative and helps to show how clever some people are at not just surviving but thriving in their new life.

In terms of whether they were doing something completely new or not, this was split about fifty/fifty. I think many initially thought they might be able to use their previous experience to find work overseas, but when they realised this might not be possible, found ways to use their existing skills to try something different.

Anjie, who was a registered nurse prior to living in Dubai, found work as a paediatrician's community liaison after approaching her own paediatrician and asking if he would employ her to follow-up on his sickest patients. In other words, she made up her own job: genius.

Maria, who lived in both Bangladesh and Vietnam, found work editing for various organisations, including the charity CARE, UNICEF and a PR company, and then later worked for an international kindergarten. She said that although she had never edited before, she did have a background in international development so 'the editing...was relevant and helped me keep up to date with what was going on in that realm'.

Sue, a midwife and health visitor, 'worked for myself in Madrid as I was covered professionally to work in Europe. Although I could not work in a hospital due to the language issue, I aimed my service at English speaking families and this worked well'.

She then found that she would have needed to sit exams to work as a midwife or nurse when they moved to the States, so managed to get a job teaching new and expectant mums with a large healthcare company. 'It was hard to find this job, but I enjoyed it and it was a great experience,' she said. 'It was also important for me to do some work to provide evidence to my registering body of continuing practice in order to keep up my registration as a midwife / health visitor.'

Other paid work examples given to me included:

- Librarian work in a school.
- Online coaching and support business.
- Four days paid secretarial work for UNDP
- Teaching English in a British school.
- Community development and health program work.
- Community liaison officer within an embassy
- Antenatal teacher.

Finding a portable career

One thing that struck me as I looked at the list of jobs people had done over the years on their various postings was how important it is, if possible, to find a career that is portable. This is, of course, not always possible and what might work well in one country may be a total dud in the next. However, there are a few things you could consider before you leave, if you have the time, which might stand you in good stead when you are looking for work abroad.

One of the most obvious one is teaching English as a foreign language. There are plenty of courses available to help you learn how to do this either before you go, or possibly once you arrive in your destination country. You don't necessarily need a recognised qualification to pick up private English teaching but it helps and you may even be able to fix yourself up with a job before arrival.

Another area that could help you find work is helping other expats – anything from career or personal coaching, to location expert or community liaison. This could be something you need to learn from scratch or it might be something you can adapt from an existing job you're already doing in your home country.

Nicola M, who was already trained as a personal and business coach in the UK, spotted a gap in the support services given to expatriates when she moved to the Netherlands and ended up setting up her own coaching business. Likewise, Louise decided to start her own online coaching business in Portugal as an extension of her work in training and personal development, and education in occupational psychology, as well as her Masters dissertation on the experience of accompanying partners.

I've also had friends who trained as music teachers, hair dressers, nail technicians, doulas…all things it is possible to take to either the expat or even the local market depending on the country you are moving to. Once you put your mind to it, and with a bit of research (including what the market will be at your destination country – would you just be catering to expats or will you be able to compete with the locals, for example), there are plenty of ideas that you could at least consider.

Unpaid/voluntary work

For many who don't have the option to do paid work, whether because they can't get the relevant paperwork, there isn't anything available or they can't get childcare, the option of voluntary or unpaid work is still a good one.

For some people, especially those who are financially more comfortably off overseas than at home, this could be an excellent opportunity to do some really fulfilling work – especially if you are lucky enough to find something that actually uses your skills, and keeps your CV up to date.

Just like paid work, voluntary work is often difficult to find, competitive, and very dependent on where you live. Gone are the days when you could swan into a school in the developing world and expect them to allow you to teach just because you've got a degree and can read and write a bit. So, creativity is again key here, and it's worth looking out for opportunities as early as possible (before you arrive is ideal).

Working in your child's school or pre-school is almost always a good option. My daughters' school in St Lucia was crying out for volunteers despite the fact that, as far as I could tell, most of the other mums spent a good proportion of their time at the gym. I ended up reading library books to the children once a week and helping out on a sweltering sports day. Others have found themselves assisting in various ways from accompanying children on school trips, to hearing children read.

Another obvious place to volunteer is with expat groups, again almost always on the lookout for helpers. Manning stalls at the International Women's Group annual bazaar might not be everyone's idea of a great day out, but if you think of it as a networking event you never know where it might lead. Louise volunteered for an expat group in Portugal as the activities co-ordinator, which involved organising their once a year activity fair for more than 300 attendees. A 'big little job' as she described it, but also a job that would look good on her CV and would stand her in good stead when she started moving to working with expats.

Others have managed to find work with local Non-Governmental Organisations (NGOs), including: Liz who worked for a Spanish charity in Benin which had opened a welcome centre for Nigerian refugees; Maria who volunteered with an NGO in Kosovo working with youths from Serbia and Albania; and Nicola who worked with a volunteer expat group in the Netherlands and then became involved with an international woman's contact group. But perhaps most resourceful of all is Hilde who over the years took on all sorts of roles, including: 'making special footwear for leprosy patients, evaluating programme proposals, undertaking needs analysis of community development programmes, yoga classes for children, vegetarian cooking classes and setting up health promotion programmes at schools'. Which certainly goes to show, if you look hard enough, there's usually something out there for everyone to do.

Problems in the workplace?

We all know work can be a tricky place, whether you're at home or in a new country. You spend a lot of time with your colleagues, you are expected to behave and not lose your temper (at least not on a regular basis) and the artificially imposed 'hierarchy' of grades, bands and pay differences can make it hard to hold on to your identity. But throw a totally new culture into the mix and there will be days when you wondered why you ever bothered.

It may be that you are working within your own culture – in an embassy or a large global company for example. But even if this is the case, you are still going to have to deal with people from your host country whether as fellow employees or as customers/clients.

Culture shock can be hard enough in normal circumstances but it can really rear its ugly head when you're also trying to remain calm, collected and professional in the face of what seems like completely ridiculous and unreasonable behaviour (never, ever returning a phone call; shutting up for two hours at lunch time; treating you differently because you're a woman – for example).

Anjie is Australian and said she finds working with Filipinos hard. 'Culture wise I find many of my co-workers lazy, and I feel relieved that I am autonomous and don't rely on others to succeed at work,' she said. Knowing what I do about the people of the Philippines (generally very hard-working and focused people) it was almost certainly not that her working colleagues actually WERE lazy, just that this was how their way of working came across to her. In other words, another version of culture shock.

In Jamaica, Nicola D also found a very different culture: 'The work ethic was completely different,' she explained. 'I found that people clock-watched and when it was time to go, they went, irrespective of workload. Not what I am used to at all as a scientist working for beans!'

On the other hand, Hilde found working in a different cultural challenging for completely different reasons: 'Working hours are much longer overseas, more intense also, more responsibilities, bigger challenges,' she said. 'Working with other cultures is enriching – but also tiresome.'

And just to even things out a bit, Louise described the positives of working in another culture: 'My first few roles working for Saudi employers were great,' she said. 'It was good to emerge in a culture which as an expat you don't really see.'

The long-term effect on your career

Whilst some will undoubtedly benefit from working overseas – in particular anyone who has a special interest in global work – there is no doubt that for a lot of us, being an accompanying partner is a one-way ticket to career suicide. Or, at least, suicide of the career we had before we followed this particular path. This is something you will need to consider, and something that, should you decide to go ahead anyway, you will need to reconcile yourself with.

There will undoubtedly be days ahead when you feel a huge amount of frustration and anger about your situation, and this anger might end up being taken out on your partner/relationship. But instead of mourning the loss of what was, look at what you have gained, see if you can use what you have learned on your travels in new ways, exploit any new skills you've learned (from your never-before-realised super organisational skills gained from project-managing three moves, to language skills, cultural awareness, any experience you have gained through voluntary work…) and put them to work in whatever life you move on to next.

And finally, just remember some of these little pearls of wisdom:

'Think carefully about what work means to you BEFORE relocating. It is your life and if you cannot imagine not working, think very carefully about making a move to a country where you cannot work or cannot work in your chosen field. If that is not the case, approach the new experience with an open mind, think re-invention and growth and it will be an exciting and hopefully rewarding experience.' Louise, Portugal and Madeira.

'Be flexible, take advantage of networking opportunities. If work is what you want, make sure you spread the word about what you're interested in doing and what your background is. Many companies and organisations are eager to find someone on site, rather than having to recruit from abroad.' Maria, France, Taiwan, Eritrea, Italy, Kosovo, Guinea, Sierra Leone, Cameroon, Bangladesh, Vietnam and Qatar.

'Be creative with your skill set and find ways to work for yourself. Know things will change as you are changing – i.e. don't hanker to return to your old job/career…let this go!' Nicola M, Ireland, the United States and the Netherlands.

'There is much more to life than work. Don't focus solely on that…always have a back-up plan with activities that you can do by yourself that bring you joy. Be aware that, more than back home, you have to build on the strength in yourself. Finding a paid job can be very difficult in some places. Don't forget this is an amazing adventure with so many other things to explore, culture, creativeness, language, social life, surroundings…' Marloes, France.

So that's the world of work and if that's left you feeling a little faint I've got just the thing for you – in the next chapter I look at another of those 'big' issues: health.

Websites That May Help You Find Work Overseas:

The 'insider's guide to expatriate recruitment':
http://expatrecruiter.com/

Making global mobility for dual career couples a reality. Apparently: http://www.partnerjob.com/

Offering career help to spouses moving to Switzerland:
http://www.spousecareercentre.com/

A 'global jobsearch tool': http://www.passportcareer.com/

Voluntary work abroad: http://www.workingabroad.com/

UK Government tax information if you work overseas:
https://www.gov.uk/personal-tax/living-working-abroad-offshore

Health, Including
Having a Baby Overseas

Although it's impossible to know in advance exactly what health issues you will face when you get to your new country (even if you already have an existing condition, living in a new place may exacerbate things) you almost certainly WILL face some sort of health crisis at some point in your stay overseas. This may be a mini crisis or a major one, but whichever it is, it's worth being as prepared as possible for medical emergencies, as well as all those everyday complaints that could well turn into an emergency if you don't know what you're doing. This chapter helps you do this, by first looking at the three I's (Immunisation, Insurance and being In-the-know); then discussing what to expect from your local facilities – and what to do if they're not up to your expectations. I also talk about how to cope with a real medical emergency; and finally we turn to pregnancy, childbirth and post-natal issues.

Perhaps the most enduring memories from my childhood as a 'trailing daughter' is the day my father nearly died.

Parts of the day are a total blur. Other parts are as clear as if they happened just a few weeks ago. As is always the case in situations like this, the things you remember are not always the most relevant (we ate mock turtle soup for lunch). And no doubt if I compared my memories to those of my brothers, we would all have a totally different account of what happened.

This is what I do remember.

We were living at the time in Lagos, Nigeria – a stiflingly hot, dangerous city without much in its favour, at least from the view of a newly-arrived eleven-year-old English girl. On the day in question, my father developed the most appalling headache. So bad that he couldn't move or even sit up. I can't recall how or why, but we ended up at the house of one of his colleagues (possibly even the High Commissioner), playing something – was it pool or table tennis? – with his children. Older than us and possibly with a greater understanding of what was going on, I remember being treated with great kindness (although I am not sure that serving us mock turtle soup could be considered particularly thoughtful – but remembering what a lack of choice there was in Lagos at that time it was possibly as good as it got).

What we didn't know at the time, but I do now, is that my father was taken to the American Embassy clinic and then almost immediately put on a flight home. He was accompanied by a colleague's wife, who happened to be a nurse, and who apparently stood holding his drip for the entire flight home. He was taken straight to St Thomas' hospital where he was diagnosed with a subarachnoid haemorrhage (bleeding in the lining of the brain) and where he remained for many weeks to recover.

In the meantime, we prepared to fly home the next day. I am assuming that somehow my mother managed to pack suitcases for us all, organised for the house staff to be paid, made sure our flights were booked, arranged for someone to take us to the airport and meet us at the other end...but all I remember is the relief when someone volunteered to look after our bald African grey parrot.

We never returned to Nigeria, but my father made a full recovery. What happened to him could have happened anywhere – it wasn't necessarily living in Nigeria that caused the bleed (although the stress of the move, the particularly difficult circumstances we found ourselves in for the first few months of the new posting and the oppressiveness of Lagos might have all been contributing factors). But had we not been lucky enough to have access to the modern clinic run out of the American embassy, and to have been in Nigeria with an organisation that was willing and able to medivac him out immediately, I don't know how this story would have ended.

This was thirty five years ago, and thankfully much has changed in the world. Medicine and medical facilities in most countries (at least for those of us lucky enough to be able to afford it) has caught up with what we're used to in the so-called 'developed' world. Yet, whilst things might have improved, there are still a lot of places where you'll need to be taken elsewhere in the case of serious medical emergencies – a quick look at an expat website for Nigeria shows that someone with a sub-arachnoid haemorrhage would probably still need to be evacuated for treatment. And even if your posting is to a 'modern' country with the sort of facilities you would expect 'back home', it's still worth finding out what's available and – crucially – where it's available in good time for the first time you need it.

Preparation

While there's no real way of being ready for the unexpected, as per the scenario just described, there are things you can do in advance of your postings to make sure you are prepared for the more run-of-the-mill medical incidents.

At some point you are almost certainly going to need a doctor, a dentist or some other medical professional – and, if you are travelling with a small child or baby, this is likely to be sooner rather than later (at one point I tinkered with the idea of taking my duvet and pillow with me to our local GP's surgery, so much time did I seem to spend there when my children were babies and I was recovering from two births).

As with most things discussed in this guide, it's always best to try and do as much research as possible about the facilities in your new country before you leave home. This can roughly be broken down into three categories:

1. immunisations;
2. health insurance; and
3. being in-the-know about what's available in the place
   you're moving to (and what do you need to take with you).

First make sure you're immune...

Immunisations should be relatively straightforward – most GP surgeries can offer a travel clinic and you can find out what you need to have from various websites (including in the UK this one run by our National Health Service: http://www.fitfortravel.nhs.uk/ destinations.aspx) or you might be lucky enough to have a company or organisation that can give you all this information. Don't forget to do this with plenty of time to spare as you may need to spread the jabs out over several months, depending on what's recommended.

Another tip is to make sure you keep a good record of what you and every member of your family have had and when – it can get awfully confusing when you need boosters to remember what you have already had.

You might also need to think about malaria prophylactics, depending on your posting. There are different ways of taking these and it's worth researching the pros and cons of each, particularly if you have children who will need to take them. Again, get advice at the earliest possibility about the risk level of Malaria at your destination (and this goes as well for travelling around once you are in your new posting) – it may be low enough that it's not worth the possible side effects from the drugs.

Then make sure you're insured...

Health insurance of some sort, if not covered by your partner's employers, is another must. We're all used to taking out insurance when we travel on holiday so it's not dissimilar to this – just on a much bigger scale.

What sort of insurance you take out does, of course, depend on where you are going and what you are already covered for when you get there. If you are a European moving to another European country, for example, you might find that your European Health Insurance Card (EHIC) is sufficient enough cover. But there will be other countries where you'll need to prove you have cover or can pay for your treatment in some way or another before they'll even start to treat you. Not ideal in an emergency (which could happen from any moment when you arrive in-country) so definitely worth sorting out in advance.

'Chickenruby' found this out to her expense (literally) when she and her family moved to South Africa: 'Despite asking the company for medical papers the minute we arrived, we found ourselves in our third week here with our eldest being rushed to hospital. We were unable to see him until we opened an account and handed over the Amex. It took a further three months to claim our money back.'

Interestingly, it was those that have lived in the States – a country notorious for its controversial healthcare policy, and for being a place where you really do need to be insured if you're going to get treatment and not need to re-mortgage your house to pay for it – that seemed to have the most to say on the question of medical insurance.

Jacqui, who lived in California with her husband and baby, said her medical insurance turned out to be 'great' but added this proviso: 'We wish someone had taken the time to explain what would be covered, as we always had a fear in the back of our minds that we would be hit with a large bill in the post.'

Another US resident, Jenny, said health insurance was a 'massive issue' in the first year they lived in Oregon in the States: 'If I was referred to a specialist, I would phone the insurers to make sure I could see that particular specialist, would be told yes, then they would send me a bill a bit later anyway. Fortunately, the company changed insurance and they have been pretty good since then. I am so pleased we have insurance and would wish to leave the US if we lost it.'

Still on the question of insurance, Nicola D, who moved to Kingston, Jamaica, said they had no support from the organisation her partner worked for (the UN), which was particularly worrying as she had a medical condition that needed monitoring. They decided to take out 'expensive and private' US medical insurance to cover themselves, which meant they had the reassurance that they could travel to the US if required for treatment and specialist care.

Finally make sure you're in-the-know...

Before leaving your home shores, it would be a good idea to find out exactly what is available in the place where you are going and plan accordingly. This could include anything from what medicines are available and what you need to bring with you, to what the local facilities are like and whether you should have any treatment/check-ups before you leave.

You might be (pleasantly) surprised by what is available in the country you are moving to – certainly, we didn't have to worry about taking much with us to Pakistan, where generic medicines were available over the counter at a fraction of the UK cost. But you will need to plan ahead if you or any of your family have any specific needs – you really don't want to run out of something potentially life-saving only to find it's going to take the local medical practice two-four weeks to order in a new batch!

In terms of medical facilities, use all resources available to you (hopefully by now you'll have a few – websites, forums, colleagues, predecessors) to find out as much as possible in advance of your posting, but it is still worth having check-ups for the whole family organised before you go. Try and do this a few months beforehand in case you need any treatment.

Hilde, a Belgian, found that asking around as much as possible got her the best info on health facilities: 'As the health facilities are not that good in Bangladesh, we found out we should go to Bangkok for serious issues. We have friends living there and they recommended us some good hospitals just in case we should need them. I also asked our dentist in Belgium if he could recommend some dentists in Asia and he told me that Malaysia was the best place to find a good one!'

If you're not lucky enough to have on-the-ground contacts to provide you with the information you need, spend as much time as you can doing it yourself when you first arrive. Nicola D, in Kingston, said she started off by looking in the phone book and on the web, and then 'immersed myself as much as I could by visiting GPs and hospitals to see what was available – which proved invaluable when we did have an emergency'.

Which brings us nicely to...

Local facilities...and what to do if they're NOT up to scratch

Of course, 'up to scratch' is very subjective. One person's luxury is another person's doss house. But generally most of us want to know that when things go really wrong, they'll know where to go and what to expect when they get there. It's also worth bearing in mind that this might be one time when your knowledge of the local language will really be put to the test – try dragging the words for 'fracture' or 'huge red spots all over her chest' out of the back of your head in the local lingo when under the stress of a trying to find help for your potentially not very well child.

How easily you find it to cope with explaining your medical emergency in another language will of course depend on where you are, and what level of the local language you can cope with – as well as whether medical staff in that country are used to using English to communicate. Katrina, for example, found that she was fine in Greece, where, despite high levels of bureaucracy and complicated paperwork she was able to get by, as she spoke Greek and they spoke good English. However, 'Italy was the worst as you had to speak Italian, there were no other options...'

Cultural issues, and just different ways of doing things, can also pose difficulties – Richelle, who has moved with her eight children between several different countries including Bangladesh and Niger, said she once drove all the way to an ER department at one of the hospitals only to find that 'no-one would answer the door and there was no information posted'.

Nicola M also found problems in Ireland, where she gave birth to her son, saying: 'Although no language issues, there were differences in culture and belief systems...for example, a Catholic maternity hospital that didn't have a single woman on the board but several priests.'

Difficulties like this aside, one thing you do want to be sure of is that when you do get to your local GP surgery or hospital you will actually be able to be treated. For some people, what they get is better than that they could expect back home (in particular if you can afford private health care either through your sponsoring company or organisation, or through insurance). Liz, for example, found a 'superb' clinic five minutes from where they live in Beijing, which is probably a good thing as she took her son there twice within the first three months of their arrival. And Maria, in Singapore, found the medical facilities to be 'excellent'.

In other places though, be prepared that things won't be quite what you are used to. Nicola D found the facilities in Jamaica to be 'old fashioned' and a lot of the staff to be 'not empathetic or supportive', although most of the medical professionals they encountered did their best to help.

Warren found that hospitals were 'okay' for basic problems in Dhaka, but that any surgery had to be done back in his home country or in Bangkok. Lizzie was particularly scathing about the facilities in Saudi Arabia, which she said were 'shocking and out of date' and where nursing care was very poor.

You also need to consider what the actual method of getting to the hospital will be – in an emergency at least. In Malaysia, Michelle found that ambulances 'could take hours to arrive, even though we were on a tiny island!' And Naomi described the ambulance service in Delhi as a 'laughing matter...our drivers could get to hospital MUCH faster than waiting for an ambulance'. Certainly we knew we could never rely on the local ambulance service to get us to the one private hospital in St Lucia – it's something you get used to, but it can be a chilling thought if you come from a country where you know all you have to do is pick up the phone and within minutes you'll hear sirens.

When emergencies happen

Hopefully, having read all of the above, you will be prepared for when/if this does happen. I have been very lucky as a parent to so far not have to deal with any MAJOR medical emergencies with my children whilst we have been overseas. I say major because it's hard for any child to get through the first few years of life without one mishap or another – but the worst we had was a head cut that needed stitches in Islamabad and an overnight stay at a hospital in St Lucia when my youngest had croup. My childhood, however, was riddled with emergencies, although strangely none of them concerning me (the only girl, with three brothers).

My mother, Rowena, reminisced with the typical understated calm of a long-term diplomat's wife: 'It was always a concern. Bill's emergency sub-arachnoid haemorrhage in Nigeria was obviously a huge worry and if it hadn't been for the Americans, I'm not sure what would have happened. However, evacuation by air to the UK was quick and efficient.

'Cuba was always worrying and when Matthew got pneumonia we had to inject him ourselves as the doctor didn't have enough petrol to come to the house. And when Toby nearly died of chicken pox, I didn't feel I had any help or support at all (Bill was out of contact in New York). On the other hand, Matthew's two broken arms were dealt with well in the Philippines and when Oliver got Malaria in Cameroon it was probably far better dealt with than it would have been in the UK.'

Hopefully your posting(s) won't be quite as dramatic as ours were, but you do need to be prepared for anything from a broken bone to a tropical disease. Depending on the severity of the accident/illness, it might be something that can be dealt with in-country, or you may need to medivac (if health cover/insurance includes this option – check!).

Haylee faced this situation within just a few weeks of moving to Islamabad, when her eldest daughter cut her nose on a coffee table and needed stitches. Not a massive accident, but one that, due to local facilities, it was felt was better dealt with out of country: 'As the local hospitals in Islamabad weren't considered safe for children to have anaesthetic, Sophie had to be flown to Bangkok to have her operation. The embassy was brilliant in booking flights/organising the hospital trip/booking a hotel for Dave to stay in (I stayed in Islamabad with Benjamin – I was too upset to go and I didn't have the confidence to go to Bangkok by myself). I did worry that Sophie had to wait nearly forty eight hours to get her nose stitched – however, the doctors were very reassuring that it was going to be okay.'

Flying a child out of country for treatment can be pretty scary, but not all medivac stories turn out to be entirely negative, as Sharon's story from her time in Rwanda proves: 'I had to be medi-vacced for an infected spider bite (!)…the process was well organised and smooth and although I was sent alone to South Africa to get it sorted out, for me it was lovely as I got to go back to Pretoria and catch up with old friends!'

For most accidents or illnesses, however, you won't need to be taken to another country for treatment. Which doesn't mean that the experience will be any the easier – even if you are in a so-called 'developed country', like Katrina: 'Sweden was the worst as they would only treat children in ONE hospital in Stockholm – and many people would find out while waiting with a bleeding child in the wrong hospital.'

It's always worth remembering that if you've lived in a tropical country, diseases that you might have picked up in one country can manifest themselves much later on. If you have lived anywhere with Malaria in particular, always be on the lookout for symptoms as it can be a very deadly disease. And if you've ever lived any-where where small creatures burrow into your toes and lay eggs...keep an eye on those small lumps on your foot you thought were veruccas. Oh yes, it happened to me.

Finally on the subject of emergencies, as well as all the usual planning there is one thing you should know from the moment you step foot in your new country – and that is the local emergency phone number, whether it be 999, 911 or whatever. In many countries you can use 112 as a 'standard' call for emergency services (see below for a link to check which countries this covers). Unless, of course, you live in one of those countries where you might be waiting an awfully long time for an ambulance to turn up. In which case, my piece of advice would be to make sure you had the number for a darn reliant local taxi service in your phone instead.

Childbirth and antenatal/postnatal care

It's perhaps not surprising that many people I have spoken to in the course of researching this book have had babies while living overseas. After all, if you've given up your job (possibly even career) to move with your partner overseas, and there isn't a whole lot of ways for you to occupy yourself in your new destination, what better way to get through the long days than to run around after a toddler or two?

Speaking to my mother about life in Cuba in the 1960s, where they had no television, no clubs, no real restaurants, no gyms or even proper shops, I suspect the reason I came along as number three was because there just wasn't anything else to do. She, in those days, had little choice but to give birth at post – from what I understand, not the most fantastic experience for her. But these days, most people can decide whether to stay where they are for the birth, or return home. Both have its advantages and disadvantages.

The ideal, especially if you have other children already, is to stay. After all, who wants a potentially long journey home when you are heavily pregnant, having to live away from your partner – and possibly in cramped conditions with your parents or in-laws –

while you wait for the birth? Then your partner plays roulette as to when he needs to come home – leave it too late and they may miss the birth; too early and they could spend their paternity leave sitting around waiting for the baby to make its appearance. It's a lot less hassle to stay – as well as anything else, you don't have to worry about getting the baby's passport sorted the MOMENT it's born.

On the other hand, going home does mean you return to a (hopefully) familiar health service, where you speak the language, where your friends and family are around you after the birth for support and where you know there will be programmes on the telly that you'll actually want to watch during those long mornings of breastfeeding.

So depending on your personal circumstances and preferences, you will at some point need to make a choice. Once you have made that choice, gather as much information as you can, in particular if you are staying put. If possible, find private antenatal classes – a great way to meet other parents at the same stage as you, as well as learning about birth and parenting. This is also a good way to get an understanding of what the birth culture is like in your country – and if the predominate way of giving birth is not the one you want for yourself (a lot of countries have a very high caesarean rate, for example), is there a particular hospital, birth unit or obstetrician who will be more understanding towards your needs?

As well as the birth itself, it's also important to think about what sort of local support there is post-natally. This is especially true if it is your first baby – and also if you are moving out to your new post fairly soon after having the baby back at home. I touch on postnatal depression below, but support is important for all mothers – in fact for all parents – as your life will go through so many changes after you have a baby.

So what is it like to actually have a baby whilst living as an expat?

In the course of researching this chapter, I heard about babies who were born in Greece, Italy, Denmark, Ireland, Malaysia, Morocco, the US, St Lucia, France, Hong Kong, Belgium and Cuba (me and one of my brothers!). I also heard about people who chose to return home from Islamabad, Cote d'Ivoire, Jamaica, St Lucia and other countries. Experiences were mixed, but I thought I would let them speak for themselves:

'Greece was overly-medical in how they treat pregnancy/childbirth... Denmark was a do-it-yourself pregnancy (even the urine and glucose tests were self-administered and self-reported during check-ups) but when I had a complicated pregnancy/delivery I got the care I needed.' Katrina, Greece, Sweden and Denmark.

'In Dublin, I had never had a baby before and it wasn't exactly as I'd have liked but it worked out well... I got choices and support through the midwives who knew how to manage the predominantly male doctor/risk averse hospital system to support the mother and baby...the midwife service was great but the postnatal service was poor. I had to sit with my lovely new born baby a couple of days old in a waiting room with drug addicts waiting for Meth at one health centre... I didn't go after the second visit as it was so awful.' Nicola M, Ireland, the US and the Netherlands with her husband and son.

'I had my second child in Kuala Lumpur and although I had no issues, there wasn't the same level of interest as in the UK. In the UK I had a midwife-led birth, in KL it was doctor led and I don't feel the midwives had the same level of confidence. There was no antenatal or postnatal care.' Michelle, Malaysia

'As far as being pregnant (in Morocco) – it was very clinical, I would go and have my check-ups, went to have my caesarean section and that was it, no follow-up, no midwives, nothing. I did my homework I tried to go to antenatal classes but it didn't exist, they didn't understand that. Clinically it was fine. But I was totally isolated – I was in a private room and would've preferred to have been on a ward to meet others.
   'After the baby was born I was stuck there and I was in agony. B went to work and, the (glass of) water was so far behind me, I couldn't reach it

and they wouldn't bring it to me – I had to wait for B to come back, they were used to people coming with families. I asked them to show me how to bathe my baby, asked first day, second day and they wouldn't. On the third day they turned the tap on her, on, off and gave her back so I gave up after that and did it my own way. She had colic, so very difficult, we had no midwife, we left hospital. She cried most nights for the three months non-stop, and she was dead, she collapsed, we rung up the doctor in a panic, and the doctor came and said she was just exhausted, it was so scary...' Anthea, Morocco and later France, now back in the UK with her French husband and three children.

'I remember being pregnant in Pristina with my first, and reading advice online that said not to get stuck in traffic while pregnant due to the pollution – while in my neighbourhood, the snow and the ice were so thick that traffic had stopped and people had set the dumpsters on fire because the garbage trucks couldn't get to them... What I mean is that American advice did not really apply to my situation and didn't make me feel at all secure...' Maria, who has lived all over the world including France, Taiwan, Eritrea, Italy, Kosovo and more.

'I became pregnant in Islamabad – I had to leave post at 36 weeks and Sophie had to leave the nursery to accompany me back to England. I flew back to England by myself with my two and three-year olds... I went to stay with Dave's parents who were superb. It was harder on Dave to be left at post by himself than it was for me – as I was having a great time and catching up with friends. Dave flew to the UK three weeks later and Emily was born in mid-July.' Haylee, who, with her family, went from Islamabad to Abu Dhabi and is now in China.

'I had a baby here (in the US). I managed to have no interventions in the birth, which is more and more unusual here. However, I saw my OB/GYN at a Billy Bragg gig so I suspect he is slightly more left-leaning than the average American!' Jenny P, British expat in the US.

'I returned home (from St Lucia) at seven months to have my second child. It was an upheaval for all of us, Chris had to take a lot of time off

but it was nice to be around family and in reassuring surroundings.' Marianne, now in Barbados.

'I became pregnant in Jamaica – and the medical welfare office were brilliant at offering me support from afar. I returned to the UK before the birth of my daughter, but this was towards the end of my husband's posting so we were not affected by having to be separated during my "confinement" (I do hate that word by the way!)'. Sharon, who is now settled back in the UK with her daughter and partner.

There are many more stories: childbirth is, after all, one of those massive life-changing experiences (a bit like moving abroad in fact!) that everyone has something to say about. But overall, leave your expectations at the door, be prepared for things not to be as you perhaps would like them to be/they would be at home and gather as much support around you for the postnatal period – wherever you are for the birth.

A word about postnatal/postpartum depression (PND/PPD)

I've already touched on depression in the Culture Shock chapter, but I thought it was worth emphasising here how important it is to understand postnatal depression in particular. Incredibly common amongst all women (statistics for the UK show up to twenty five per cent of mothers get PND), what many people don't realise is that it is not caused by hormone changes. After giving birth, your 'feel good' hormones do plummet and cause what is commonly known as the 'Baby Blues'. This affects nearly all women, but usually it passes fairly quickly and is a momentary blip on that scary journey into parenthood.

PND, however, is caused by a mix of things that includes your environment, your social situation, isolation, lack of support...many of the same things that can effect women who have recently moved overseas in fact. So if you are pregnant or thinking about getting pregnant after you move, especially if it is both your first baby and your first move, I would strongly advise you both (you and your partner) to read up on PND.

If at all possible, arrange postnatal support for after the baby comes – can your mum or another friend or relative come over? How much time can your partner get off work? Track down as many postnatal groups and services as possible. Say YES to all the invites to those dreadful sounding 'mummy and me' classes. They're not dreadful at all – you might feel silly at first singing endless rounds of 'The Wheels On The Bus' but you'll soon be grateful for the chance to swap notes with fellow exhausted parents. Talk to your partner, make sure they understand what you are going through – and remember dads can get PND, too. If all else fails, do go and see your doctor. Counselling or anti-depressants can certainly help in these situations – although if you are breastfeeding make sure you take the drugs that are compatible with this.

Whilst I touched on the possibility of a medical emergency in this chapter, what I haven't really talked about yet is what happens in a major emergency of another sort. Bombings, civil war, terrorist threats – all these and more are sadly part of life in many countries these days. Add to this list weather 'events' such as hurricanes or typhoons and you'll see why my next chapter is called If It All Goes Wrong.

Websites to Help You Deal with Health Issues Abroad:

Travel health information for people travelling abroad from the UK: www.fitfortravel.nhs.uk

Lots more information for travellers, as well as health professionals, from the UK's National Travel Health Network and Centre: www.nathnac.org

You can find out more about the 112 emergency number and which countries use it at http://en.wikipedia.org/wiki/112_%28emergency_telephone_number%29

Echo 112 is an app that sends your location to local emergency services, world-wide: http://www.echo112.com/

Some great suggestions to help you deal with unwanted creepy-crawlies in your house, wherever you are in the world: http://www.partselect.com/JustForFun/Diy-Pest-Home-Hacks.aspx

Find healthcare providers near where you are, wherever you are: http://www.medihoo.com/

Health and nutrition advice from a former-expat, with an understanding of the particular stresses of global living: http://www.take-your-health-to-new-horizons.com/

UK Foreign Office advice on staying healthy abroad: https://www.gov.uk/knowbeforeyougo

A blog featuring women's experiences of having babies all around the world: http://www.mummyinprovence.com/global-differences-having-baby-abroad

CHAPTER SEVENTEEN

If It All Goes Wrong

No-one likes to think of disaster when they're preparing for their overseas move, but I urge you to take very seriously the possibility that something may go wrong. This is true wherever you are moving to – terrorism is sadly everywhere these days: even in the course of this book I have seen the terrorist threat expanding across the globe into places we might once have felt safe. And bad weather can also happen anywhere, although in some countries (the Caribbean, the Philippines etc.) a major storm or earthquake is more likely to happen to you at some point than not. So in this chapter I will describe from a personal viewpoint what it's like when the worst does happen; list some of the types of emergencies you might need to be ready for; go through ways you can prepare for these emergencies; and finally give some first-hand examples from people who have faced living through a disaster – and survived.

'Rhiannon came around to me and said: 'Should we get under the table now?'

The above very short extract is from the excellent blog written by Carole Hallet Mobbs, the owner of the Your Expat Child website about living through the devastating 2011 earthquake in Japan.

The blog chronicles in a compelling, first person style not just the first, terrifying few hours during and immediately after the main quake itself, but also the many, many aftershocks and then onto the weeks that followed: the confusion, the uncertainty, the questions about what they as a family should do, should they stay or should they do as so many others were and leave the country.

To find out more about what happened to Carole and her family, you can read the full fascinating (and well written) blog for yourself here - http://japanory.typepad.co.uk/japanory/2011/03/j apans-big-earthquake.html – but I was particularly moved by not just the description of the terror they as a family must have gone through, but the aftermath – the bit that people often don't think is going to affect them in the same way as the event itself but that is often in many ways the hardest part of the whole incident. This resonates so strongly with me because this is exactly what it was like for us following the Marriott bombing when we lived in Islamabad.

The bombing happened on a quiet night in for my husband Keith and myself. We were meant to be going to friends for dinner that evening, not far away, just on the other side of the British High Commission compound, where we lived with our two young daughters at the time. But illness had forced us to cancel, and so I remember clearly we were sitting in our living room watching one of our box sets of DVDs (probably Grey's Anatomy – we were half way through the first series and I know we never completed it), the girls asleep upstairs, when there was a whumph sound that I had never heard before. Keith understands these things better than me, having worked in law enforcement for most of his working life, and he immediately jumped up and said, 'That was a bomb, a large one.'

Now had we been living in almost any of the other places I've lived, either as a child or an adult, I would have thought he was losing his mind. Gunfire in Kingston, sure, but I've never lived anywhere before or since where it was perfectly possible that a bomb so large and so destructive could explode a few miles from where we sat, and we could hear the distinctive noise it made even whilst sitting indoors with the television on.

What must have been only a split second later, we heard screaming from the back of our house and ran out to find out what was going on. We eventually found out that one of Keith's colleagues had been in the Marriott picking up a takeaway from the Chinese restaurant within the hotel when the bomb went off. He had actually been on the phone to his wife when it happened – hers was the screaming we heard as the phone was blown out of his hand by the blast. She of course had no idea what had happened to him (luckily he was fine, he turned up later at the High Commission bar with a few cuts and bruises but otherwise unharmed; sadly this wasn't true of so many others in the hotel that night – fifty four people, many of them hotel workers, died and 266 were injured. Amongst those injured were some of our colleagues, including the single mother of two young children who had only just arrived in the country).

The rest of that night was a blur of radio contact between all staff and dependents, with our head of security establishing everyone's location and trying to decide whether it was safer for a group who were at a leaving party at one staff member's off-compound house to all stay there or to return to the safety of the diplomatic enclave. I managed to call home to let my family know I was safe and put a message on Facebook – it wasn't long before the press were reporting that two British children were among the injured and I wanted everyone to know we were all safe.

But whilst the immediate concerns were the safety and security of all staff (including local staff) and their families, we knew that our lives had changed forever.

We'd only been in Pakistan for a few weeks when the bomb went off. Our heavy baggage had very recently arrived and we'd just unpacked and managed to sort the children's rooms out. I'd ordered wall stickers for their rooms and we had finally had carpet laid in the living room to protect our youngest daughter from the cold marble floor as she started to toddle her way around the house. It had been a very, very hard start to our posting but I was beginning to feel settled. The weather was cooling, my eldest daughter had finally stopped crying every morning on the way to pre-school and we had all begun to make friends. I even had hopes of getting a part-time job and had recently discovered a new supermarket with a supply of frozen lamb!

But this bomb was just the latest in a series of increasingly violent episodes in that troubled country and knowing as we did that we were already on 'last warning' I knew in my heart that they would be sending families home.

Unfortunately, although we all felt it was inevitable that it would happen, it took the powers-that-be around two weeks to make the final announcement – all families had to leave, although spouses without children were allowed to stay. Two weeks of massive stress and uncertainty, two weeks of not knowing what was going to happen to us – where would we go if we had to return home? What would happen to my husband, would he be able to come with us?

In the end, we did all leave Islamabad (although Keith returned briefly to do a handover) and moved into a holiday let in England, while we waited for the tenants in our house to move out. I managed to get my eldest daughter into the local pre-school and eventually our lives returned to some degree of normality. But without a doubt, those few months – from arriving in Islamabad, living through those difficult early weeks with no baggage and no friends, the bomb, the period of uncertainty and then having to pack everything up and return to the UK to start all over again – were amongst the most stressful of my life. It changed us; it affected everything about us, our lives, our relationships, our outlook. It is something I hope I never have to go through again.

In response to questions about whether they had ever experienced any sort of emergency whilst living overseas, one of my respondents, Viktor, said he didn't believe it mattered whether you were living in another country or your home country – unexpected events could happen anywhere. Well, yes, of course they can: floods, bombs, water shortages, even tornadoes and droughts – these are all things that have happened right here in the UK within the last few years. They have all been scary, life threatening and stressful. But imagine how much worse these events are if you are a long way from your family, if you don't know the local system or if you are suddenly told sorry, you're going to have to leave the country – right away!

Be prepared for anything.

As you will know if you have already read this far, as well as the evacuation from Islamabad I have had a few other emergencies to deal with in my time living overseas. As a child, my father was medi-vacced home with a brain aneurism. Visiting my parents in Cameroon in the 1990s, we had to be escorted out of a town by the Red Cross after local unrest started to get out of hand. Living in Jamaica, we dealt with a whole string of violent hurricanes including the particularly deadly Ivan, which left us for days without water or electricity. And in St Lucia we were hit by yet another hurricane – Tomas, which stranded us in the States for days as we tried to find a flight to take us back to our flooded home.

Although all very stressful events, we came out of each one relatively unscathed. In some cases due simply to good luck but in others because we planned ahead. And I can't emphasise enough how important this is. You really don't know what is round the next corner.

Of course, the sort of event you might need to prepare for will differ according to where you are heading for. But here are a list of just some of the emergencies that could affect you:

- Local unrest.
- Civil war.
- Catastrophic weather events (hurricanes, typhoons etc.).
- Floods.
- Earthquakes.
- Terrorist-related activities (including threats).
- Major accidents, illness or even, sadly, death.
- An outbreak of a deadly disease (I actually don't know of this happening to anyone to the extent that they had to leave but it's always a possibility in this day and age).

I am sure there are others I could add to the list, but these are the ones that I know have happened either to me or to someone I know.

So how do you prepare for something like this?

Well, first of all have a think about which catastrophe or catastrophes, if any, are most likely to affect you and plan accordingly for that. If you live in, or are moving to, a hurricane zone, think about what you would need if a hurricane hit, or if your property was flooded. What about terrorist activity – will the safest option be to bunker down, or to move elsewhere very quickly? At what stage does it become safer to leave than to stay – how will you know? What is the security like at your property – will you move/be moved if your lives are endangered by civil unrest?

To help you think this through, here's another check list – this time of things you might want to consider doing in advance in the event of some sort of crisis:

- Keep a cupboard or box of emergency rations that would cover your whole family (including pets) for at least four days – tins, dry food that doesn't need cooking or that doesn't go off too quickly. Keep it topped up, check use-by dates etc. Also keep as many bottles of drinking water as you can – especially if it looks like something might happen, or for example during hurricane/typhoon season.
- Do you have a camp stove or some way of at least boiling water if you lose electricity?
- Other things worth considering include supplies of torches and spare batteries, water purification tablets and buckets to fill with water for washing in if it looks like the water supply might be cut. You might also want to keep a stock of wet-wipes and hand sanitiser.
- Who and how would you keep contact with each other (e.g. your partner at work, his colleagues etc.)? Are you going to be provided with radios (which might be the case in some countries)? If not and losing phone lines/mobile

signals is a real possibility, could you set this up with a colleague or friend?

- Try and remember to keep cars at least half filled with petrol at all times, or at times of particular risk (e.g. hurricane season). Lines will be long at petrol stations if there is the possibility of needing to evacuate.
- Do you and your children know the drill for what to do if there is an earthquake or another natural disaster?
- Do you know what the school procedures are in the event of an emergency? How will they let you know if they need you to pick the children up?
- Are you registered to get updates from your local consulate – which could be vital in a crisis? Have you read up on travel advice?
- Do you know where to get the latest weather advice? In some countries this is relatively easy – the Weather Channel in the US (and broadcast throughout the Caribbean area), for example, or the excellent US-based NOAA (National Oceanic and Atmospheric Administration) website, which tracks all weather 'events' in the region. But what about local papers, television channels, websites etc. – find out where local people get their advice from and follow suit.
- If you live within a hurricane zone do you know the evacuation route and where emergency shelters are located?
- Do you know where you would go if you had to leave the country? Whether back home or to a nearby country, assisted or not, this is always going to be difficult. Particularly so if your partner is a different nationality from you and you are evacuated to their home country – where you might know no one and have no support network.
- Do you have local friends or neighbours, anyone who you can trust, who can help out if needed? This is tough when you first move somewhere but even if it's a colleague from your partner's workplace, it's always useful to have

some local assistance when it comes to what to do or where to go in an emergency.

- Do you have access to cash if you need it? It might be difficult to get to a bank or ATM in a crisis situation – think about keeping some notes in an easy-to-reach safe, along with things like your passports and other important documents.
- Consider keeping a list of things that you need to take with you if you had to leave with very little notice – passports, money and bank cards, contact lenses, medicines, children's favourite toys or blankets, all the things that you can't buy if you forget them. Keep this list somewhere safe. Then when your mind goes blank when you're told you've got ten minutes to pack and get out, all you have to do is try and remember where you put that list.
- How would you let people at home know what's going on? As well as immediate family, other relatives and friends might be worried about you. If you don't use Facebook or other social media, or can't use it due to power issues, could you set up a cascade and make sure whomever you do manage to tell can get the message out?
- Make sure if possible that your friends and family have the real picture of what is going on: the media back home have a habit of over-sensationalising events overseas and only showing what they think will make a good story. They might see a picture of total devastation, whereas in reality only a small part of the country or city where you are living may be affected. What they won't be able to see however is how something like this can affect your lives: you might not be involved in the actual incident itself, but the 'aftershocks' such as the lack of coherent information, the uncertainty of knowing what is going to happen to you, the fear that something might happen again may have a much bigger impact than others will realise.

Most people find that in the immediate aftermath of an emergency situation, they run on adrenaline. This will keep them going for the first few hours or even days, however long the immediate incident lasts. But be prepared for reality to hit at some point – you will be exhausted, you may find yourself crying or getting very angry, you may also end up sliding into depression when everything is over and 'normal' life carries on.

Don't underestimate how stressful an emergency situation like this can be, especially if you are living overseas without your normal support networks. Recognise that it is a highly traumatic event and that you may need to seek help in its aftermath. Don't be afraid to admit it if you find that you're not coping. And give yourself and your family time and space to recover if you possibly can.

Some more stories...

Haylee

Haylee and her husband Dave were living in Islamabad at the same time as us when the Mariott bomb exploded. They were also evacuated, but unlike our family, they were separated while Dave had to return to work in Islamabad and Haylee took the children back to live in the UK.

'This was a very, very emotional time for us all. I remember breaking down in tears in the kitchen,' she recalled. 'We didn't want to go, to leave our happy bubble...the unknown was awful, of not knowing where our life was going to lead. It was a very sad way to leave our friends who were all in the same boat as us.'

Originally, Dave accompanied his family back to the UK, where Haylee moved into his parent's three-bedroom bungalow with her five-month-old baby, four and three year old. Dave then returned to Islamabad – they had no idea how long this set-up would be for but in the end it lasted for a further three months as they waited to hear whether Dave would be cross-posted to Abu Dhabi along with other staff from the British High Commission, or whether he would be posted elsewhere.

'I lived in the UK for three months by myself with the children but I wasn't too bad – I had my friends and family,' said Haylee, 'but Dave especially was put under immense pressure.

'He was now living in Islamabad with no family, missing watching his newborn daughter grow up. The post environment was miserable – lots of drinking going on to excess. He became very withdrawn, which is why we said enough was enough, come back to England and we'll see where our life goes. This is when Abu Dhabi were then able to offer Dave a posting and we then had three very happy years there.'

Ange

Angela and her husband Neil were in Jamaica at the same time as us.

'We endured two hurricanes. We took up residence in our basement along with some neighbours from the High Commission when Ivan passed close by,' Ange told me.

'The hurricane was never the worst part, the aftermath without clean running water and huge queues at supermarkets, was much worse. I remember diplomats at the high commission being very angry at the lack of support – but expecting the High Commission to provide bath plugs seemed trivial! We had radio contact and I felt a well organised plan. When people had lost homes, we were in a privileged position.

'If I had to go through it again, I would certainly think hard about planning a last minute trip home, if possible, but only for the lack of running water. I remember people did pull together in times of crisis, offering use of bathrooms when they had their water back on before ours (thanks Clara).'

Penny

Penny also lived through a series of hurricanes, although this time in the States: 'In Florida there were four hurricanes while we were there. And of course many, many fantastic thunderstorms.

'One afternoon I was watching Judge Judy (that's how bored I was!) when suddenly this voice came through the TV, barely intelligible. I thought it was a nuclear war announcement or something. Eventually I managed to make out "Brevard County, Brevard County, storm warning" and realised what was going on. Still a bit puzzling, as you can quite clearly see the storm clouds approaching, so why you need an announcement through the TV I don't know.

'We evacuated only once for a hurricane, although most people evacuated for three of them. The first one was just like a bad storm to me – in the UK we wouldn't have had much to talk about. A few branches brought down and that was pretty much it.

'But the Americans love a disaster. Every time a hurricane was coming the supermarkets would be emptied of food within a nano-second and there would be twenty four hour news coverage for days on end – for a bit of a windy day, really. The strongest one we did evacuate for, and we had to go nine hours' drive up to Georgia to find a hotel that would take the dog. We stayed on Jekyll Island for nine days as we didn't want to return until the electricity had been put back on.'

Sharon
'In Rwanda we had a volcanic eruption in the neighbouring state which caused earthquakes in Kigali. Along with a general feeling of Rwanda being a "fragile state" (due to a new government), the office had an emergency contingency plan in place that each member of staff knew about. Simple things like knowing where to meet up, an agreed route to the border and keeping a stash of dollars in the house in readiness for a quick evacuation gave a sense of security and safety knowing there was a plan in place.'

A final word on emergencies: don't try and be the hero. At least, not unless you actually ARE the best person to go out in the middle of the storm to try and fix the electric cable that's come loose and needs tying down for you to get your power back… There are too many stories of people getting electrocuted or standing too close to waves during hurricanes – these are the ones who are really in danger. If you are sensible, follow instructions, evacuate when you are advised to, don't worry too much about leaving your precious 24-piece dinner set behind and take up all offers of non-working partners and children first then you will be fine. You know those people in all the Vietnam war movies who were the last to leave in the helicopters from the top of the American Embassy? You really don't want to be one of them.

After reading this chapter, I hope you feel more ready for any kind of emergency you might encounter while living abroad – whether serious or relatively minor. Up until now, though, all my advice has been aimed at anyone, whatever kind of a partner they are. In the next chapter I look at the needs of two, smaller but almost certainly growing, sub-sections of the expat partner community: the male trailing spouse, and the same-sex partner.

Websites and Information to Help You Deal with Emergencies Abroad:

The UK Foreign Office's advice on dealing with a crisis overseas: https://www.gov.uk/how-to-deal-with-a-crisis-overseas

US Passports and International Travel website Getting Help in an Emergency: http://travel.state.gov/content/passports/english/emergencies.html

Australian government advice for dealing with an earthquake: http://www.smartraveller.gov.au/zw-cgi/view/TravelBulletins/Earthquakes

Emergency evacuation planning: http://www.expatexchange.com/article/2823/Security-Issues-Evacuation-Planning

More advice for coping with an emergency evacuation:
http://www.shelteroffshore.com/index.php/living/more/expats-
living-abroad-prepare-for-emergency-evacuation-10992

When You Don't Quite 'Fit In': The Male Trailing Spouse and the Same-Sex Partners

I wasn't sure what to name this chapter. I wanted to write about two sets of 'trailing spouses', which were slightly different from the 'norm' but at the same time I didn't want to single them out as being 'abnormal'.

I think it is important to acknowledge that whatever type of partner you are, whether you're male or female, gay or heterosexual, black, white, pink or yellow, most of the issues I have discussed so far in this book will affect you all. Everyone worries about being lonely, or not finding work, or their children not settling. But for these two groups, there may be some issues, which will be peculiar just to them and this is what I wanted to explore in this chapter.

Unfortunately, I don't really have space to do this subject justice: a little research has shown me just how much information there could be about both these groups and their particular needs. However I hope I can show that there is a place for all types of partnerships in the expat world and that, in this day and age, as we become more accepting of same-sex partnerships and as more women become the main breadwinners and their male partners the accompaniers, these two types of trailing spouses are going to become more and more common. I hope that, one day, they won't need a separate chapter.

The male trailing spouse

'I was in my early thirties and in a long-term relationship. Relocation for the wife's job was just a sabbatical from my own in London. But it was tough. I went from being in a two-career relationship and experienced the themes of the male trailing spouse crisis at first hand; no recognition that I had given up a career, lack of cultural support, inability to maintain social identity in a new environment, reduced self-esteem, alienation from my "friends" and "peers". Despite talk in Western Society about gender equality and househusbands, the majority of people are conventional. I was seen as the jobless partner. And tolerated a great deal of sexism from both men and women. I was used, abused, bemused but amused!' From the refreshingly honest blog by Alexander Reynolds (http://maletrailingspouse.blogspot.co.uk/), which chronicles his life as the spouse of a Department for International Development, and later UN, worker in Bangkok.

I'm not going to start this section by talking about how a man, finding himself as the accompanying partner, suddenly has to get used to his new identity. Prepare his answer for when he's asked 'what do you do?' Start making his excuses about how hard he works looking after the children, or how he's looking for work once his visa comes through … gets used to the glazed-over look and the over-the-shoulder peering as his interlocutor tried to find someone more interesting to talk to at the Ambassador's reception. Nope, you'll get no sympathy from me here. As female accompanying partners, this is what we have had to deal with for years. Get used to it, that's life.

However. I'm not going to be completely mean. Whilst I will not be sympathetic to men having to endure the same indignities as their female counterparts, I will, grudgingly, admit that they are likely to be disadvantaged in some ways. Like being ignored or even rejected by other non-working partners for being the wrong sex, or finding it harder to meet people and make friends.

Google the term Male Trailing Spouse and you'll get plenty of hits – from personal blogs (some of which I list below) to in-depth studies. It's a relatively new phenomenon, and it's hard to know exactly how many there are out there – but it's certainly one that seems to have caused some interest.

One study by Dr Nina Cole, Associate Professor of the Ted Rogers School of Management at Ryerson University - which you can read more about here http://www.iorworld.com/trailing-expat-spouse--a-man-s-perspective-pages-250.php – talks about how men socialise differently, how they network differently and how they find their friends in a different way from women. Whilst female partners tend to meet others more casually, at the school gates or through coffee meet-ups, men like to 'network around a common activity, especially something physical' – in other words, they often bond while playing sport.

So whilst most expat daytime social life is aimed pretty squarely at women, it is now becoming more commonly acknowledged that men require something a little different.

To meet this (albeit still fairly limited) demand, there are network groups aimed specifically at men being set up in many of the larger expat communities – for example the Spouses Travelling Under Duress (STUD's) group which started in Brussels, and Secret Men's Business set up by a group of Australians and New Zealander's in Singapore.

Warren, who accompanied his wife to a posting in Dhaka, Bangladesh, was told by his CLO (Community Liaison Officer) about a group of men who got together to play golf on Tuesday afternoons. Known as the 'Dhaka Hackers', the 'golf was secondary to the real purpose of the afternoon, socialised drinking'.

Warren also found friends – both male and female – through other routes, including through expat clubs, but found that while he was the accompanying spouse he actually spoke to the women more as found he had more in common with them. He was also invited to monthly coffee mornings and all in all seems to have been widely accepted as one of the accompanying partners, despite being a man.

Even though men might find it harder to meet friends via their children than women (who are more likely to be used to doing this if they were stay-at-home mums already; this might of course be less natural for women coming straight from a full-time job into the accompanying partner role), this is still always going to be an option.

James, who moved to Switzerland with this wife and two children, said it took him a year to find any other dads like him – and had to really push himself to make friends. This included joining a local ladies 'Anglophone' group, where he was the only man in a group of sixteen women, and starting his own weekly playgroup with some of the mothers. But he must have been pretty happy when a fellow male trailing spouse turned up about a year after he arrived.

'We meet regularly and share experiences,' he said. 'But generally I have always been accepted by other trailing spouses/mothers etc. I have never really experienced any form of rejection or criticism.'

However, not every male accompanying spouse wants to make 'mum' friends or join in the 'expat lifestyle' – and of course, that's fine, too. Chris, who moved to California with his wife and baby, said that although he enjoyed spending time with his daughter and did meet some people through baby groups, he had 'no interest in meeting people or making friends and so was quite happy'. And why not?

Same sex partners

While it may be slightly harder for male trailing spouses to settle into an expat life than their female counterparts, the problems faced by same sex partners could be on a different scale altogether. Of course, if you are accompanying your partner on a posting to a liberal country with no more prejudice towards you than you might expect in your own country, then you could find things all relatively straightforward. Other than all the usual issues that any trailing spouse faces (including, for men, those of being a male accompanying partner), your sexuality may not pose any particular challenges. However, if you are travelling to a country where you're not likely to be so accepted, even where your life might be in danger if you are overtly 'out', then things might be very different for you.

It's only fairly recently that the issue of same-sex accompanying partners has started to be talked about, and their needs acknowledged by employers. It's not that long ago that being gay was a 'bar' to a career as a diplomat in the British Foreign Office – it was thought to be too much of a security risk. Of course, it was more of a risk that they were secretly gay and therefore open to blackmail, but it wasn't until the early 1990s and under John Major's government that this sensible argument won the battle and anyone who was gay, lesbian, bisexual or transgender now has the same rights as all other staff.

There have since been postings at high levels of gay officers both in the UK and in other countries – Barack Obama, in particular, seems to be making a point of posting gay ambassadors to countries which recognise same-sex marriage; although his appointment of gay ambassador James Brewster to less-liberal (and Catholic dominated) Dominican Republic caused outrage in that country (you can read more about that outrage here: http://www.theguardian.com/world/2013/nov/29/dominican-republic-gay-us-ambassador).

What's interesting to me, though, about the Brewster storm, isn't just that the American president appointed a gay ambassador to a Catholic country, but that the ambassador took his husband with him. Whilst the ambassador will have the security of knowing he's going to work in a little bit of America every day, with all the backing they have publicly afforded him, his partner is in a very different situation. Everyone will know who he is, and everyone will know that he's gay. But he'll be trying to make a life for himself, trying to do a job or take part in sports or make friends within the local community. And all of it he'll have to face on his own.

Of course I don't know anything about James Brewster's husband, apart from he's called Bob and he featured in a little video that Brewster made and put on his Embassy's website when he first arrived. For all I know, Bob might live in the US and commute out at weekends, or he might be happy slobbing all day on the sofa at home, eating cookies and keeping himself to himself.

But let's face it, gay or not gay, this isn't the life most accompanying partners want for themselves. Most of us want to get out there, meet people, maybe get a job, do things with the kids if we have any. Have a life. And not have our sexuality be an issue in any of these things.

A good starting point if you are in this situation and want to find out more about what your life will be like is the FCO travel advice. If nothing else, this can give you a hint as to how welcome you will be made to feel in your host country. Under the section 'local laws and customs', you can find out whether there is likely to be an issue around homosexuality. If there isn't, there won't be anything in this section about it. But if there is likely to be any problem at all, this is where you should find some information.

Each country is slightly different and, I suspect (without going through each and every one of them) some of them will be open to interpretation whilst some of the advice will be clearer.

Jamaica, for example, states fairly unequivocally: '*Jamaican laws make certain homosexual acts illegal. The attitude of many Jamaicans to gay, lesbian, bisexual, transgender and intersex people is hostile.*'

And for Saudi Arabia: '*Homosexual acts and adultery are illegal and can be subject to severe sanctions.*'

In most, if not all, Muslim countries homosexuality is illegal – although I assume that some countries will be more tolerant than others. However, the advice for India, as an example, is slightly more ambiguous: '*On 11 December 2013, the Indian Supreme Court set aside a 2009 ruling of the Delhi High Court that decriminalised homosexuality. Although prosecutions of gay people are rare, conviction for engaging in a homosexual act could lead to a prison sentence.*'

And for Sri Lanka: *'Same-sex relations are illegal but the FCO is not aware of any prosecutions.'*

As well as individual country advice, the FCO also has a page on general advice for the LGBT community travelling abroad – https://www.gov.uk/lesbian-gay-bisexual-and-transgender-foreign-travel-advice – which includes general tips for travelling overseas if you are gay. The US State Department's travel advice has a similar page: http://travel.state.gov/content/passports/english/go/lgbt.html, as does Australia's Department of Foreign Affairs and Trade: http://www.smartraveller.gov.au/tips/lgbti.html.

Another useful website is the International Lesbian, Gay, Bisexual, Trans and Intersex Association (ILGA), which has a map that clearly shows the laws on different issues that may affect gay couples – including where there are laws that prohibit discrimination on grounds of sexual orientation, where it's illegal to be gay and where not only is it illegal, but it is punishable by death. You can also click on each individual country to find more information. The website can be found at: http://ilga.org/ilga/en/index.html.

Of course, as well as how welcome you will be made to feel, whether you will be safe etc., there are many other questions a gay or lesbian couple might have about taking an overseas posting. Will your same-sex marriage be recognised? Will the partner be able to get a visa, or a work permit? These are all questions you will probably want to find out before you commit to a posting. Some employer's (including the UK's Foreign Office) will be able to provide you with this sort of information, but for others the best advice is to find out directly from your country's embassy or consulate in the country to which you are moving.

You may also find some re-location businesses that have specific knowledge or expertise to help LGBT couples or families to relocate. One company that I found, just through a quick Google search, is Relonavigator (http://relonavigator.wordpress.com/tag/trailing-spouse/), which features a story of how it helped a lesbian couple relocate from the Netherlands to the US – including immigration and employment issues.

So what is it actually like to move overseas as part of a same-sex couple? Brooke has been a family member with the US Foreign Service in both a heterosexual marriage and in a same-sex relationship. She and her children from her first marriage have accompanied her partner to various postings to Europe and southeast Asia. Her main considerations when bidding for a new job were accreditation/visa issues, whether or not a country recognised same-sex partners and their children, safety and tolerance of the host country and ease for a woman to travel alone. And then when they arrived in the country of posting, the main change in the way they lived their lives was to 'be more aware of cultural sensitivities. We never threw it all out there. No PDA (public displays of affection).'

Brooke said she felt the support of her partner's employers was 'mixed', with some wanting to use her as a 'flag waving best practice test case', especially as they had children. Others ignored her as a partner. She herself preferred to keep her head down, for the sake of her children, and had this advice for others in a similar situation: 'Do your homework and conduct a thorough host country research. Take heed of countries that do not recognize same-sex orientation. Be prepared to keep a low profile and perhaps be considered "relatives" or "friends". Don't go to places that would bring you in on a "domestic staff" visa. It shows a general lack of underlying tolerance. Don't make assumptions – fully research not only about living there, but also our own employment options.'

Another respondent, who wished to remain anonymous, found that although in the country they moved to they were able to live openly as a gay couple, they were not made to feel welcome. 'There is a lot of negativity from the locals, they do not invite us to their houses, etc.,' she said. 'Also, I can tell there is a lot of surprise in their faces when learning about my sexual orientation and the fact that I am sharing that.' She said her employers had tried to be helpful but were up against a difficult situation as the country they had moved to didn't recognise same-sex marriage. 'By the end I felt it was a hands off attitude,' she added. 'We cannot have a joint bank account, we cannot have rights as a couple in this country, so the visa and everything else is a mess. So it is like we are two single people and one has a child. Very uncomfortable.'

Hopefully the day will come sooner rather than later where same-sex partners can feel comfortable moving anywhere in the world (although I fear it will be a lot later with many places – including parts of Africa, the Middle East and huge chunks of the United States). But until that time comes, my best advice is re-search, research, research – and don't be afraid to say no if you don't think your life would be a happy one if you did go to a par-ticular country.

I've now covered pretty well as much as I possibly can about mov-ing and living overseas, about making a new life for yourself and your family, settling in, making friends, finding work, dealing with emergencies. Now all there is left to do is look at what happens when it's time to move on – either to another country or back home. In the next chapter I look at that often-overlooked issue of repatriation, and how hard some people, now they've come this far, find it to go back to where they started.

Websites and Articles for Male Trailing Spouses and Same-Sex Couples

An article about male trailing spouses:
http://iwasanexpatwife.com/2012/11/12/sometimes-its-the-guy-who-trails/

Male trailing spouses – an 'inconvenient truth':
http://expatriateconnection.com/male-trailing-spouses-an-inconvenient-truth/

Challenges facing the expat male trailing spouse:
http://www.iorworld.com/trailing-expat-spouse--a-man-s-perspective-pages-250.php

Understanding a new phenomenon – the male trailing spouse:
http://www.expatica.co.uk/hr/hr-careers/Understanding-a-new-phenomenon-The-male-trailing-spouse_20270.html

Pension advice for expat same-sex couples:
http://www.worldofexpats.com/blogs/same-sex-marriage-expat-community-what-about-your-pension

Relationship advice for gay couples moving overseas:
http://www.huffingtonpost.co.uk/richard-adams/gay-couples-rights-overseas_b_2449401.html

An article about the days before it was okay to 'come out' in the British Foreign Office:
http://www.independent.co.uk/news/uk/this-britain/the-love-that-dared-not-speak-its-name-in-the-foreign-office-1931127.html

The world's worst places to be gay:
http://www.takepart.com/article/2014/11/06/worlds-worst-places-be-gay?cmpid=tp-ptnr-upworthy

UK Foreign Office advice for LGBT travelers:
https://www.gov.uk/lesbian-gay-bisexual-and-transgender-foreign-travel-advice

Article about global mobility and the gay worker:
http://www.brookfieldgrs.com/knowledge/sa_global-mobility-for-lesbian-and-gay-assignees/

CHAPTER NINETEEN

Moving On, Coming Home

Repatriation – moving back home – is one of those subjects that most people don't even think about when they're preparing to move overseas for the first time. But, often all-too-quickly, the time to move on comes around and in this chapter I consider how it feels to move back home for both adults and for children; just exactly what is 'reverse' culture shock; what the long-term effect of living overseas for a period of time can mean for you; and ways to help you cope with re-integrating back into your home life.

'Moving back home was profoundly disorienting in a way I wasn't expecting. I thought I'd be able to slip back into the life I'd left behind, but I didn't take into account how much I'd changed in the five years I'd been away. It was extremely hard to settle back in. I'd say it was two years before I felt comfortable in my own skin again.' Maria, Singapore and Bordeaux.

For many people the hardest thing about being an expat isn't the moving abroad – it's the moving back home again. It's something that few are prepared for, and it's something that can actually have a more lasting impact on your life than the original move.

As a child, I remember coming home after four years in the Philippines. For me, time had frozen back in our small village in north Kent. My best friends would still be my best friends. I would slot straight back into the life we'd left behind.

However, life for everyone else obviously had moved on. My best friend had a new best friend. We were all four years older, and four years is a long time when you're only eight. Why should everything wait for you? It was a hard lesson for me to learn and, when we went away on another posting a few years later (this time to Nigeria) and the same thing happened again, I think a little bit of my trust in other people died forever.

Repatriation and the feelings it brings are quite hard to categorise, as it will be so different for everyone dependent on how long you've been away, where you have been living, whether you wanted to come home or it's been forced upon you, whether you're moving back to a place you know well, near to friends and family, or somewhere completely new, what's waiting for you when you get there in terms of work and schools.

A good way to look at it is to think of all the things you went through when you first moved overseas and then understand that you will probably go through them all again, albeit often (but not always) on a lesser scale. You may have to make a decision to leave (and then tell people); you will have all the practicalities of a major move; you will have to ensure the children have a school place and you'll have to make sure you are registered back with the local doctor etc. You will also, almost certainly, get culture shock in one way or another – which can be quite unexpected for some people. Who knew you could be thrown by your own culture in the same way that you could by alien cultures?

To deal with this, some treat coming home just as if it was in fact another overseas move. Certainly this is what helped Nicola when she moved back to the UK from the Netherlands: 'I don't think I felt reverse culture shock as I stayed in the not knowing, and treated my new home as a new location overseas. I'd been away ten years and this was a whole new location to me (I'd never lived here before).'

Magda, who moved back to her home country of South Africa after living in the UAE, Penang, Hanoi, Bangkok and Mumbai, said she probably would have found it easier to have moved back somewhere completely new. To try and help her transition, she went exploring to a nearby city at the weekends. As expats, we're so used to being surrounded by the unfamiliar, we sometimes find the familiar hard to cope with.

I think I have been lucky coming back to live in the UK as an adult. We own a house in a town in the west of the UK and have a good group of friends around us, as well as family not too far away. I have always felt I have slotted back in reasonably easily to my previous life, possibly because we weren't away in Islamabad for very long and my oldest daughter started school immediately after we came back from St Lucia and I made friends through that. The children were also young enough when we left that they didn't really have any memories of their time in the UK or close friends to re-connect with.

It also helped that we wanted to come home from St Lucia, and initiated the move ourselves. But for others, making the decision isn't so easy.

Adele, returning to the UK from Qatar, recalled what a difficult time this was for her family: 'I got quite depressed and tearful. I was very scared to go home alone (her husband had to stay behind in Qatar for work reasons, although he tried to come back to the UK as often as possible to see them), and also to go back to work, after a year out. I ended up taking anti-depressants to try and help the anxiety. We stayed until the end of the school year. I got quite a lot of hostility from some that I was leaving, like it wasn't good enough for me, which it wasn't! I think some people were jealous, some thought we were splitting up as a couple. I had one lady who was quite nasty saying how could I take the kids away from their daddy.'

In a way this just mirrors the reaction many get when they first decide to leave their home country to move abroad. Making a life-changing decision like this is always a brave thing to do, and brave decisions often attract hostility in those who are too scared to make a similar decision for themselves.

Haylee, leaving a very happy life in Abu Dhabi (where they ended up after being evacuated from Islamabad at the same time as us) said they were very sad to leave: 'We had an amazing three years there, life was easy – no DIY or gardening, a healthy salary – it was like we were on holiday for three years. The children had a great education, surrounded by many friends. Given the chance I would have loved to have stayed for a few more years.'

But it wasn't just sadness at leaving that was hard for her – it was getting the children settled into school: 'Benjamin went to school on his first day in the UK with a smile on his face, then came out beaming – he settled in brilliantly. We got offered a nursery place for Emily. Forward planning on my part – knowing that we were coming back to the UK. But I was more concerned for Sophie, who was seven years old. Although she had been to (the local) Infant school with some of the children for three months when she was four, she didn't really remember them and girls being girls form close bonds. Sophie did have a couple of weeks when she wasn't sure about going to school – I did feel for her.' Luckily two terms on and Sophie was completely settled. The family are now on a new posting, in China.

Adele had similar schooling worries returning to the UK from Qatar with her three children, including a set of twins. 'Back in UK, our elder child wasn't able to get into the local (state) schools, so he goes to the local private school,' she said. 'He still, one year on, can't get a place.' He is, however, happy at his school and with her husband's company paying the fees, she feels that as the schooling issue was the main reason they moved back it was the right decision.

As well as the 'big' issues of things like schooling and settling the children back in, some people find it difficult simply coping with the way of life once they are home: 'I think for me it was the general feeling of being overwhelmed – by the speed and busyness of life, the decisions which needed making (from the massive things like what next? to the buying a new toilet seat),' said Helen, who moved from Kyrgyzstan back to Oxford in the UK.

Jackie, who also lived in Kyrgyzstan but whose home country was New Zealand, agreed: 'Sometimes it was overwhelming just going to the supermarket or the bank,' she recalled.

Judy, who lived in Azerbaijan, believed this does very much depend on where you have come from: 'When we repatriated from Azerbaijan, I too found the "stuff" overwhelming, sickening even. I remember having to leave the supermarket only half way through my weekly shop because I just couldn't handle it. But coming back from Dubai was easier in that respect, in fact it was a relief to get away from all the consumer excess!'

Hopefully most of the time the decision to leave a post, move on or home, will be a relatively happy one. Many of us, of course, have no say in this decision – the contract or the posting comes to an end and it's time to either go home or find another job. In this case though, even if the accompanying partner is ready to go, it's once again the lack of control over the decision – a decision which will have an impact on the life of the partner and any children as well as that of the worker – that is so difficult to deal with.

It was getting control of her life back that made coming home for Sue (who had lived in Madrid and Washington with her husband and two sons) such a positive experience: 'It was lovely to have my life back and to be back in control of my home and my own and my children's health care. Whilst there are many positive experiences about being abroad, not feeling in control of these issues is very hard. We had missed the family and friends so it was nice to be back with them, and I was very pleased to have my old job back, too.'

Another up-side of coming home for many is finally realising how special that home is. Just like the story of the bluebird, or Dorothy in Kansas, it's only by going away from it that sometimes you understand how much you love the place where you come from. This was certainly true for Adele: 'We had looked at expat life in New Zealand. But this experience has made us very much home birds – we want to be in England, where there is a police force, proper laws and accountability. Freedom of speech, all the things you take for granted, until you don't have it!'

Whilst the initial period after you return home can be the most intense, as you find a house, a school, see friends and family, rediscover your country, enjoy the supermarkets or the countryside or the weather or whatever it is that you've been missing while you've been away, it's often later that things can get tough.

Speaking to fellow ex-expats (also known as re-pats), I have realised that the effect of having lived abroad and then returned to your home country can be far more long-lasting than some may realise. Initially you might fit back in with your friends, enjoy catching up with them, get caught up in the school-gate gossip. But after a while you might feel there's always a bit of you that's going to be different from everyone else, that none of your 'home' friends are ever going to really 'get' you. They may be interested in hearing about your travels and your overseas adventures for a while, but eventually you'll realise that you've had your time and from now on they don't want to hear about your 'other' life. Which can be very difficult, and quite isolating.

'I found it very difficult to recalibrate friendships when I returned home,' said Maria, returning from France. 'Some had drifted, and I didn't know how (or even if I wanted to) rebuild them. But there was definitely a sense of "now your great adventure is over, so let's not talk about it anymore" that was hard to swallow. I felt that I was expected to flip a switch and return to the life I had and the person I was five years earlier. That caused a bit of resentment on my part.'

Naomi, who lived in India and Singapore, said she felt she almost had to change her personality in order to 'fit in' when she returned home: 'For me, the hardest thing was no longer having a group of people who "got me",' she said. 'The women I was meeting were gossiping about their neighbours and talking about back to school events. I found myself desperately wishing for someone that understood me. I even (I am surprised at myself with this one) stopped wearing my "funky" and unique clothes that I acquired when overseas because of the comments I would get.'

Danielle, moving back to America, agrees: 'It was hard coming back to the US because the people I was meeting had no idea what my family and I had just been through,' she said. 'I felt like I had to limit my "When we lived in Australia" stories to avoid boring them.'

For Magda, she actually found some of the people she'd left behind were openly hostile to her on her return: 'Our best friends and even family became our worst enemies – they saw us as the very same people they knew from decades past and simply were unable to realise that even though the physical voice and laughter remained the same, the mental voice and laughter was now something completely different. These are people who instead of embracing our changes, fought against it every single time we connected and it really became a massive challenge having a normal conversation without it ending up in arguments. All I wanted was for people to acknowledge that repatriation for us was not easy and all they wanted to do was to reinforce why our passport country is the best place in the whole world.'

So what can you do in these circumstances?

For some, it's about finding ways to occupy yourself, a new challenge to help you transition. Just like when you first moved abroad, you will almost certainly have been so caught up in the move – at an estimate, six months either side – that it's only when the dust has settled a bit that you start to think what on Earth you're going to do with the rest of your life. Some people are lucky and can get back into whatever they were doing before they left, or they may have children to care for or other caring responsibilities (e.g. elderly parents, which may have been the reason you returned home). But for others it may be a case of finding something completely new.

When I returned from St Lucia, I was at a bit of a loss. Although my youngest daughter was still at home with me, I knew it wouldn't be long before she would also be off to school and she was already going to a pre-school three mornings a week. I hadn't had so much time to myself since I gave up work after having my first daughter and I knew running the house wasn't going to be enough for me. I had been thinking about this for months before we returned home and still wasn't sure what I was going to do with myself. But, as it usually does, some voluntary work led to an idea, which led to a query and before I knew it I was training part-time to be an antenatal teacher. And not long after that, I started writing this book.

Seeking out others who have lived overseas or at least travelled is another solution. Just being able to understand where someone is coming from when they talk about the difficulties of finding decent bread or yoghurt in the local shops, how to settle children into a school where everyone else speaks a different language or what to do in the summer holidays when you need to spend eight weeks away from your house because it's fifty degrees in the shade and every other family has gone away, can really help you feel less alone.

For Magda though, it wasn't the expat equivalent of small talk that she missed, but the global outlook on life that she just didn't find back home: 'Conversations with expat friends are much easier and revolve around all sorts of interesting global issues. Conversations are not just based on opinions, but real experiences and critical understanding of dilemmas within, for example international politics and the economy. I find that back home, people hardly had any insight into global matters and conversations were about local issues, viewpoints were often one sided with sweeping statements and ethnocentric behaviour leaving me feeling frustrated. One might feel excluded when discussions are about the daily grind, it feels like constant small talk.'

Unfortunately not everyone has the opportunity to seek out fellow re-pats. If you're moving back to a city or a large town you may find others who have lived abroad, some of whom might even want to be your friend.

But what if your hometown is a small country village in the middle of nowhere? Or if the only people you interact with are your basic, bog-standard haven't-ever-travelled types? Luckily, in this day and age, there is another way and it's called modern technology.

Thanks to the Internet, you don't have to lose touch with the friends you made abroad. Just like your kids, you can continue to interact with them through Skype, Facebook, emails, FaceTime, iMessage – whichever method you both prefer. And not only that, but in this globalised age there are plenty of websites, forums and other social media groups out there filled with people just like you.

And if all else fails, you can always start planning for that next overseas move…

Websites and Information to Help You with Repatriation:

Defining repatriation – an interesting blog article: http://iwasanexpatwife.com/

Coach, who specialises in repatriation issues: http://www.wattsyourpathway.co.uk/about.html

A whole page of articles about repatriating on the Expat Exchange website: http://www.expatexchange.com/returning.cfm

Interesting article about repatriation which explains why the writer thinks she is a triangle: http://naomihattaway.com/2013/09/i-am-a-triangle-and-other-thoughts-on-repatriation/

And the Facebook page she set up following her repatriation experience: https://www.facebook.com/groups/IAmATriangle/

CHAPTER TWENTY

Okay, So What Have We Learned?

So that's it, you're ready to go. Or, if you've read this far, perhaps you're already there – maybe even preparing to come home again. I hope you've learned as much from reading this book as I have from writing it; certainly one thing I now realise is that however much we travel, however many times we move, we're never experts because everyone's experiences are unique. I have been struck in particular by how different people cope with whatever it is that expat life throws at them – and how whilst some people always seem to remain positive, others find the accompanying partner life a lot harder. Whichever it is for you, it's fine: I have always believed we shouldn't feel guilty if we don't love our overseas lives, but I do hope that by reading this book you can at least survive it!

In this final chapter I want to go over again some of the most important points in this book, remind you of those things I be-lieve you should particularly bear in mind when you are preparing your overseas move (or even if you are preparing your move back home again); and guide you to where to find further resources from me, should you need it, and can feed back your thoughts on the book.

But before I do I just want to talk briefly about something that has come out of the experience of writing this book for me, and that is the importance of technology and the online community.

When I moved overseas the first time as an expat partner, back in 2008, Facebook was in its infancy. We posted messages and photos and people could reply. But there weren't groups or pages in the same way that there are today. Instead, I found online forums of like-minded people to be the best way to find support – Mumsnet in particular got me through the early years of parenting.

Then by the time I left St Lucia, and certainly since I have been back in the UK, the Internet has exploded. The way we interact with people has changed immensely – I would say I have as many online conversations in a day as I do 'real' face-to-face ones. I belong to Facebook groups, I blog, I use Twitter. All day long I can keep up with people all over the world, and I have re-connected with dozens of people from my childhood, teenage years, even those early days of living overseas when it wasn't so easy to keep up with each other after we parted.

I have been working at home for the last year or so and on some days I go six hours straight without seeing another fellow human being, unless they're passing my kitchen window or delivering something to my door. But this doesn't mean I feel lonely because I am constantly communicating with my online friends, a combination of people I have met in real life and people I have only ever known on the 'screen'.

And the beauty of all this? It doesn't change when you move abroad! You can take all your friends with you.

So, yes you will be saying goodbye to a lot of people who are very near and dear to you. It will be hard not to see them in person for months, possibly even years, at a time. But this doesn't mean you won't be constantly in contact with them. As a child at boarding school, I was lucky to speak to my parents more than once every few weeks on the phone. Nowadays, I would be able to text or email or message them every day. Or speak on Skype or Face-Time. Technology really has changed things for the better for expats and I am so glad that when we move, this time my children will be able to keep in touch with their friends and their grandparents as often as they like.

Not only this, but there are now more and more communities for expats like you. Facebook groups, blogging communities, forums. Lots and lots of people going through exactly what you are. So when you can't get your friends back home to understand why you're feeling a bit low despite the fact that it's 30 degrees outside and you've got a swimming pool in your back garden (or you live in Manhattan; or a glass of wine costs less than a cup of tea…), you know there will always be someone, somewhere you can contact who will give you sympathy. Because they will be going through exactly what you are. Or they will have been through it at some point.

And now, to wrap up, here are the most important points from the book to help remind you what you have learned. They may not be what you think are the top points, but this is my list:

1. Give yourself plenty of time to prepare. Don't be afraid of starting earlier rather than later, and also don't be afraid of writing lists. A lot of them.

2. Develop a thick skin when you tell people about your plans. Ignore any negativity. Block on Facebook if necessary. Or change the settings for the particularly negative people so that they only ever see pictures of you with a cocktail at sunset. Even if you're moving to Greenland.

3. Pick your moment to tell your children (if you have any), dependent on their ages and personality. And make sure you get it the right way round: don't tell your toddler you're moving to the other side of the world 12 months before you actually go (and if you do, prepare for a year's worth of where's Greenland mummy/daddy questions). And don't tell your sensitive teen they've got to say goodbye to their best friends the night before you leave…

4. Don't forget to separate out what you need to keep with you and what you want to send ahead when the packers come. And please don't let them pack the bin still full of rubbish.

5. Consider sending your partner ahead. He/she can get settled in to their new job, as well as sort out those all-important issues for your first few weeks like transport, a phone and internet access, before you arrive.

6. Remember, you might be on a high for the first few days or weeks after you arrive in your new home. At this stage, everything is wonderful and your messages home will probably convey this feeling loud and clear. Many people will therefore think you are fine and stop worrying about you. This is the honeymoon period – it's just the start. It will almost certainly get worse before it gets better...

7. But it WILL get better. This will be different for everyone and sadly, for some, it may not get better enough. Or at least quickly enough. However, for almost all of you, life will improve – probably within 3 to 6 months of arrival. When you're having a bad day, just keep repeating this mantra: It will get better. It will get better.

8. You will also make friends. Again, it's very difficult to generalise as everyone is different when it comes to friendship – some people like a wide, social group who they can see regularly. For these people, I would suggest getting out as much as possible, accepting every invitation. Others prefer a smaller, more select group of friends and I would say these people will very possibly take a little longer to make those bonds. But all of you will eventually meet someone or some people that you click with – and often in the most unexpected places.

9. Try and get your house right from the start. This is a tricky one as many of you won't have much choice – but if you do, choose wisely. You are probably going to be in that home a lot, possibly on your own. You want to be happy there. And try and get the location right, too – school runs in heavy traffic are not the best way to start any day.

10. Safety should be a priority right from day one. Apart from in countries where you feel particularly secure (and it's getting harder to know which these countries are nowadays), don't go out on your own until you know your way around a bit. This is especially so at night. Take up any offers of security briefing you might be offered through your partner's work.

11. Find a way of getting around independently as soon as possible – preferably from the day you arrive. There is nothing worse than being stuck at home alone (or with moaning children) because it's too dangerous to walk anywhere, there's no suitable public transport and you only have one family car – which your partner needs for work. Even if it's just a number for a reputable taxi company, find some way of getting out.

12. Accept that you won't be able to eat in exactly the same way as you are used to at home. If you are lucky, all you will have to do is swap a few of your usual ingredients for the local equivalent. If you're unlucky, your entire diet might have to change. But embrace the newness – one of the most fun things about living in another country is discovering the local cuisine.

13. Treat your domestic staff as you would wish to be treated were you doing their job. Or in fact, as you would like to be treated whatever job you were doing. Just treat them with respect. There is definitely a bad karma thing with domestic staff…

14. Find something to do that's just for you, particularly if you are not working. This is good advice whether you're an expat or not – but there is definitely something about expat life that has the potential for your to lose sight of yourself a bit. If you can do something that makes you happy and makes you feel like you are more in control of your own destiny, then do it. Blogging, writing, studying,

gardening, photography, art, cooking. Or it doesn't have to be creative – you could volunteer with a local charity or help out at your children's school. If you have the time (and for the first time in your adult life, you might actually have more time than you can fill) then use it as a fantastic opportunity to do something new.

15. Listen to your children. Don't dismiss their fears, talk to them. Tell them it's okay to feel a bit afraid, and in fact you are also nervous about the move. But try and end these conversations on the positive. You want them to think you want to move – even if inside it's the last thing you want to do.

16. If your children are older, in particular teenagers, look out for any specific issues they might be having with the move. Leaving their friends behind is a difficult thing to do at this age and they might be feeling very insecure. If necessary, get counselling – for them and for you.

17. If you think you are going to want to work, then start looking into this AS SOON AS POSSIBLE. Don't leave it to chance that you'll be able to breeze into a job the day after you arrive. You may need to get a working visa or permit and this can take months. You might also want to think about learning a new trade, or even a new language, before you go.

18. Don't overlook voluntary work as a way to gain experience, meet people and get involved in your local community.

19. A health emergency can happen to anyone, at any time. Be prepared from the day you arrive. It's no good waiting until you've been there for a week before working out the best way to get to the local hospital.

20. Don't expect the same level of health care in your host country as you do back home. In some cases, of course, it will be 'better' – but in almost every case it will be

different. The systems will probably also be different so make sure you have an idea of what to expect. Will you need to pay in advance for treatment, for example? Do you need to prove you have health insurance?

21. Just the same as health emergencies, other emergencies can happen anywhere, to anyone. Terrorism is sadly on the rise everywhere in the world and expats are becoming increasingly common targets. Weather events are also something to be prepared for. Speak to the local community, watch the local news, keep abreast of developments.

22. If you are part of a same-sex couple, make sure you do your research about what life will be like for you – unless you are going to a very gay-friendly part of the world. But don't forget, in some countries tolerance levels change the further you get from the larger, urban areas.

23. Repatriation can be as hard as the initial move – and this can come as a complete shock to many people. Be aware that there will, again, be a honeymoon stage but that you may not feel completely settled back in for a year or two – or even longer.

And finally – if you only remember three things what should they be? This is hard as there are so many important messages I want you to take away. But having thought about it long and hard, these would be my top three:

- **It will almost certainly be hard at the start but it will also almost certainly get easier.**
- **Don't worry if you don't make a bunch of friends immediately; this will come.**
- **If you have children, don't move at the start of the summer holidays.**

I hope you have enjoyed reading the Expat Partner's Survival Guide. I would love to hear your views – in particular if you think I've missed anything out or got something completely wrong. Hopefully by now you will have received the message loud and clear that my experiences will not be your experiences, and things I loved you might hate, or things I found hard might be a breeze for you. Nevertheless, please do tell me if you think there is something so way off mark in the book that it needs changing. And of course, times move on – there will be ways to improve our lives in the future that I don't even know about yet so do let me have any of your ideas, tips and thoughts on how others in your situation can makes things easier for themselves in the future.

You can do this by emailing me clara@expatpartnersurvival.com, or via my website http://expatpartnersurvival.com/ or Facebook page https://www.facebook.com/home.php .I am also to be found on twitter at @strandedatsea.

So finally all it remains for me to say is good luck, have a ball, you'll be fine! And don't pack your passport in your sea freight...or forget to get your mail forwarded...or....

Meet Some of My Contributors

Adele – *Adele moved to Qatar with her husband and three children in 2010. She and her children are now back in the UK, whilst her husband commutes between the two countries for work.* 'Expat living can be exciting and scary. I would try to go into it with your eyes open, make sure it works well for ALL the family. Make sure school provision is acceptable, and think about what your children will do when not at school. Swimming, soft play and park, might not seem so exciting after 3 months. What about after school care if you intend to work? Do employers accept the sort of work schedule which you can manage? Where I was based, work was full time, or no time. Consider medical care – are you insured, and what really is the quality of the practitioners? Do you need an exit permit to get out, even in an emergency? The most important thing to pack, is a sense of humour – it's the one thing you will REALLY need!'

Angela K – *Angela was in Jamaica from 2002 – 2005 with her husband Neil and daughter Molly.* 'My favourite part of being abroad was experiencing a different culture, meeting people from different backgrounds and travelling. I made a lot of friends away from the (British) High Commission through my daughter and families on the compound. Definitely try lots of different groups and take up any invitations at first, you'll soon find out what you enjoy and how you want to spend your time. Through my daughter's nursery, I got together with a group of mums and made a memory book for my daughter. It brought out my creative juices, but also ensured I saw other mums regularly for a chat.'

Anthea Dufour – *Anthea spent two years in Casablanca, Morocco. Her first child, a girl, was born in Morocco.* 'I was unusual as I am English married to a Frenchman. I had no contact with the British community and only knew my husband's work colleagues, French and Moroccan. I was very isolated and made the most of my time by painting and giving English lessons from home (I didn't have a car and cycling wasn't practical over there!). I should have reached out to the British embassy – but didn't think of it! And also I prefer to mix in a country as I had done in France – but it wasn't so easy in a Muslim country.'

Belinda Zauner – *Belinda lived from 1999-2001 in Germany (with husband); from 2001-2003 in USA (with husband and oldest child, who was born there; living there until she was 15 months) and from 2003-present in Austria (with husband and three children – two girls and one boy; younger two born there; children now aged 13, 10 and 8.)* 'The most important thing you can do when moving abroad is to keep an open mind – and, it may sound obvious, but not to expect things to be the same as in your home country. Since living in Austria, I have had to take up running to counteract the effects of a Kaffee und Kuchen lifestyle. My favourite part of living abroad is when abroad stops feeling like abroad and becomes home.'

Benedicte Franchot – *Benedicte has been a long-term expat in three countries (Poland, Japan, India) after leaving France about 17 years ago. She briefly returned to Paris for three years in the middle of her travels, so has experienced repatriation and reverse-culture shock first hand.* 'I have been following my husband's expatriations for his company (but it's always been me in the first place who wanted to move, so I reject the label of 'trailing spouse'!) and have raised 3 'TCK's, now almost all off across the globe for their studies. I have been struggling with keeping up some professional activities for all these years, with different levels of success depending on the countries I lived in, and found that the best solution for me was to be a consultant and coach in my field, which is HR and project

266

management. More recently, I joined some professional women groups (Chennai Expat Expertise in India, Femmes Actives Japan in Tokyo), to share my experiences and pass on some of my skills to other women who are foreigners and wish to keep up with their careers and professional skills while abroad. Thanks to living a life and working abroad, I have now a quite significant experience of expatriation and cross-cultural adjustment, both in personal and professional life. I am always glad to help, discuss and share on these subjects.'

Carole Hallet-Mobbs – *Carole lived with her husband and daughter in Tokyo 2006-2011, where her daughter Rhiannon was aged 5-10; Berlin 2011-2013 and Pretoria from 2013-present (2015). Her daughter is now 13. Carole is the owner/writer of the* Your Expat Child *website - http://expatchild.com/.*

Catherine D – *Catherine lives near Utrecht; she has lived in the Netherlands for 7 years.* 'I still can't speak Dutch, I still can't ride a bike well, I still can't ice skate – but I make a mean pancake!'

Chellie E – *Chellie's many years living abroad between 1986 and 2013 have included trailing after her military husband and then later taking her 2 children to Kerkrade in Holland, Bracht in Germany, Berlin in Germany, the fantastically named Medicine Hat in Canada, Celle in Germany, Kingston in Jamaica, Monchengladbach, in Germany and Riyadh in Saudi Arabia.* 'My favourite part of living abroad was being able to experience the different cultures and being able to explore different foods and trying new flavours, sometimes not always successfully. One tip I was given decades ago which has never failed to assist in integrating in new environments was always say yes to any invitation made. Tip number two, which has helped meeting a wide variety of interesting individuals is the Hash House Harriers a running/walking/social group which have events all over the world.' *You can find out more about the Hash House Harriers here: http://www.hhh.org.uk/index.cfm.*

'Chickenruby' – *Chickenruby moved from UK to South Africa January 2011 with her husband and their two children aged 11 and 15. In December 2014 they moved again, to Dubai. Again for work but this time with a cat and a dog, the eldest child has left home since and the youngest returned to boarding school in the UK in 2013. Chickenruby (not her real name!) can be found blogging at: https://www.chickenruby.com.*

Chris Boulton and Jacqueline Hall – *Chris and Jacqui lived together for one and a half years in California, arriving with their 3 month old girl.* 'We mostly loved treating it as a big holiday filling our weekends with exploring (near and far). Oh and the food, namely locally grown avocados and figs, plus getting orange juice from the trees in the garden.'

Elizabeth El-Abed – *Elizabeth lived in Saudi Arabia from 2010-2013 and then moved to Dubai in 2013 with her husband and two girls aged 3 and 2 when they first moved. Her third daughter was born whilst in Saudi (they travelled to the U.S. for the birth).* 'Our move to the Middle East provided me with the opportunity to be a full time stay at home mum, finish my studies and start a business. The conditions in Saudi compound life were perfect for a mum with young children, everything in walking distance, parks and swimming pools and the school. It was a hassle free life. Do not be lured by the attractive salaries of Dubai, it will never be enough to live on and save. The cost of living is extortionate! We were lucky and achieved what we set out, 5 years, a permanent move to the US and mortgage free.'

Evelyn Simpson – *Evelyn lived in the US from 1989 - 1997 (where she met her Aussie husband at the Columbia Business school in 1996); Hong Kong from 1997-2000 (her daughter was born there in 1999); Zurich from 2000 - 2004 (her son was born there in 2002); Shanghai from 2004 - 2007; Michigan, USA from 2007 - 2009; Brussels from 2009 - 2014; and is now in Edinburgh, UK.* 'I've always been curious about what it is in people that makes us decide to take the plunge and move overseas while others are content to stay put and wouldn't dream of living anywhere else. My favourite thing about living overseas is that there's always something new to learn, whether it's a language, a new way of doing something etc. Something people wouldn't necessarily know – I met my business partner, Louise, online. We had worked together for 8 months before we finally met in person!' *Evelyn and Louise's website Thriving Abroad, which helps expats create lives they love, can be found here:www.thrivingabroad.com, their Facebook page here: www.facebook.com/thrivingabroad, and they can also be found on twitter here: @thrivingabroad.*

Farrah Ritter – *Farah, who is originally from South Carolina in the US, has lived in Oisterwijk, Netherlands since 2012. She lives with her husband and three sons – her twins are 4 years old and her oldest son is 6.* 'My favourite thing about living overseas is easily our village in North Brabant and its location, which makes it easy to jump to France, Germany, Belgium and Luxembourg. Our kids experienced more countries in our first six months than I had in 37 years!' *Farah blogs at Three Under Three -http://thethreeunder.com. She can also be can be found on Facebook at: https://www.facebook.com/TheThreeUnder.*

Haylee Morath – *Haylee lived in Islamabad, Pakistan from July 2007-October 2008, with her husband and two children aged 4 and 3 years old. While they were there, Haylee had a third child, a daughter, who was three months old when they left Islamabad. They lived in Abu Dhabi, UAE from January 2009-December 2011 and then moved to Guangzhou, China in August 2013. Their children are now aged 10, 9 and 6 years.* 'Dave and I love living abroad, the hardest step was leaving the UK for the first time, but we haven't looked back since. I think being an expat makes you a stronger person, you have to integrate, learn different cultures. I have seen many children of different ages moving around and they settle in so quickly. It amazes me how well the expat children adapt. It's hard saying goodbye, but once a new day starts in a new country, whether it be a new posting or back home, another exciting adventure starts. My favourite part about living abroad is the quality time we have been able to spend together as a family. I have also had the opportunity to work in the Visa sections in two of our postings, now the children are at school this gives me an identity and something to structure my day. It's always good to have something on my CV for when I do return back to the UK! There are positives and negatives about living abroad, you can't have everything in life! However I can honestly say the positives far outweigh the negatives.'

Jenny P – *Jenny has lived in central Oregon, USA, from 2008 onwards; she went with her husband and her children – a girl aged 2 when they moved and a boy of 8 months. Her second son was born there in 2011.* 'Known as the playground of the Northwest, living in Central Oregon has provided many leisure opportunities on the doorstep such as skiing and snowshoeing which would have been much harder to access at home. I think my tip would be to try to take advantage of new and different opportunities if you can, as you never know when the expat situation might end or change! It might help to know that we were on an L1B visa (intra-company transfer) and as a spouse my visa entitled me to work. I don't think those visas have changed, but it certainly helped to know I could volunteer and work, as other visas don't allow that.'

Josine van Heek – *Josine, with her husband Steven was in Singapore from 1995-1998; Shanghai in 2006; Taipei from 2007-2012 and will next we heading to Boise in Idaho.* 'This will be really exciting as this will be the first experience for us outside Asia and that is actually rather scary.' *She blogs at: www.dutchgirlidaho.blogspot.com*

Judy R – *Originally from the UK, Judy has called Canada home for more than 35 years. She's lived with her family for 3 years in Azerbaijan, 1 year in Egypt and 8 years in total in the UAE (on 3 separate occasions).* 'My son, who was 9 years old when we expatriated, dealt with one repatriation as a young teenager and then another when he returned to Canada for university. In total I've repatriated 3 times and they have been the most difficult periods of my expatriate life, but the experiences I've had and the friends I've made were worth it. We expats ARE a third culture and the bonds that unite us defy race, colour or creed. I'd do it all again in a heartbeat.'

Julia Simens – *Julia is an educator, speaker, author and consultant for 'global nomads', supporting global families. She first went abroad as an elementary school teacher in the South Pacific. She then returned to the USA to get her master's in Clinical Psychology, fell in love and went back abroad with her husband. They have lived in Singapore, Australia, Indonesia, the USA, Nigeria and Thailand. She is the mother of two TCKs. Julia can be contacted through her blog www.jsimens.com.* 'We have been lucky enough to see so many places in the world. Each and every location, vacation and trip have given us a lifetime of memories.'

'K' - *K came to Switzerland 7 years ago with her ex-husband and young son (who was 2.5years old at the time). Her husband left and she and her son stayed.* 'Living here is a roller coaster – ups and downs all the way. You embrace the highs and get through the lows. Your friends become your family. Most of us expats are women living in the real world of being abroad whilst the men go to work in an English speaking environment. It's the women who live it, have to cope with a foreign language, culture. It's us that go to the shops, schools etc. A lot of time is invested by companies in bringing the man and his family over, but once here that's it! As an employee the man has support, the woman nothing, but in all that it shows strength of character to stay and to live the life to integrate to make friends. Something I don't think men are as strong at doing...'

Katrina M – *Katrina moved to Vienna in 1994 and lived there for a year. She then lived in Zug, Switzerland until 1997, when she moved to Athens, Greece with husband Costas and had her first son Kiriakos. In 1999 until 2006 they lived in Milan in Italy, where their second son, Pavlos, was born in 2000. Their next move was to Copenhagen, Denmark, where Anna was born in 2007, and then in 2008 they moved to Stockholm in*

Sweden. They moved back to Athens in 2013, where they still live. Her husband works in Milan. 'My life is filled with the challenge of living outside my comfort zone. I liken moving away from a home to being a baby bird that has to jump from the nest – it is only when we take that leap of faith that we find we have the wings to keep us in the air. Home is where your family is.'

Liz Rodriguez-Notley – *Liz first moved to Abidjan, Ivory Coast in 1997 and lived there until 2000. Her son Tristan was 18 months when they arrived, her son Matthew was born while they were there. The next move was to Cotonou in Bénin, from 2000 to 2005, then Tel Aviv, Israel from 2005 to 2009. By the time they left for Nice in France in 2009, they had a third son, Tom. In 2013, the family moved to Beijing in China. Their eldest son has now left home, Matthew is 15 and Tom is 9.* 'What can I say about my expat life? Well as far as my boys are concerned, I do find it strange, and somewhat sad, that they don't have any roots. When you ask them where they're from, they can't really answer! Their mum is English, their dad is French, they've never lived in the UK, they were all born in Paris because I went back to the same hospital every time, they don't feel Parisian whatsoever... I lived in the same house in Kent until I was 18 years old! I go back to my hometown every summer and see all my old friends who never moved away, it's very comforting actually to have this sort of continuity in my life; my sons will never have that, and yes, it does make me sad sometimes (I don't think they really care, though, to be totally honest because they've never known a "normal" life have they?) Every summer we go back to France and to England, travelling between the two countries, changing "hotels" (aka friends' and relatives' houses) every week or so, it's no fun. Our house in Paris has been rented out for years so we couldn't go there. At last we've bought a "summer home" in the south of France, where this summer we will be able to put our cases down and stay there for the duration of the school holidays; maybe this is the house that they will consider "home" eventually, who knows?'

Louise Wiles – *Louise has lived abroad for most of the last 20 years, returned to the UK August 2014. She has lived in Spain and Portugal both before children and then with them. Louise runs the website Thriving Abroad: www.thrivingabroad.com.* 'Story One: Moved abroad the third time when I was four months pregnant. Certainly this was one way to get to know the medical services on the island of Madeira. Though my language deficiency at the time certainly added to the challenge, never quite sure what test was being performed, or whether the two hour wait was because the doctor was overworked or I was in the wrong place. But I survived and lived to tell the tale which actually was one of real kindness, care and warmth. Story Two: Having repatriated home in August 2014, I realise in retrospect what a special community my expat circle of friends were, and are. The sense of support and understanding that comes from people who know and understand what it means to pack up your whole life and start again somewhere new every four years is something I truly miss back home. Everyone assumes coming home is the easy bit – it is not.'

Maria French – *Maria has lived in four states in the US as well as France (as a teenager in 1990-91), Cameroon (as a student in 1993), Eritrea (as a student in 1995), Italy (as a caretaker of an Arabian horse farm in 1997), Taiwan (as an English teacher 1998-99), Northern Ireland (grad student in 2000-2001), Kosovo (as accompanying partner in 2001-2002, pregnant for most of that), Guinea and Sierra Leone (with partner and infant son 2002-2003), Bangladesh (with partner and 2 year old son and infant daughter 2004-2006), Vietnam (with partner and kids 3 and 5, 2007-2009), and moved to Qatar in 2013 with her then 3, 8 and 10 year olds (now 5, 10, and 12). In between there were a couple of separate years in Burlington VT, three years by Atlanta GA, and 1 1/2 in San Francisco.* 'I'm surprising myself at the moment by starting to enjoy Doha, against all expectations. And no surprise that it finally happened when I stopped caring what I was supposed to do (as an expat of a certain class, as a woman, mom, etc.) and just started doing, respectfully, what makes me happy. I've been drawing on the street, talking to strangers, taking a ton of pictures, spending time wherever I can to find camels, taking long walks through old neighbourhoods that are a world away from the sterile compounds where many of us expats here live.' *Maria blogs at Far Flung Home – manyhomesmanymoves.blogspot.com and also throws pictures onto tumblr at farflunghome.tumblr.com.*

Marianne D – *Marianne has lived abroad for 11 years, in the Turks and Caicos Islands, St Lucia, Tortola in the British Virgin Islands and is now in Barbados. She lives with her husband and two children under 6.* 'The best thing about living abroad is it makes you broader minded. It also helps you meet good friends from all over the world and all walks of life. I notice the "can do" attitude of expats compared to the "oh, it's too far to travel there" grumblings of people who have not lived abroad. It gives you and your children so many more life experiences and changes you as a person for the better, I would say. I would recommend spouses who do not work to join classes and be involved in things they would not get a chance to do back home as they would be working. I would recommend getting involved with as many groups and activities as you can to meet friends and enjoy your experience.'

Michelle Officer – *Michelle lived in Malaysia for 5 years 6 months. She went with her oil field worker husband and baby of 10 months, and had her second child there.* 'I HATED the first 2 years of our time! Ended up loving it and met one of my best friends there. Now miss the place! Thanks to two wonderful women, the three of us got a great group of women together, which is still running 2.5 years after we left. My most favourite thing about Malaysia was the ease in which we could travel, as a family, mums and kids or just as single females.'

Morwenna Lawson – *Morwenna has lived in Singapore with her husband and son since August 2012.* 'Having taken at least a year to find my feet, I now like the tropical lifestyle, am enjoying a spot of freelance journalism, have graduated as a museum guide and take far too many holidays. I still can't stomach durian, though (and yes, I miss home).'

Naomi Hattaway – *Naomi has lived in Delhi, India and Singapore (2009-2013), with her husband and three children (ages 3, 6 and 15 when they left).* 'My proudest expat life moments? Moving our family to India without the help of a relocation company or HR department! I'm now an expert! Also, I truly loved all of the amazing volunteer opportunities I was given in India. Irreplaceable moments! My not so awesome moment? Going to the open air meat market (INA) in the dead of hot, hot Delhi summer, fresh off the airplane and terribly jet lagged with two small children. NOT a smart idea!' *Naomi's relocation assistance company can be found here: http://8thandhome.com.*

Nicola D – *Nicola lived in Jamaica for 11 years with her husband.* 'I would hugely recommend finding something for just you; without husband/children/known friends whilst you are overseas. I learnt and qualified to be a yoga teacher, I learnt to speak Spanish etc. and I strongly believe it kept me sane! Expat life can be incredibly incestuous and it will send you mad! Take the opportunity to do something different/travel somewhere new and whatever you do, don't feel sorry for yourself. Look at it as an adventure and an opportunity to do something very few people could ever hope of experiencing.'

Nicola McCall – *Nicola was an expat spouse for 10 years from 2002 to 2011, as well as the child of an expat. She left a HR career in London to go on maternity leave in 2002 and never got the time to go back. Her son was born in Dublin, went to Dutch kindergarten and US PreK and then to an international school in the Netherlands. In 2006, Nicola created Live Life Now Coaching to coach and support expats to find fulfilment in their life overseas. In 2011 she and her son repatriated whilst her partner continued working in the Netherlands and she found herself being the stay at home partner her mother had been – a role Nicola had never thought she* *wanted! Now back working part time in a HR role, manning the home fortress and homework schedule all week alone and then trying to have 'us' time at the weekend, Nicola is experiencing another 'expat' lifestyle.* 'My tip for it all is pick your friends you confide in wisely, have humour and accept the challenge of new perspectives readily and of course drink GIN regularly.'

Nicola P – *Nicola lived in Dubai from 2004 until 2010 with her husband, three kids aged from 0 – 9, plus Alex and Safa, desert cats. In 2010, the family moved to The Hague where she still lives with her husband, her three kids now aged 13, 11 and 7, plus Merlin and Ninja, witches cats and Holly the Sprocker Spaniel.* 'Best things about being an expat – the adventures and having a swimming pool in the garden! Worst things about being an expat – the time it takes to make good friends, then having to say goodbye to them…then repeat…'

Olga Mecking. *Olga is a Polish woman living in the Netherlands with her German husband and three trilingual children. She is a translator, blogger and writer. The European Mama is a blog about her life abroad, raising children and travelling.*

Penny Knight (nee Johnson) – *Penny lived as a child between the ages of 0 and 2 in Sudan, then Nigeria (3-5), Indonesia (5-20). As an adult, she has lived with her husband and her dog in the US in 2004, and in France from 2004-2009 with her husband, son Luke (born in 2005) and their two dogs. They are all now back in the UK, along with another child, a daughter.* 'Favourite part of living abroad was the general experience of life in a different culture, climate, flora, fauna; meeting and making friends with different nationalities; the party lifestyle (as a child!). As an adult, I feel privileged to have had a different experience in life to that of most of my peers back in the UK.'

Philippa P – *Philippa lives the South of France and has been here for 2 1/2 years. She lives with her husband and 2 children – M is 6 years and B is 4 years.* 'Living in France has been both a challenge and great fun.

Bilingual children is an achievement until they start talking amongst themselves. Learning about your immediate family is fantastic but extended family staying with you for long periods needs to be thought through.'

Rachel Andrews – *Rachel moved to Hong Kong in 2009, intending to stay two years.* 'I'm now only months off permanent residency, have finally stopped translating the cost of everything into sterling and now think "same-same but different" makes perfect sense. I have two children, aged 4 and 2 and am famous for having wangled a part time job.'

Richelle W – *Richelle lived for 14 years in Niamey, Niger. She arrived with four children ages: 5.5 years, 4 years, 2.5 years, 6 months and left with 8 children: 17.5 years, 16 years, 14.5 years, 12.5 years, 10.5 years, 8.5 years, 7 years, 4.5 years. Their next stop was Quebec, Canada.* 'I'm terrified of flying and our big joke was always that when the day came when I told my husband I couldn't get back on another plane, let it be on the right side of the Atlantic Ocean. The "right side" still remains to be seen.' *Richelle can be found at: http://www.ourwrightingpad.blogspot.co.uk/*

Rowena Quantrill – *Rowena (also known as my mum!) is a third generation expat partner. She has lived all over the world: Belgium, Cuba, the Philippines, Nigeria, Venezuela, Gibraltar and Cameroon. She now lives in a small town in the west of England.* 'My grandmother lived in Ceylon (Sri Lanka) with her colonial service husband and passed her time in 'good works' and playing mah jong (as far as I can make out). It must have been very tough though, not seeing her children for years at a time when they were sent 'home' to boarding school. My mother met and married my father in Sierra Leone during the war, having gone out as a nursing sister. Once married she spent her time dressmaking (great materials obtainable from the Syrian run shops apparently), attempting to grow 'English' flowers, keeping chickens and fighting mould. Keeping the tradition I married a diplomat and lived in seven different countries constantly inventing a 'new' life for myself – it was hard (especially before the Internet age). But looking back I feel incredibly lucky to have experienced so many different cultures and places and made friends of many nationalities. I recommend birdwatching as a fantastically portable hobby and a great way to get to know locals and get off the beaten track.'

Sharon Lewis – *Sharon accompanied her partner on postings to Dhaka, Bangladesh from 1992-1995; Pretoria, South Africa from 1995-1998; Kigali, Rwanda from 2001-2003 and Kingston, Jamaica 2003-2006.* 'I enjoyed trying to avoid the temptation to introduce myself at receptions as "Plus One" when it was written on the invitation!'

Sue Behan – *Sue lived for one year in Madrid and 18 months just outside Washington DC in Northern Virginia with her husband and two boys, who were 4 and 6 when they arrived in Madrid.* 'I don't miss the mosquitos of Washington DC or the language barriers in Madrid. But I loved the adventures of being in a new country and meeting lots of wonderful people. I would do it again, but now the boys are settling into high school it won't be until they are much older.'

Viktor and Olenka Rozenburg – *I met Olenka in my home town in the UK; her husband and she had been living here for a while but he had already moved on to their next posting, Saudi Arabia, to get things started.* 'I am not already considering myself as expat. An expat, in my view, is someone who lives at home and one day moves abroad to work and eventually comes back. My scheme is little bit more complicated and I hope that final stage will not happen. I can say that I consider myself as a global citizen.'

Warren D – *Warren was first posted overseas to the Far East with his wife Jacqui, where their first child was born, then later to South Asia and southern Europe with two children of primary school age.* 'I enjoy playing sport and that has always been a good way for me to meet people and make friends. Apart from football, and as someone who is not into running, I have found a willingness to try new sports or activities helps. Depending on location, that might be squash or tennis, skiing or sailing, whichever have some popularity locally or among expats. In addition to the social benefits, they provide new sets of goals to work on and also compensate for indulging in the local food.'

Acknowledgements

Firstly I want to thank all my wonderful contributors who gave me their experiences, tips, anecdotes and advice about living overseas. From every corner of the globe, I received so much help with this book I can't thank everyone enough. Some of these women and men are listed in my appendix, others aren't, but their names can be found in the pages. And then there were others still, who spoke to me, emailed me, answered my pestering questions and gave me the background information that helped form the Guide. Without them this would be a very different – and very slim – book.

I also want to thank all the expat friends I have made along the way, both as a child, as an adult and as a mother. There are too many to mention, but hopefully you will all know who you are. In particular I want to thank those who got me through the early days as a trailing spouse. I will never forget the kindness of Kairi, Haylee and others in Islamabad, and the relief of meeting Donna and the Twilight sessions with Marianne, in St Lucia.

I want to also thank my editor, Gary Smailes, of Bubblecow, for not only helping me turn this into a readable guide but also for giving me the confidence to publish. Also to Andrew and Rebecca Brown at Design for Writers for knowing what I wanted for the cover even before I did. It's perfect, thank you.

Many people encouraged me along the way – just the occasional 'you're doing brilliantly' truly did help. Deborah Dooley at the fabulous Retreats For You for telling me I was good enough. Elizabeth el-Abed, just for that one time you said 'keep going' when I needed it most. And Lorna Syred and Carole Hallet-Mobbs for all your constructive feedback.

Finally thank you to my husband Keith for having a job which allowed me to be able to write this instead of doing proper work.

Made in the USA
Coppell, TX
30 May 2020

26725510R00164